The publication of *New German Critique* is made possible by funding from Cornell University's College of Arts and Sciences and the support of Cornell's Department of German Studies.

New German Critique is published three times a year by
Duke University Press, 905 W. Main St., Suite 18B, Durham, NC 27701.

Visit the editorial office at ngc.arts.cornell.edu
and Duke University Press Journals at dukeupress.edu/journals.

Submissions

Texts submitted to *New German Critique* should adhere to *The Chicago Manual of Style*, seventeenth edition. Short-form citations are provided in footnotes, while a reference section at the end of the manuscript contains the complete bibliographic information of works cited. The journal accepts both electronic and paper submissions. Send electronic submissions as email attachments to new_german_critique@cornell.edu. Send paper submissions in triplicate to *New German Critique*, Department of German Studies, Cornell University, 183 Goldwin Smith Hall, Ithaca, NY 14853.

Subscriptions

Direct all orders to Duke University Press, Journals Customer Relations, 905 W. Main St., Suite 18B, Durham, NC 27701. Volume 49 of *New German Critique* corresponds to issues 145–147. Annual subscription rates: print-plus-electronic institutions, $330; print-only institutions, $315; e-only institutions, $246; individuals, $38; students, $22. For information on subscriptions to the e-Duke Journals Scholarly Collections, contact libraryrelations@dukeupress.edu. Print subscriptions: add $11 postage and applicable HST (including 5% GST) for Canada; add $14 postage outside the US and Canada. Back volumes (institutions): $315. Single issues: institutions, $105; individuals, $16. For more information, contact Duke University Press Journals at 888-651-0122 (toll-free in the US and Canada) or 919-688-5134; subscriptions@dukeupress.edu.

Permissions

Photocopies for course or research use that are supplied to the end user at no cost may be made without explicit permission or fee. Photocopies that are provided to the end user for a fee may not be made without payment of permission fees to Duke University Press. Send requests for permission to republish copyrighted material to permissions@dukeupress.edu.

Advertising

Direct inquiries about advertising to
Journals Advertising Coordinator, journals_advertising@dukeupress.edu.

Indexing

For a list of the sources in which *New German Critique* is indexed and abstracted,
see dukeupress.edu/new-german-critique.

© 2022 by New German Critique, Inc.
ISSN 0094-033X

NEW GERMAN CRITIQUE

An Interdisciplinary Journal of German Studies

NUMBER 145 · FEBRUARY 2022

HANS BLUMENBERG AT 101

Special Issue Editor: Hannes Bajohr

Introduction: Hans Blumenberg at 101
Hannes Bajohr. 1

Intermittent Legitimacy: Hans Blumenberg and Artificial
Intelligence
Leif Weatherby. 11

A Well-Tempered Modernist
Colin Lang 41

Hans Blumenberg and Leonardo
Johannes Endres. 67

Working on the Myth of the Anthropocene: Blumenberg and the
Need for Philosophical Anthropology
Vida Pavesich. 97

The Vanishing Reality of the State: On Hans Blumenberg's
Political Theory
Hannes Bajohr. 131

Decoding Aesop: Blumenberg's Fabulistic Turn
Florian Fuchs 163

New German Critique is the leading journal of German studies. It covers contemporary political and social theory, philosophy, literature, film, media, and art and reads cultural texts in light of current theoretical debates.

No More Than Seeing: Hans Blumenberg's Poetics of Spectatorship
Daniela K. Helbig 185

In Memory of Ernst Cassirer: Speech Delivered in Acceptance
of the Kuno Fischer Prize of the University of Heidelberg, 1974
Hans Blumenberg 215

Unburdening from the Absolute: In Memory of Hans Blumenberg
Odo Marquard 225

Introduction:
Hans Blumenberg at 101

Hannes Bajohr

The philosopher Hans Blumenberg (1920–96) must count among the most prolific thinkers of postwar Germany. He also remains one of its most enigmatic figures and one of the last to enjoy the "transatlantic theory transfer" in which *New German Critique* has engaged over the last half century.[1] Compared with the reception of other members of what one could call "German theory" in America—Martin Heidegger and Hans-Georg Gadamer, the Frankfurt School, or even Niklas Luhmann and Friedrich Kittler—Blumenberg's has gathered momentum only slowly. This special issue aims to contribute to its acceleration and place Blumenberg's insights into dialogue with contemporary discourses.

While the erudition displayed in Blumenberg's weighty tomes and dense essays may stagger the reader, the breadth of their topics is equally astounding, as is apparent from a survey of his most famous works. *The Legitimacy of the Modern Age* (1966/1975–76, trans. 1983) not only defends modernity against its detractors from both right and left but also offers a functionalist theory of historical reception. *The Genesis of the Copernican World* (1975, trans. 1987) recounts the momentous loss of earth's—and humanity's—central position in the cosmos and reflects on its philosophical consequences. *Work on Myth* (1979, trans. 1985), beyond developing a theory of the persistence that mythical

---

1. See Huyssen and Rabinbach, "Transatlantic Theory Transfer."

New German Critique 145, Vol. 49, No. 1, February 2022
DOI 10.1215/0094033X-9439587   © 2022 by New German Critique, Inc.

thought enjoys alongside the rationalism of modernity, is also a highly original contribution to "philosophical anthropology," the study of the world relation of humans. To this list we might add *Paradigms for a Metaphorology* (1960, trans. 2010), a theory of the uses of metaphor that suggests a surplus content irreducible to mere concepts, as well as more literary, late-style volumes like *Care Crosses the River* (1987, trans. 2010) or *St. Matthew Passion* (1988, trans. 2021) that place Blumenberg into a lineage of aphoristic philosophers such as Friedrich Nietzsche or Walter Benjamin.[2]

The overwhelming breadth of his output has made Blumenberg hard to place, a solitaire among the factions of Frankfurt School thought and Heidegger-inspired hermeneutics that dominated the German philosophical scene after World War II. Trained as a phenomenologist, he remained at a distance to this school, nor did he found one of his own, even if many of his former pupils now hold chairs in German philosophy departments. And while he was intent on growing his readership, and often complained to his publisher about its, as he thought, too modest size, he retreated from the public toward the end of his life and relegated the greatest part of his writings to his archive, to be edited posthumously.

As a result, there is a mystique surrounding Blumenberg's name that extends beyond academe: a film about the notoriously reclusive thinker, *The Invisible Philosopher* (2018), as well as a novel by Sibylle Lewitscharoff, simply titled *Blumenberg* (2011, trans. 2017), testifies to a popular interest usually reserved for public intellectuals of towering stature and (at least relative) accessibility, like Hannah Arendt or Benjamin—as do the surprisingly brisk sales of some posthumously published books.[3] As the celebrations occasioned by his hundredth birthday in 2020 made amply clear, this mystique has also made Blumenberg a target for intellectual cathexis: he is feted in the feuilletons as one of the last true universally learned scholars, a paragon of a bygone era of philosophers untethered from the drudgery of grant writing and managing "research clusters,"[4] ignoring the fact that already in the 1970s, Blumenberg complained to Reinhart Koselleck about the *Betrieb* of his profession.[5]

---

2. Blumenberg, *Legitimacy*; Blumenberg, *Genesis*; Blumenberg, *Work on Myth*; Blumenberg, *Paradigms*; Blumenberg, *Care*; Blumenberg, *St. Matthew Passion*. Missing from this list of titles available in English are Blumenberg, *Shipwreck*; Blumenberg, *Lions*; Blumenberg, *Laughter*; Blumenberg, *Rigorism*; and, most recently, Blumenberg, *History, Metaphors, Fables*. More translations of his work, such as *Lesbarkeit* and *Lebenszeit und Weltzeit*, are planned.

3. Rüter, *Hans Blumenberg*; Lewitscharoff, *Blumenberg*. Denis Trierweiler called Blumenberg's *Beschreibung des Menschen* (*Description of the Human*) a "quasi-bestseller" ("À propos de Hans Blumenberg"). See also Zill, *Der absolute Leser*, 365–78.

4. As only one example of this tendency, see Steinmayr, "Das große Ganze und dessen Reform."

5. See Vowinckel, "'Ich fürchte mich vor den Organisationslustigen.'"

Even now, a quarter century after his death, rarely a year goes by without a new publication under Blumenberg's name. Indeed, the posthumous books now outnumber those published during his lifetime three to one. Peculiarly, this situation has partly hampered Blumenberg's reception by fostering the impression that a comprehensive picture of his scholarship remains to be discovered—not least in the vast and seemingly endless *Nachlass* of publication-ready manuscripts and in a slip-box catalog that rivals that of Luhmann.[6] But as the archival well slowly but steadily runs dry, Blumenberg's work has—at least in Germany—begun to resolve into a coherent and abiding whole, and the work of canonization has taken up speed: two extensive biographies, several new volumes dedicated to his work and life, and a generous *Handbuch* make his status as classic unmistakably clear.[7]

Yet as Paul Fleming remarks, Blumenberg's recognition in the United States has seen many delays.[8] While his major tomes have been available since the 1980s, anglophone readers have only begun to appreciate the breadth of his work in the past decade. Now, the wave of more recent translations mentioned above has made available Blumenberg's versatility, both in substance and in style. That his extended oeuvre has awakened academic interest among anglophones is evidenced by special journal issues, of which the latest was the *Journal of the History of Ideas*, devoted to the fiftieth anniversary of *Legitimacy of the Modern Age*, which remains Blumenberg's most influential book in the English-speaking world.[9] With the publication of *History, Metaphors, Fables: A Hans Blumenberg Reader*, it is now possible to survey the vast body of essays, glosses, and feuilleton pieces that extends the range of topics from those he is known for—modernity, myth, and the history of science—to themes

---

6. The centenary alone saw two new books appear under Blumenberg's name: *Realität und Realismus* and *Beiträge zum Problem der Ursprünglichkeit*. For an overview, see Bajohr, "Gebrochene Kontinuität."

7. Zill, *Der absolute Leser*; Goldstein, *Hans Blumenberg*; Müller and Zill, *Blumenberg-Handbuch*. Important contributions to interpreting his work, albeit predating the centenary, are Flasch, *Hans Blumenberg*; and Nicholls, *Myth and the Human Sciences*. Among the increasingly numerous volumes devoted to Blumenberg's work, the last two years alone saw the following: Heidenreich, *Politische Metaphorologie*; Lederle, *Endlichkeit und Metapher*; Waszynski, *Lesbarkeit nach Hans Blumenberg*; Attanucci and Breuer, *Leistungsbeschreibung*; Steffens, *Auf Umwegen*; and Bajohr and Geulen, *Blumenbergs Verfahren*.

8. Fleming, "Verfehlungen." Commenting on the situation in France, where Blumenberg's work was subject to a similar delay, Trierweiler spoke of "un autisme de la réception" ("Autisme").

9. See Gordon, "Introduction"; Campe, Fleming, and Wetters, "Hans Blumenberg"; Savage, "Hans Blumenberg." In most publications, however, *Legitimacy* remains the center of attention, as in the recent volume by Bielik-Robson and Whistler, *Interrogating Modernity*.

he is less associated with, such as art and literature, fables and nonconceptuality, and politics and a theory of historical *episteme*.[10]

The publication of the *Reader* is the ideal occasion for this special issue of *New German Critique*, which examines his lesser-known contributions and invites a broader engagement with the complex whole of his oeuvre. It is not entirely inappropriate that this issue comes a bit late. The slightly ironic title, "Hans Blumenberg at 101," reflects both the delayed reception that Fleming noted as well as the fact that anniversaries can only ever be a contingent occasion to consider a thinker's work. This issue opens up a broad range of topics that defined Blumenberg's writings, spanning technology, aesthetics, language theory, poetics, and politics, and brings his insights to bear on current debates, be it the Anthropocene, artificial intelligence, liberalism, spectatorship, art-historical modernism, or the uses of a specifically fabulatory philosophy for life. Finally, the issue includes two historical texts in translation, one by Blumenberg's friend Odo Marquard and one by Blumenberg himself.

Leif Weatherby's opening contribution, "Intermittent Legitimacy: Hans Blumenberg and Artificial Intelligence," expands on Blumenberg's philosophy of technology by investigating a little-known text on what one can plausibly call the first chatbot: Joseph Weizenbaum's program ELIZA. For Weatherby, Blumenberg is instructive for second-wave AI philosophies, as he connects a phenomenological notion of consciousness to theories of the computer: both are the product of rhetorical interactions. The intermittence of consciousness—constituting itself, as Edmund Husserl had argued, but also continually restituting itself and correcting its interruptions—is for Weatherby structurally comparable to the intermittence between data and instructions in the otherwise unified architecture of computers. Bypassing the fruitless effort to distinguish between human and artificial semantics, Weatherby mobilizes Blumenberg for a critique of AI in which semiotics and rhetoric, not functional or anthropological theories, are the common plane of operation.

Technology and art, both rooted in the concept of techne, share for Blumenberg a close connection in Western intellectual history, as they both gain their autonomy in a postnominalist modernity. Yet while Blumenberg cites a surprisingly wide spectrum of topics in art, including pop art and abstraction, Barnett Newman and Paul Klee, little has been said about Blumenberg's own conception of art history. In "A Well-Tempered Modernist," Colin Lang shows that Blumenberg's use of art to gain insight into the formation of epochs also

---

10. Blumenberg, *History, Metaphors, Fables*. For an accessible introduction to Blumenberg's life and thought, see Bajohr, Fuchs, and Kroll, "Hans Blumenberg."

includes a connection between his immanent theory of modernity and a philosophy of art that reveals him to be a theoretician of aesthetic modernism parallel to contemporaneous US formalist art critics like Clement Greenberg and Michael Fried. Reading, among other things, Blumenberg's contributions to the Poetik und Hermeneutik research group of which he was a member, Lang investigates this surprising commonality that rests in a shared sense of the autonomy of the artwork and the distance its observer has to take on.

Blumenberg's aesthetics were, as for many other German postwar academics around the Poetik und Hermeneutik group, heavily influenced by Paul Valéry. In "Hans Blumenberg and Leonardo" Johannes Endres shows that Blumenberg's reading of Valéry aims at an aesthetic as well as at a scientific appraisal of the modern age. Both of these aspects are represented in the figure of Leonardo da Vinci, to whom Valéry repeatedly returned, as did Blumenberg through his study of Valéry. Focusing on the "window image," Endres demonstrates that at the center of Blumenberg's pictorial theory lies a critique of a mimetic aesthetics of images that contradicts both Valéry and Leonardo. The focus on textuality that Blumenberg cannot shed is, in Endres's estimation, in the end too uncharitable toward these thinkers and misses the mark of a truly comprehensive theory of the image—Blumenberg was an eminently textual thinker.

Since the posthumous publication of *Beschreibung des Menschen*,[11] the development of a "phenomenological anthropology" has emerged as a major project of the late Blumenberg. In her contribution "Working on the Myth of the Anthropocene: Blumenberg and the Need for Philosophical Anthropology," Vida Pavesich reconstructs this undertaking and its genesis and shows how it can be brought to bear on the planetary politics of climate change and the dawn of the Anthropocene. She makes this point by arguing for the necessity of engaging philosophical anthropology to theorize humanity's impact on earth. Against the backdrop of Blumenberg's *Work on Myth*, Pavesich both reads the Anthropocene as unprecedented and draws on Blumenberg's critical resources for separating modernist myths from necessary narrative.

Before he turned to his "phenomenological anthropology," Blumenberg worked on something he called a "historical phenomenology." Based on a historicized understanding of Husserl's life-world, it aims at reconstructing past realities not in their material content but in their "concept of reality," that is, the conditions of the possibility of their being experienced. Blumenberg applied this approach most famously to the theory of the novel, but also in the less-

---

11. Blumenberg, *Beschreibung*.

well-known "Concept of Reality and Theory of the State,"[12] his only direct engagement with political theory. My essay, "The Vanishing Reality of the State: On Hans Blumenberg's Political Theory," offers a detailed reconstruction of this rich and complex text and finds within it an anti-Schmittian, post-sovereigntist theory of liberal politics based on a non- and even antiperformative theory of language: "how to do nothing with words," as Blumenberg puts it, becomes the central political question in the age of technology.

Blumenberg's concern with language is attested most notably by his *Paradigms for a Metaphorology* from 1960. However, in Blumenberg's studies of fables and their rewritings, begun in the early 1980s with the speech "Pensiveness"[13]—delivered when he received the Sigmund Freud Prize for academic prose—one finds an overlooked and radical reformulation of the metaphorology project, as Florian Fuchs argues in "Decoding Aesop: Blumenberg's Fabulistic Turn." In reading anecdotes and fables from the late work, a "fabulatory philosophy" emerges that surpasses even Blumenberg's early opposition to the systematization and full terminologization of philosophy. Writing an alternative genealogy of thought that begins with Aesop, Blumenberg reminded his postmodern present that philosophy is always indebted to and in need of recourse to the primordial, antitheoretical *Unverstand* recorded in fables.

Blumenberg not only analyzed small forms like fables or anecdotes but also made them part of his writing practice. From the dense essays of his early career to the massive tomes of his middle period to the short forms of the late Blumenberg, he commanded a variety of genres, giving a formal complement to the thematic scope of his writing. In "No More Than Seeing: Hans Blumenberg's Poetics of Spectatorship," Daniela K. Helbig reads Blumenberg's formal and genre choices alongside those of his contemporaries, chief among them Heidegger, and shows how these choices changed his conception of philosophy throughout his career. During his late phase, Helbig argues, the figure of the spectator becomes both a theoretical focus and a means of self-stylization for the increasingly withdrawn philosopher.

The issue concludes with two translations, both of them speeches. Blumenberg gave "In Memory of Ernst Cassirer" as the acceptance speech on the occasion of his receiving the prestigious Kuno Fischer Prize for philosophy in 1974. One of Blumenberg's few explicit self-reflections on his intellectual

---

12. Blumenberg, "Concept of Reality and the Possibility of the Novel"; Blumenberg, "Concept of Reality and the Theory of the State."

13. Blumenberg, "Pensiveness."

genealogy, the text gives a leading role to Ernst Cassirer and his philosophy of culture. Blumenberg both criticizes the particular execution and affirms the general impetus of this project and relates it to his own ideal of an anthropologically informed historicism. The speech, an ideal introduction to the late Blumenberg's self-understanding, illuminates an ethical approach to the history of philosophy that forgoes "the mediatization of history" for the sake of the present. That Blumenberg insists on the "elementary obligation of forsaking nothing that is human" puts him in surprising proximity to more left-leaning thinkers of history, such as Benjamin and Siegfried Kracauer. Joe Paul Kroll, who thoughtfully translated *Rigorism of Truth* and parts of the *Reader*, has rendered the speech into English.

The second translation, too, is one "in memory of"—this time, Blumenberg himself. The philosopher Odo Marquard wrote it as a eulogy after Blumenberg's death in 1996. Marquard, who had been a colleague for many years, gives one of the most well-known interpretations of Blumenberg's thought—that his main concern was the "unburdening from the absolute." Humans, as misfits of evolution but also as cosmological outcasts, need to conceive of devices to keep the "absolutism of reality" at bay, as Blumenberg put it in *Work on Myth*. Marquard, taking this idea as a shorthand for the theoretical stakes of Blumenberg's complete oeuvre, argues that it can be found in all of his texts in one guise or the other. Willfully reductive, Marquard's interpretation needs to be read with a grain of salt, as it ignores the early Blumenberg to whom the anthropological world relation is not yet a pressing concern. Marquard is perhaps responsible for some of the mystique surrounding Blumenberg, painting him as a driven recluse, sleeping only six days a week to make up for time lost during the war. Yet Marquard's text is also perspicacious and deeply sympathetic to his subject; it has drawn many into the orbit of the "Blumenberg galaxy."[14] It is a fitting conclusion to this issue, which hopes to bring into view a few of its multitudinous constellations.

Hannes Bajohr is a postdoctoral researcher in the Department of Arts, Media, Philosophy at the University of Basel.

14. Brague, "La galaxie Blumenberg."

References

Attanucci, Timothy, and Ulrich Breuer, eds. *Leistungsbeschreibung: Literarische Strategien bei Hans Blumenberg / Describing Cultural Achievements: Hans Blumenberg's Literary Strategies*. Heidelberg: Winter, 2020.

Bajohr, Hannes. "Gebrochene Kontinuität: Neues über Hans Blumenbergs Werk." *Merkur*, no. 860 (2021): 71–81.

Bajohr, Hannes, Florian Fuchs, and Joe Paul Kroll. "Hans Blumenberg: An Introduction." In Blumenberg, *History, Metaphors, Fables*, 1–29.

Bajohr, Hannes, and Eva Geulen, eds. *Blumenbergs Verfahren: Neue Zugänge zum Werk*. Göttingen: Wallstein, 2022.

Bielik-Robson, Agata, and Daniel Whistler, eds. *Interrogating Modernity: Debates with Hans Blumenberg*. Cham: Palgrave Macmillan, 2020.

Blumenberg, Hans. *Beiträge zum Problem der Ursprünglichkeit der mittelalterlichscholastischen Ontologie*, edited by Benjamin Dahlke and Matthias Laarmann. Berlin: Suhrkamp, 2020.

Blumenberg, Hans. *Beschreibung des Menschen*, edited by Manfred Sommer. Frankfurt am Main: Suhrkamp, 2006.

Blumenberg, Hans. *Care Crosses the River*, translated by Paul Fleming. Stanford, CA: Stanford University Press, 2010.

Blumenberg, Hans. "The Concept of Reality and the Possibility of the Novel." In Blumenberg, *History, Metaphors, Fables*, 499–524.

Blumenberg, Hans. "The Concept of Reality and the Theory of the State." In Blumenberg, *History, Metaphors, Fables*, 83–116.

Blumenberg, Hans. *Die Lesbarkeit der Welt*. Frankfurt am Main: Suhrkamp, 1981.

Blumenberg, Hans. *The Genesis of the Copernican World*, translated by Robert M. Wallace. Cambridge, MA: MIT Press, 1987.

Blumenberg, Hans. *History, Metaphors, Fables: A Hans Blumenberg Reader*, edited by Hannes Bajohr, Florian Fuchs, and Joe Paul Kroll. Ithaca, NY: Cornell University Press, 2020.

Blumenberg, Hans. *The Laughter of the Thracian Woman: A Protohistory of Theory*, translated by Spencer Hawkins. New York: Bloomsbury, 2015.

Blumenberg, Hans. *Lebenszeit und Weltzeit*. Frankfurt am Main: Suhrkamp, 1986.

Blumenberg, Hans. *The Legitimacy of the Modern Age*, translated by Robert M. Wallace. Cambridge, MA: MIT Press, 1983.

Blumenberg, Hans. *Lions*, translated by Kári Driscoll. London: Seagull, 2018.

Blumenberg, Hans. *Paradigms for a Metaphorology*, translated by Robert Savage. Ithaca, NY: Cornell University Press, 2010.

Blumenberg, Hans. "Pensiveness." In Blumenberg, *History, Metaphors, Fables*, 525–30.

Blumenberg, Hans. *Realität und Realismus*, edited by Nicola Zambon. Berlin: Suhrkamp, 2020.

Blumenberg, Hans. *Rigorism of Truth: "Moses the Egyptian" and Other Writings on Freud and Arendt*, translated by Joe Paul Kroll. Ithaca, NY: Cornell University Press, 2018.

Blumenberg, Hans. *Shipwreck with Spectator: Paradigm of a Metaphor for Existence*, translated by Steven Rendall. Cambridge, MA: MIT Press, 1997.

Blumenberg, Hans. *St. Matthew Passion*, translated by Helmut Müller-Sievers and Paul Fleming. Ithaca, NY: Cornell University Press, 2021.

Blumenberg, Hans. *Work on Myth*, translated by Robert M. Wallace. Cambridge, MA: MIT Press, 1985.

Brague, Rémi. "La galaxie Blumenberg." *Débat*, no. 83 (1995): 173–86.

Campe, Rüdiger, Paul Fleming, and Kirk Wetters, eds. "Hans Blumenberg." Special issue, *Telos*, no. 158 (2012).

Flasch, Kurt. *Hans Blumenberg, Philosoph in Deutschland: Die Jahre 1945–1966*. Frankfurt am Main: Klostermann, 2017.

Fleming, Paul. "Verfehlungen: Hans Blumenberg and the United States." *New German Critique*, no. 132 (2017): 105–21.

Goldstein, Jürgen. *Hans Blumenberg: Ein philosophisches Portrait*. Berlin: Matthes und Seitz, 2020.

Gordon, Peter E., ed. "Introduction: Reflections on the Fiftieth Anniversary of Hans Blumenberg's *The Legitimacy of the Modern Age*." *Journal of the History of Ideas* 80, no. 1 (2019): 67–73.

Heidenreich, Felix. *Politische Metaphorologie: Hans Blumenberg heute*. Berlin: Metzler, 2020.

Huyssen, Andreas, and Anson Rabinbach, eds. "Transatlantic Theory Transfer: Missed Encounters?" Special issue, *New German Critique*, no. 132 (2017).

Lederle, Sebastian. *Endlichkeit und Metapher: Studien zu Hans Blumenberg und Eugen Fink*. Würzburg: Königshausen und Neumann, 2021.

Lewitscharoff, Sibylle. *Blumenberg*. London: Seagull, 2017.

Müller, Oliver, and Rüdiger Zill, eds. *Blumenberg-Handbuch: Leben—Werk—Wirkung*. Stuttgart: Metzler, forthcoming.

Nicholls, Angus. *Myth and the Human Sciences: Hans Blumenberg's Theory of Myth*. New York: Routledge, 2015.

Rüter, Christoph. *Hans Blumenberg: Der unsichtbare Philosoph*. Real Fiction Filmverleih, 2018. DVD.

Savage, Robert, ed. "Hans Blumenberg." Special issue, *Thesis Eleven*, no. 104 (2011).

Steffens, Andreas. *Auf Umwegen: Nach Hans Blumenberg denken; Studien, Essays und Glossen*. Wuppertal: Arco, 2021.

Steinmayr, Markus. "Das große Ganze und dessen Reform: Hans Blumenberg und die Universität." *Frankfurter Allgemeine Zeitung*, September 9, 2020.

Trierweiler, Denis. "À propos de Hans Blumenberg: Entretien avec Denis Trierweiler." *Cahiers philosophiques* 123, no. 4 (2010): 101–9.

Trierweiler, Denis. "Un autisme de la réception: À propos de la traduction de la 'Légitimité des temps modernes' de Hans Blumenberg en France." *Esprit* 24, no. 6 (2000): 51–62.

Vowinckel, Annette. "'Ich fürchte mich vor den Organisationslustigen': Ein Dialog zwischen Hans Blumenberg und Reinhart Koselleck." *Merkur*, no. 781 (2014): 546–50.

Waszynski, Alexander. *Lesbarkeit nach Hans Blumenberg*. Berlin: de Gruyter, 2020.

Zill, Rüdiger. *Der absolute Leser: Hans Blumenberg; Eine intellektuelle Biografie*. Berlin: Suhrkamp, 2020.

Intermittent Legitimacy:
Hans Blumenberg and Artificial Intelligence

Leif Weatherby

> Only in language is the fateful incongruence of action and consciousness reconciled, which becomes more and more decisive for our current situation. Machines can help us to skip levels of consciousness, and we often have to respond to the overexertion of objective demand by automatizing ourselves—for example, by using formulas that we do not fully grasp [*durchschauen*]. Thus, our consciousness is "bypassed" by a set of behaviors and actions that result from the inherent laws of our areas of life, which are objectivized and have become autonomous, and are constantly forcing themselves on us. From the conditions and necessities of circumstances we immediately obtain achievements to master the physical world.
> —Hans Blumenberg, "World History and World Models"

Artificial Semantics

We spend a lot of time today in a space of artificial semantics, in which even the most banal communications are partly generated by digital machines. Chatbots and algorithms organizing the flow of communications data behind the scenes not only provide a platform for the movement of speech, money, and labor throughout the globe—they also shape the meaning of that movement, in real-time interaction with human deeds. Both what we mean and the way that

New German Critique 145, Vol. 49, No. 1, February 2022
DOI 10.1215/0094033X-9439601   © 2022 by New German Critique, Inc.

11

meaning takes hold beyond our control result from this incredibly complex set of human-machine interactions. With recent shifts in artificial intelligence (AI) making use of the vast amounts of data generated by those interactions, we can recognize a situation described by the phenomenological critique of technology, a world papered over by automatically generated and perfectly repeatable actions distant from any experiential grasp, opaque yet efficient. Whether machines are "intelligent" is not the point for such an account. Instead, the digital role in the constitution of meaning—what I am calling artificial semantics—must be taken into account. For that, the work of the philosopher Hans Blumenberg is crucial, since he came to the conclusion that meaning is always artificial, regardless of the question of machines. Although he never completed his intended study on technology, he pushed the phenomenological critique rooted in Edmund Husserl's *Crisis of European Sciences and Transcendental Phenomenology* and Martin Heidegger's "Question Concerning Technology" beyond its technophobic moorings. In what follows, I consider a fragmentary piece of writing, "The Phenomenologist Can Only Correct Himself" ("Der Phänomenologe kann sich nur selbst berichtigen"), in which Blumenberg addresses the problem of AI in a characteristically dense manner that compares the project of making machines think to Husserl's and Immanuel Kant's theoretical philosophies. Taking as his example the first chatbot, Joseph Weizenbaum's ELIZA, Blumenberg adumbrates a phenomenological critique of large-scale, interactive AI data systems. ELIZA was one of the first AI systems to interact successfully with humans, and Blumenberg's treatment of it is surprisingly relevant to today's much more powerful artificial intelligence. For Blumenberg, intelligence of any kind is "intermittent," only unreliably and periodically connected to a world outside itself. This characterization allows Blumenberg to compare human consciousness to a computer. But rather than model the brain on the logical capacity of hardware, Blumenberg shows how the computer shares epistemological limitations with us. This move is a step toward a critique of AI that is not mired in dualisms about human and machine, consciousness and action, the abstract and the embodied. What Blumenberg describes as the "reconciliation" (*Versöhnung*) of action and consciousness in language is always a sort of simulation. AI shares in modern "legitimacy," to use one of Blumenberg's signature concepts, and must be allowed this participatory role before a critique can take root.[1]

---

1. The modern period, for Blumenberg, comes to claim a legitimacy lacking metaphysical roots or even the univocity of concepts over time. See Blumenberg, *Legitimacy of the Modern Age*, 65.

The problem of technology is deeply entwined with the highest theoretical flights of epistemology.[2] The goal of the phenomenologist may be to reduce consciousness to "things themselves" and to become a "pure observer" by bracketing all presumptions and additions, but the phenomenologist will always fall back on the self-correction of the fragment's title, interrupting the very experience to be purified, and mistaking the correction for the desired purity. Weizenbaum's chatbot illustrates the same complex self-delusion: designed to pass the Turing test—to trick humans into thinking they were interacting with other humans—it worked too well. Named for George Bernard Shaw's Eliza Doolittle, ELIZA had a prepopulated list of keywords causing semantic "transformations," leading to output replies. To Weizenbaum's horror, his secretary asked him to leave the room while she talked with the sub-program DOCTOR, which imitated a Rogerian therapist—a comparatively easy programming task, since this style of therapy relies on repeating the patient's words and associative links. But it drew its interlocutors in too easily, invoking the uncanny feeling of success where Weizenbaum knew there was none. The ELIZA incident illustrated a fault in modern epistemology more generally:

> To delimit this intervention Joseph Weizenbaum's "Eliza" suffices, which was thought up in order to provide the counterproof for what its performance ironically proved. The patients were not fooled, but forgot the computer as quickly as they were supposed to forget the analyst according to Freud's original notion. But the analyst for the most part cannot bear this mute role—just as little as the phenomenological subject can bear the pure role of the observer, and must instead by its very description [of the activity of consciousness] instruct, inform, form dogma, and in the end treat the *Crisis*.[3]

The apparent success of the phenomenologist is similar to ELIZA's: both assume that intelligence is available to be witnessed or recorded. When this assumption proves wrong, the phenomenologist doubles down, while the algorithm generates meaning, spinning out of control. Yet for Blumenberg, knowledge had never been in the kind of control the phenomenologist wanted.

Just like the phenomenologist, Weizenbaum both wanted to purify dialogue and assumed that he was far from doing so. When people entered into

---

2. They even share an anthropological origin, in which the targeting of an animal with a rock or a spear is the origin of the concept. See Blumenberg, "Theory of Nonconceptuality." Cf. Zill, "Von der Atommoral zum Zeitgewinn," 312.

3. Blumenberg, "Der Phänomenologe," 36 (hereafter cited as DP).

dialogue with the chatbot anyway, it demonstrated the opacity of everyday speech, simulating "reconciliation" where the designer knew there was none. The bot, after all, is empirically artificial—it *cannot* be a knowing agent, a true dialogue partner. Weizenbaum, according to Blumenberg, immediately wanted to "treat" rather than observe the problem at hand. What for Husserl had been a "crisis" in the split between experience and science repeats itself in a crisis about the very concept of the artificial with ELIZA. The machine was "of the 'rhetorical' type," Blumenberg wrote (DP, 39–40)—AI puts us in a space of artificial meaning, or better, it shows us how artificial meaning is in the first place.

ELIZA is a complex example in the history of AI, because it was meant to illustrate a core assumption of the early movement—that meaning is first formulated and then distributed—but actually provided the counterproof that rhetorical situations first generate meaning. Blumenberg compares the first assumption to the phenomenological attempt to establish neutrality with respect to his own intentionality. Recalling Husserl's formulation that *"the point is not to secure objectivity, but to understand it,"*[4] Blumenberg argues that no amount of introspection can account for the genesis of consciousness. Likewise, as ELIZA demonstrates, no amount of reflection can draw a bright line between authentic and artificial semantic space. In comparing the chatbot and the phenomenologist, Blumenberg draws a parallel between "psychophysical dreamers" and neuroscientists following brain waves to make a "film of *Dasein*" (DP, 35–36) and Husserl's notion of experience. What they share is the belief in a "disinterested spectator," who may be the experiencing subject (Husserl), the analyst (Freud), the technician at the electroencephalogram machine, or "the least interested of all witnesses, the computer" (DP, 36). For Blumenberg, Weizenbaum's horror at the machine's success demonstrated the "pathological function" (DP, 36) in the idea of this disinterested spectator. Neither the introspective phenomenologist nor the machine's alleged intelligence can produce a transcript (*"Protokoll"*) of experience. Blumenberg writes that "not to be able to master the *epoché*" is "essential" to the subject just as it is to artificial intelligence: "There can be no machine that determines what is self-evidently true [to the subject]" (Eine Evidenzfeststellungsmaschine kann es nicht geben). The self-evidently true, Blumenberg argues, must be within the bounds of a formal symbolic language (he invokes Ludwig Wittgenstein's *Tractatus* here, which we may take as an example of the sort of logical language systems, such as Bertrand Russell and Alfred North Whitehead's *Principia Mathematica*, that led to the development of the computer), but any *user*

4. Blumenberg, *Beschreibung des Menschen*, 183.

of that language, machine or human, exceeds the bounds of its formal system, opening semantic space uncaptured by its syntax. What appears as success is alarming error—yet error is the normal semantic space in which we live.

Where Weizenbaum saw human failure, Blumenberg saw the opportunity to integrate cutting-edge computer science into his conspectus of intellectual history. His proposal brings human and artificial intelligence close together, allowing AI to illustrate the precarity of knowledge in general. Both, Blumenberg suggests, function *intermittently.*[5] Both *seem* to synthesize radically heterogeneous "sequences"—perception and reflection, data and program. Yet both are limited by the form of legitimacy that modern knowledge has come to adopt: an intermittency able to achieve neither neutral self-transparency nor externally grounded certainty. Contact with "the world" comes only intermittently—intelligence, artificial or otherwise, carries no papers, no absolute warrant.[6] Objectivity might be "just a temporary form of assistance for a consciousness reliant on memory, one that can only organize its experience in discrete episodes—an *intermittent consciousness* [*eines intermittierenden Bewußtseins*]?"[7] This proposal brings the digital computer and human consciousness into theoretical proximity, but not in the way that AI scientists imagined. Artificial intelligence of any thinkable sort may share the limitations of human knowledge.

Blumenberg's treatment of ELIZA can help us update our own critical stance toward AI in the present. Critiques of artificial intelligence have relied heavily on the phenomenological framework, suggesting that digital programs have no "experience," or are not "embodied," in the way that phenomenology accounts for in humans. Yet these critiques are largely aimed at the first wave of the AI project, sometimes called "GOFAI" (good old-fashioned artificial intelligence).[8] These are closed-symbol systems designed to take specific inputs and

5. The theory of "intermittent consciousness" is mentioned three times—each time without elaboration, and twice in connection with Husserl—in Blumenberg, *Beschreibung des Menschen*, 183, 421, 609. Intermittency means that the possession of knowledge is irregular rather than constant and transparent (or completely false, as in skepticism). Marion Schumm argues that the wider critique of Husserl is at least partly aimed at Husserl's notions of "retention" and "protention," since these building blocks are meant to ensure the continuity of the self-transparency of consciousness to itself for Husserl ("Blumenberg und die Intermittenz des Bewusstseins"). Schumm does not deal with technology. An intriguing parallel could be drawn to Bernard Stiegler's use of these terms to elaborate a philosophy of technology.

6. See Kirk Wetters's suggestion, which I follow, that we use Blumenberg's refusal of any "absolute" to read him ("Working Over Philosophy"). Paul Fleming carries out a similar reading of Blumenberg on stylistic grounds ("Perfect Story").

7. Blumenberg, *Beschreibung des Menschen*, 183.

8. Coined by Haugeland, *Artificial Intelligence*, 112.

manipulate them expertly in a given syntax, or set of transformational rules. Their successes throughout the 1970s and 1980s were remarkable in isolated areas—chess and high-order logic, in particular—but a barrier was quickly reached due to an almost total lack of flexibility. A program that can beat a human at chess may be completely unable to play checkers—or, for example, make sense of recipes, making the term *intelligent* seem generous at best. The research program of these first-wave systems began to struggle as successes thinned and funding disappeared, in what is known as the "AI winter" of the late twentieth century. In the new millennium, however, a different model of AI has come to the fore. Known broadly as "machine learning," this research program employs nonlinear algorithms known as "neural nets," into which massive amounts of data are fed.[9] These systems have become more proficient than humans at many tasks, especially perceptual ones—image recognition, including facial recognition, the deciphering of handwriting, tumor detection in medical imaging, among others. Nets detect patterns where symbolic systems applied rules, and pattern detection allows for greater openness, establishing a wider margin to participate in the artificial semantic space of human-machine interaction. The phenomenon of online "personalization," for example, in targeted advertising, relies heavily on this kind of data-heavy, feedback-based AI, which has become crucial to the infrastructure of capitalism today.[10]

ELIZA was a first-wave AI product, but Blumenberg's critique is forward-looking.[11] The phenomenological account of technology in general sought to find a clear distinction between the technoscientific picture of the world and something else, which Husserl called the "lifeworld." This line of attack easily collapsed in popular accounts into data skepticism and even denial of the role that digital systems were quickly coming to occupy in our societies. But Blumenberg ceded the crucial point to ELIZA where even its designer, Weizenbaum, balked. By admitting that ELIZA was genuinely rhetorical, actually participating in a kind of semantic space that typified modern consciousness more generally, Blumenberg provides us with a way to move forward into a critique of a more worldly, flexible AI in the present. Although Blumenberg never embraced a single philosophy of technology—even abandoning his

9. A good nontechnical overview can be found in Kelleher, *Deep Learning*; for a general technical account, see Lecun, Bengio, and Hinton, "Deep Learning."

10. According to the most convincing Marxist account to date, learning systems have become part of the "general conditions of production." See Dyer-Witheford, Kjosen, and Steinhoff, *Inhuman Power*, 49–56.

11. Nearly all AI critique relies on the model established in the first wave, as shown graphically in a network visualization in Cardon, Cointet, and Mazières, "Neurons Spike Back," 179.

early plans for an "intellectual history of technology" (*Geistesgeschichte der Technik*)—he never stopped treating technology as a problem, construing it as part of anthropology and rhetoric.[12] This turn in Blumenberg's thinking situated him uniquely to address systems that were quickly becoming rhetorical actors. AI did not force us farther from a "lifeworld" innocent of technology but instead illustrated the very precarity of "legitimacy" that dogged the entirety of modernity in rhetorical form. We could even put AI in the column of what Blumenberg calls "Copernicanism,"[13] the project of finding new seams to tear open in the fabric of seemingly secure truth. In "The Phenomenologist Can Only Correct Himself," we see Blumenberg mix his characteristic high-flying intellectual history with the immediate concerns around quantification and digital systems in the 1970s. His proposal that intelligence, artificial or otherwise, is "intermittent" may prove to be a crucial step in the development of a second wave of AI critique.

ELIZA's Intermittency

Writing about the Pentagon Papers at the height of Richard Nixon's domestic struggle over the Vietnam War, Hannah Arendt castigated Robert McNamara for the introduction of data analysis into Defense Department decision-making: "The problem-solvers did not judge; they calculated."[14] What was more or less likely according to data, she argued, was not the problem at hand, since forms of "incalculable risk" were involved in war. The story goes something like this: computers calculate—in fact, they were designed to automate this allegedly lowest contribution to judgment. But they do not perform judgments themselves, the qualitative tool of reason. This division became a common diagnostic tool with the integration of data processors into large-scale social phenomena like war, policy, and market analysis.[15] The putatively

12. This point is widely acknowledged in the literature. See Campe, "From the Theory of Technology"; Zill, "Von der Atommoral zum Zeitgewinn"; Recki, "Auch eine Rehabilitierung der instrumentellen Vernunft"; Haverkamp, "Die Technik der Rhetorik"; Müller-Sievers, "Kyklophorology"; and Mende, "Histories of Technicization."

13. Especially what Blumenberg calls the "Copernican Comparative" in the eighteenth century—the quest to become "*more* Copernican," which characterizes Kant's philosophy among others—underlies this point. See Blumenberg, *Genesis*, 524–614. For an excellent account of Blumenberg's philosophy of technology in its midcentury context, see Bajohr, "Hans Blumenberg's Early Theory"; and Campe, "From the Theory of Technology," 110. See also Flasch, *Hans Blumenberg*.

14. Arendt, *Crises*, 37. Arendt's critique here is obviously related to Husserl's and specifically Heidegger's focus on "calculation" as a metaphysical dispensation of the modern world.

15. A similar division drives the narrative of Erickson et al., "Enlightenment Reason." See the compelling critique of this framework in Mirowski and Nik-Kah, *Knowledge We Have Lost in Information*, 1–31. Brian Cantwell Smith provides one of the best philosophical accounts of AI but leaves just this division intact (*Promise*).

bright line this story draws reads as little more than a defensive humanism, a rear-guard division between judgment and calculation. It is derived from phenomenological thinking and remains a dominant form of critique today.

Weizenbaum put Arendt's judgment/calculation distinction front and center in his retrospective account of ELIZA, suggesting that AI be limited to calculating and strictly kept out of the realm of judgment.[16] Tracing a "vision of rationality tragically twisted so as to equate it with logicality" to Francis Bacon, Weizenbaum argues that "we [have] very nearly come to the point where almost every genuine human dilemma is seen as a mere paradox, as a merely apparent contradiction that could be untangled by judicious applications of cold logic derived from a higher standpoint" (*CP*, 13–14). By inputting high-risk items like military strategy, Weizenbaum argues (following Arendt), we arrive at an utterly irrational use of a set of instruments that were meant to be the very crystallization of rationality. Algorithms can perform nothing more than "instrumental reason," a term Weizenbaum borrows from Max Horkheimer (*CP*, 250–52). The computer manifests the dialectic of enlightenment, but critique fails to do more than resist the onset of the digital age.

The first generation of phenomenologists did not live to confront the digital revolution. Husserl's consequential claim that Galileo had confused "being" with "method," and inserted a repeatable pattern of measurement—a "symbolic veil of ideas"—into the "universe of self-understood things" Husserl would dub the "lifeworld," gave both impulse and theoretical tincture to subsequent efforts.[17] The stakes were set at the highest possible pitch: technology was a matter of the possibility of knowledge itself, of our ability to make sense of the world. Heidegger would, if anything, raise the stakes even higher, claiming that technology was its own form of metaphysics, a "sending" or "destiny" (*Geschick*) that competed with the poetic (or poietic) "worlding" that was its alternate from the scientific revolution to the twentieth century. Heidegger did live to see the digital revolution—although not its consumer variant that began in earnest in the mid-1980s—and he scattered references to cybernetics throughout his later work. Computing exacerbated technology's tendency to make spontaneous energy into a "standing reserve," making being, once "methodized" in Husserl's account, into "pure plannability" (*Planbares*), calculation instead of *poiesis*.[18] The self-genesis of being—physis—became mere control, a notion Arendt varied in claiming that the modern human "acts into nature," denaturing the cyclical idea of history in the ancient and

---

16. Weizenbaum, *Computer Power*, 13–14 (hereafter cited as *CP*).
17. Husserl, *Die Krisis*, 55. The "veil" is a set of symbols that stands in for the lifeworld.
18. Heidegger, "Die Herkunft," 143, cf. 141. See also Hörl, "Die offene Maschine."

introducing linear, goal-oriented action into nature. Calculation and method corrupted lifeworld, being, and judgment, making ecological and social systems manifestly dangerous.[19]

The phenomenological status quo remained throughout the middle of the twentieth century, a period of intensive technization. Just as Heidegger was developing his theory of technology, the theory of number and the problem of communications engineering combined, resulting in the theory of "new automata" and eventually the canonical digital computer.[20] The phenomenologists did not often write in concrete terms about these machines,[21] even as computers were recruited into the management of corporations, economies, and societies.[22] Where digital systems outstripped human experience, outdoing the speed and scope of previous calculation by many orders of magnitude, the phenomenologist wanted to draw a line in the sand.

The engineer Weizenbaum had absorbed crucial elements of this narrative, including the broad strokes of phenomenology's diagnosis of modern philosophy and science, and wanted to isolate the effects AI systems could have. Programs, for all their abstraction, contain some information about the "real world," he knew, and they were increasingly going to occupy social and semantic space. The alarm was patent in his best-known work, *Computer Power and Human Reason*, which bears the summary Arendtian subtitle, *From Judgment to Calculation*. Weizenbaum had assumed that he was playing in a semantic sandbox, but the subprogram DOCTOR provoked real conversation that seemed genuinely therapeutic. Looking back, Weizenbaum wrote that some "subjects have been very hard to convince that ELIZA (with its present script) is *not* human. This is a striking form of Turing's test."[23] What had fooled the subjects were transformation rules in the algorithm that could respond, for example, to "everybody hates me" with "can you think of anyone in particular?" (ELIZA, 43). The script therefore both contained what Weizenbaum called "in a loose way, a model of certain aspects of the world," and the ability to provoke reactions with incomplete questions that had only a diagonal rela-

19. See Arendt, "Modern Concept of History." Blumenberg himself argues that this introduction allows a view of "the relation between the human and the universe as a quantitatively graspable proportion" to emerge (*Genesis*, 30).

20. See Campbell-Kelly et al., *Computer*; and *High-Speed Computing Devices*.

21. Perhaps this is what Blumenberg had in mind with his "intellectual history of technology." See Recki, "Auch eine Rehabilitierung der instrumentellen Vernunft"; and Haverkamp, "Die Technik der Rhetorik."

22. See Campbell-Kelly and Garcia-Swartz, *From Mainframes to Smartphones*; Mirowski, *Machine Dreams*; Medina, *Cybernetic Revolutionaries*; and Peters, *How Not to Network a Nation*.

23. Weizenbaum, "ELIZA," 42 (hereafter cited in the text as ELIZA).

tion to the world. The program's lack of understanding caused, rather than prevented, the interaction.

Therapy was the perfect type of conversation for this uncanny effect, Weizenbaum points out, since it is focused on lack of information. This means that the algorithm can identify keywords and then run transformations without needing to make perfect sense, leaving it free to "assume the pose of knowing almost nothing of the real world" (ELIZA, 42). If the bot responded to "I went for a long boat ride" with "Tell me about boats," Weizenbaum continues, "one would not assume that he knew nothing about boats, but that he had some purpose in so directing the subsequent conversation. It is important to note that this assumption is one made by the speaker" (ELIZA, 42). The reckoning system can simply push semantically related elements forward, while the judger—in this case a self-judger—makes of them what she will, operating "inferentially" to the benefit of the programmer. Therapy "eliminates the need of storing *explicit* information about the real world" (ELIZA, 42). The goal of *concealing* the computer's lack of knowledge about the real world was turned on its head: to engage in conversation, a half-strategic *revealing* of its lack of understanding was crucial. Weizenbaum concluded that this switch was a "precondition to making an ELIZA-like program the basis for an effective natural language man-machine communication system" (ELIZA, 43). The pragmatics of human-machine interaction materialized the relative semantic indifference of the therapeutic situation. Artificial semantic space can only exist because actual semantics are always blurry in the first place.

Blumenberg notes, following Weizenbaum's exoteric presentation in *Computer Power and Human Reason*, that the conversation "relies on a thin tolerance of 'initiators'" (trigger words) that form the kernel of the interaction in combination with the expectations of the analysand. Steering the conversation are the "securely efficacious 'trigger words'" that are "generically 'rhetorical' [*im Typus 'rhetorisch'*]," but which allow consensus to be reached nearly immediately by avoiding saying anything against the grain of the analysand's flow of speech. But "this is precisely . . . the role of the 'pure' subject of the therapist," Blumenberg concludes (DP, 39). The reconciliation that speech performs for us, but never actually completes, is presented as a possibility in the artificial semantic space presented by ELIZA. The algorithm is genuinely in the slipstream of the rhetorical situation, just as much as the analyst—or consciousness itself—is.

Weizenbaum's technical account of ELIZA illuminates Blumenberg's epistemological interpretation. The program was implemented in 1967 in SLIP (Symmetric LIst Processor), a programming language that Weizenbaum

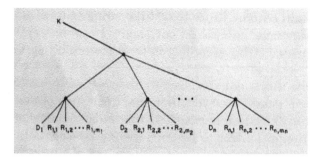

Figure 1. Keyword and rule list structure.

himself developed. SLIP is a member of the LISP family of programming languages, so called because they are "*LISt Processors.*" The "initiators" Blumenberg refers to are "keywords" that direct the program to search within its data, structured as lists. The lists are hierarchized by a ranking procedure within each key, so that any input sentence triggers a search for a correct association. Having identified the "correct" list, the program decomposes the sentence and then transforms it into a response based on rules also contained in the relevant list. The association of data points with fixed symbolic expressions and grammatical transformation rules attached to them allows the sequencing to deliver semantically proximate responses in good syntax (ELIZA, 38–39).[24] Figure 1, taken from Weizenbaum's initial exposition of ELIZA, is a diagram of the tree structure of the lists, with K representing a single key. Figure 2 is a relatively complete flowchart of the operation of the program.

Weizenbaum notes that each line in the diagram in Figure 1 is a list, as is each node. The decomposition and transformation rules are also contained as data lists (or vectors) in the lowest row in the figure. Lists of this sort can have any number of data points added to them, meaning that any number of desired rules can be added. The dimensions of these lists are potentially unlimited, with minimal programming friction (ELIZA, 38). Weizenbaum writes that

> keywords and their associated transformation rules constitute the SCRIPT
> for a particular class of conversation. An important property of ELIZA is that
> a script is data; i.e., it is not part of the program itself. Hence, ELIZA is not
> restricted to a particular set of recognition patterns or responses, indeed not
> even to any specific language. ELIZA scripts exist (at this writing) in Welsh
> and German as well as in English. (ELIZA, 37)

24. Weizenbaum notes that he is using "transformation" in the sense given to that term by Noam Chomsky.

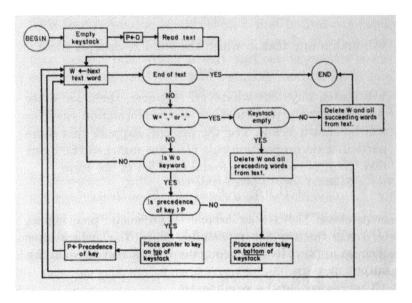

Figure 2. Basic flow diagram of keyword detection.

In other words, the lists form subroutines based on previous input. A large collection of such lists is called a "script," such as the DOCTOR program. DOCTOR's lists are, of course, tied to the symbolic expressions it is dealing with, but because the symbols and the functions are listed as data, DOCTOR can be reset to recognize different patterns, including different languages, always obeying the flowchart in figure 2.

LISP was created by John McCarthy and a team of MIT researchers. It belongs to the first generation of symbolic programming languages, and it was created for use in artificial intelligence research, where it was immediately clear that symbolic expression would be crucial. Using Alonzo Church's "lambda-calculus," McCarthy created a language in which the representation took the form of lists. The lists store symbolic expressions, which McCarthy defines as "an ordered pair, the terms of which may be atomic symbols or simpler s-expressions."[25] This intentionally circular definition simply means that any list contains instructions and data, both the terms—in ELIZA, words— and the rules for manipulating those terms. Whenever a command comes in, the program searches the lists for relevant keys and immediately decomposes and reassembles those keys for output. McCarthy designed LISP program-

25. McCarthy, "LISP Programming System."

ming to contain not only s-expressions and atomic elements but also "associations" stored in the bit structure of the lists. This allows items like the *print name* ("the string of letters and digits which represents the symbol outside the machine") to be stably associated with the list.[26] For ELIZA, this means that the keys can be mutually cross-referenced for responses as meaningful as "can you think of anybody in particular?"

LISP languages, and programs implemented in them like ELIZA, exploit a principle of the hardware design that allowed computers to run software in the first place. In creating the now canonical stored-program computer, John von Neumann and his team combined what had usually been two units, one for programs and one for data, into one. This necessitated an "active" memory in which the data and the instructions could interact and the results could be registered. There is one type of input, not two, making the computer programmable, in the sense that the relationship between instructions and data can be reset without restructuring the hardware.[27] LISP mimics this feature. One type of input is treated as two—atomic elements and s-expressions—giving wide flexibility to the language, a potentially "infinite dimensionality," as Weizenbaum had put it. These features in both hardware and program design are intimately tied to the "Turing universality" of computers, their ability to compute any computable number. Turing's theory of computation implies that there must be in intelligence the ability to treat rules and data as a *single* type of entity, but *also* the ability to disaggregate instructions from "atomic" items (data). In other words, for linguistic applications as for computation in general, computation must be both unified and divided. In the computer, a tiny interval of time registers that the unification is never complete but instead intermittent. The computer, and the language, must distinguish the program and the data in discrete steps. But when the program is run on the data, the result must be *represented* as unified, *as* the result of a single process—in a symbol. If it is not, then no answer can be given in human-readable form. This is what makes the exchange "generically rhetorical" for Blumenberg. Whether the program is intelligent or not, it mechanically presents the same results as intelligence does: symbols or words. Words seem to reconcile data and program, simulating intelligence. And intelligence, Blumenberg argues, looks a lot like simulated intelligence in the first place.

Human consciousness reconciles two heterogeneous inputs too, and like the computer, it has at best partial control over the timing of the reconciliation.

26. McCarthy, "LISP Programming System." My summary here also reflects McCarthy, "LISP Session."

27. See Dyson's magisterial *Turing's Cathedral*.

"The Phenomenologist Can Only Correct Himself" presents consciousness as an "organ" that both constitutes and "restitutes" itself.[28] Having desultory—or intermittent—contact with the world forces this consciousness to "idealize" experience and exaggerate it (Blumenberg here makes a pun on the German *übertreiben*, which literally means "to drive over," almost "to put into overdrive"). The result is neither a closed nor a truly open system but one that opens periodically, and not on its own terms, to adjust for survival. Adjustment of this sort resists the purity of the phenomenological reduction: "The products of consciousness corresponding to 'purity' are standardized medications for the 'accidents' that consciousness must suffer in the performance of intentionality, since if it had perfect programming it would be free of disappointment, but also, unable to have any experience at all, it would be delivered helpless up to every change in reality."[29] The paradox is both classical and digital. The output of consciousness to itself—the content of our experience that we can reflect on—*appears* transparent. If our cognitive efforts, or achievements (*Leistungen*, "performances"), did not seem to harbor their own genesis, to be clear and distinct all the way down, then consciousness would be opaque to itself—a sort of internal contradiction. Yet if consciousness really possessed this self-transparency all the way down, then the world would come to us only as accident, chaos, or perhaps not even at all. The system must be both closed and open to appear as it does. Blumenberg introduces ELIZA into the fragment for this precise reason.

The impasse about consciousness resembles the data-program framework. Experience appears to present us with "atomic" elements, perceptions, and symbolic "reflections" of the former. When we reflect on any mental content, we present it to ourselves as atomic, but the presentation itself is reflective. Anything I can claim to know must have both of these features. Blumenberg compares this issue to Kant's "transcendental deduction," which famously argues that consciousness of objects *is* self-consciousness, since we are able (and must be able) to append an "I think" before any mental content. Both Kant and Husserl begin from the premise that the "atomic" elements in consciousness cannot simply be ascribed to an "outside" world. What we present to ourselves is content *in reflection*, not pure content. And we can, like the LISP language, present reflection (or the results of reflection) as content (s-statements can contain other s-statements). In fact, this metareflective capacity is at the root of the ability to reflect in the first place. Data and perception can be

28. Dyson, *Turing's Cathedral*, 19.
29. Dyson, *Turing's Cathedral*, 21.

curated, forced to give consistent answers to systematically posed questions, but they give no answers freely, and therefore no warrant to describe consciousness, intelligence, or even computation from the outside.

Blumenberg uses this epistemological paradox, which he presents as the essence of philosophical modernity, to reject the phenomenological approach. The subject's "unity" is merely "given presumptively in every phenomenological act of intuition [*Anschauungsakt*]." The assumption is rooted in the self-transparency of consciousness, but Blumenberg argues that this does not justify the premise that consciousness can be described from within: "Descriptively this is a copout." The *appearance* of transparency—our security in knowing that we are thinking what we are thinking—does not constitute a meta-awareness of ourselves as conscious beings: "The subject *exhausts itself* in its immediate act of experience, and even if it had a mirror, it would not be able to watch itself in this act." There are states of synthesis and states of "accident" or adjustment, but there is no account of the difference between these states. Blumenberg writes:

> The only plausible solution for me is a schematic one, that of intermittency. The subject *interrupts itself* in reflecting, to add just as immediately the act of reflection to its already immediate affectedness [*Affektion*], such that in the same dimension two discrete, but with respect to each other strictly homogeneous experience-sequences [*Erlebnisreihen*] arise: that of perception and that of reflection. It is the same identical subject that switches over between these sequences and can do this without break in its felicity [*Seligkeit*]. Intermittency is no mechanical interjection. It is genuinely something like the *testing* of impressions to see if they are commensurate with one another, the homogenization of the *stream of consciousness*. (DP, 42–43)

Affection and reflection form two homogeneous sequences that are nevertheless permanently discrete. The one must interrupt the other for there to be experience at all. Data and program are also homogenized in algorithmic execution, providing procedural but not epistemic certainty. Because consciousness can treat its own products as experience, it appears to be genetically self-transparent, leading to the phenomenological method. But ELIZA shows us otherwise. In imitating one crucial feature of intelligence—the ability to present the results of experience (or computation) as more data—Weizenbaum's bot definitively proves that reflection's capacity does *not* extend to a proof of contact with the world, since we know where ELIZA's data come from. Weizenbaum himself acts as a mechanical check on the system. And his inability to intervene, to show his secretary that she is not having a "real" dialogue, shows Blumenberg what is missing from nonartificial intelligence. Intermittency is not a mechanical check; it does not allow us to know how things are going with our knowledge of the world. It merely allows us to check whether the homogeneous space of synthesis in which affection and reflection are combined is commensurate with *whatever* we get from the intermittent opening of the system of consciousness. We can introduce as much regularity as we want, but we can never create an architect for our own intelligence. We are like a digital program, not as a powerful symbol-processing machine, but as an artifact participating in the rhetorical production of uncertain meaning. It is this move that allows Blumenberg to move beyond the first wave of AI critique.

AI's Situation

Blumenberg was not the first to bring phenomenology into what might seem an unlikely conversation with AI. That distinction probably belongs to the American philosopher Hubert Dreyfus, who wrote throughout the 1960s and 1970s in a deeply skeptical vein about artificial intelligence. The term had been coined only a decade earlier, in the summer of 1955, by a group of early computer scientists, including John McCarthy, at Dartmouth College. Their promise was not exactly modest: in applying for funding, they had claimed that "significant progress" would be made toward the robust imitation of human intelligence by a ten-man team by the end of summer 1956.[30] Dreyfus was hired by the RAND Corporation in 1966 to study the problem, which led to a series of withering philosophical assessments of AI that culminated in his 1972 book, *What Computers Can't Do*. This book brought phenomenology to bear on digital systems, setting the standard—and the limits—of a critique that is still practiced today.

Dreyfus, like Blumenberg, thought that Husserl and AI had similar problems, relying on an "uncritical objectivism" that ignored the embodied, "prerepresentational" context in which humans know.[31] He attacked the picture of intelligence that the early discipline evinced, which relied on formalization as its primary technique (the symbolic closed-system approach described above). Breaking the assumptions down into four areas—biological, psychological, epistemological, and ontological—Dreyfus argued that in every case, proposals for machine intelligence simply missed the mark. Each area of the world was assumed to be digital: the brain was built of binary switches, the psyche

30. McCarthy et al., "Proposal," 1.
31. See the excellent account by Agre, *Computation and Human Experience*, 239.

was built on a type of knowledge that was at base formalizable in symbols. The adequacy of that symbolic knowledge implied that the world—really any object that could be known—could be construed in symbolic form.

Dreyfus was withering in his attacks, suggesting that all human knowledge relies on having a body, demonstrating time and again where implicit and informal rules were too important to allow artificial knowing to take off.[32] He claimed that embodied human intelligence is "being-in-a-situation," a variant on Heidegger's notion of "being-in-the-world." Computers, he wrote, "are not in a situation," giving rise to the problem: "how to program a representation of the computer's environment."[33] Humans, Dreyfus argues, do not apply rules to data. Instead, they select and understand data based on holistic settings, embodied frameworks in which cues count *as* pointing to something. Computers can't do that.[34]

Dreyfus argues that "we never encounter meaningless bits in terms of which we have to identify contexts, but only facts which are already interpreted and which reciprocally define the situation we are in. Human experience is only intelligible when organized in terms of a situation in which relevance and significance are already given."[35] In the "process of living in the world," man becomes the "source of facts . . . a being who creates himself and the world of facts" that "computers can only deal with."[36] Computers operate in a linear fashion on fixed data, which they merely move around. They do not *select* those data. We humans are "always already" in a situation, whereas computers are not in a "situation" at all, which would require the calibration of whole and part to form the context in which we always find ourselves.

And yet these machines relate to humans. Lucy Suchman, a pioneer of the study of "human-machine interaction," seems to follow Weizenbaum's assessment of Eliza when she writes that "the more elaboration or justification is provided, the less the appearance of transparency or self-evidence. The less

---

32. Alan Turing had given the name *the argument from the informality of behavior* to this objection five years before the term *artificial intelligence* was coined, in his influential "Computing Machinery and Intelligence," 452–53.

33. Dreyfus, *What Computers Can't Do*, 211.

34. The usual story line is that Dreyfus contributed to, if he did not cause, the "AI winter," in which GOFAI, or "symbolic AI," hit a wall in terms of the extension of technical capacities and its funding environment. Whether Dreyfus's approach would have anything to say about the recent turn to data-heavy pattern recognition techniques that is known collectively as "deep learning" remains in question. For a recent appraisal that also connects Weizenbaum and Dreyfus, see Gill, "From Judgment to Calculation."

35. Dreyfus, *What Computers Can't Do*, 200.

36. Dreyfus, *What Computers Can't Do*, 202–3.

elaboration there is, the more the recipient will take it that the meaning of what is provided should be obvious."[37] Human-machine interaction relies on the Turing-universal computer's ability to replicate the apparent identity of transparency and obscurity, which is both a characteristic of consciousness (and intelligence) in general, and a crucial feature of rhetoric. Sherry Turkle, another central figure in the study of human-machine interaction, argued that "Eliza prefigured an important element of the contemporary robotics culture in that it was one of the first programs that presented itself as a *relational artifact*, a computational object explicitly designed to engage a user in a relationship."[38] She would go on to describe the deep-fabric relationship that humans developed with computers in the 1980s, which she saw as creating a "greater sense of mutual relating than Eliza" while still having "no greater understanding of the situation of the human being in the relationship."[39] The "rhetorical type" of this interaction would become smoother, removing obstacles to human-machine intimacy.

Weizenbaum was bearish. The "contextual understanding" he and others were aiming at relied heavily on the confusion of "man's capacity to manipulate symbols" with his linguistic capabilities (*CP*, 184). In every interaction, in every train of thought, "data" could become information only "in the light of some hypothesis" (*CP*, 189). The pragmatic element of human-human interaction was anticipatory induction, a type of prediction that involved the unification of rules and data and the reflection of another such combination in the projected mind of the other. Prediction, as he pointed out, had become central to linguistic AI by the late 1960s. Since it is "in his language, above all, that man manifests his intelligence and, some believe, his unique identity as man," it is precisely in the use of language that the human either can or cannot be distinguished from the machine. Weizenbaum thought that Terry Winograd's SHRDLU, among other projects, had made this advance without recognizing that they had accidentally assumed that "the laws of the universe are formalizable in mathematical terms" (*CP*, 197). But as we have seen, algorithms can be set to represent the data-program relationship dynamically. Computers may not be in a self-constituting "situation," in Dreyfus's terms, but they have been inserted into the situation of *human knowledge*. To deny this feature of AI is to draw a nearly dualistic division between machines and humans, one that must fail to make sense of the channels of communication that exist

37. Suchman, *Human-Machine Reconfigurations*, 48.
38. Turkle, "Authenticity," 502.
39. Turkle, "Authenticity," 503. See also Turkle, *Second Self*.

between humans and computers (symbols, words, etc.), these relational, rhetorical artifacts. Now that deep learning systems have proved that they can participate in those channels, any such dualism will severely hamper critique. In separating too cleanly between human situations and digital spaces, we effectively deny the need to explain why artifacts can be "relational" in the first place.

In a note reprinted in facsimile at the end of the *Writings on Technology*, Blumenberg speaks of "consciousness-analogous machines," contrasting them to "producing machines."[40] The first type, he says, produce "irreal objects . . . we call them simulators." These machines, he writes, are already capable of simulating outer space, but "what we need and will have, is not a space simulator, but instead a world-simulator, which doesn't produce objects, but simulates indeed a complete 'world.' This would be a sort of more developed television." This extraordinary passage goes on to predict both virtual reality and the video game, imagining virtual car courses and soccer games. The "orderability" of the world would become entirely preferential, Blumenberg predicts: "Every person gets his favorite world delivered on order into his house." The result is metaphysical, but there is no hint of disapprobation, no sense of loss of some premachinic world. The manuscript reads: "There follows on the unburdening of the human through technology the unburdening of the world itself by ~~technology~~ a perfect variant [*die Entlastung der welt durch ~~Technik~~ perfekte*]." The correction leaves unclear whether technology, the relief it provides, or the world itself has been perfected. Perhaps all three amount to the same thing. By predicting Turkle's "relational artifact," Blumenberg opposed the rigid difference that Dreyfus saw between machines and humans. Machines can be rhetorical. To say that a computer is "not in a situation" is to deny it a place in the all-too-human situation that leads to any technology in the first place.

In acknowledging the human imprint on designed devices, Blumenberg is not subscribing to the so-called extension thesis, which holds that technology is merely the replacement or intensification of human functions.[41] The most influential rejection of that thesis is that of Friedrich Kittler, who suggests that technologies have their own logic, establishing a nonhuman set of a priori conditions.[42] To see technology as extending or replacing human needs or

---

40. Blumenberg, *Schriften zur Technik*, 523. The quotations in the rest of this paragraph all come from this page. Recki, "Auch eine Rehabilitierung der instrumentellen Vernunft," and Zill, "Von der Atommoral zum Zeitgewinn," are illuminating both on this fragment and on the short archival sketch "Automation," which discusses feedback-based machines.

41. This thesis is most often ascribed to Marshall McLuhan and, in a very different way, to Arnold Gehlen. See DP, 39–40.

42. Kittler, *Gramophone*, 117–18.

functions is to miss the vocation of technology altogether.[43] Kittler agrees with Dreyfus, although their views are nearly perfectly opposed: the computer is not in a human situation. Although Blumenberg allows that technologies are partly extensions of anthropological need, he cannot conceive of that need as "human" in the anthropocentric sense. This is because, in the modern era, the human is not a unified "center" at all, lacking in principle the ability to suture together function and goal, means and end—concept and intuition—into a single warrant for truth.[44] Blumenberg's critique of Husserl avoids the dualism of machine and human and provides the basis for a second-wave critique of AI.

Performance and Insight

Blumenberg takes Husserl's notion of a "veil of ideas" that modern technology casts over the world and, undermining the notion that there is any final distinction between the "lifeworld" and the veil supposedly covering it, shows that technology and rhetoric are nearly identical. Both make meaning out of things, replacing a concept of intelligence "purely" gazing on things with a fundamental artificiality in the makeup of meaning. This argument pushes us beyond a critique of AI that is based on questions of authenticity and into a recognition of the reality of the conventions and institutions that AI participates in realizing through symbols and signs. AI critique 2.0, we can begin to see, must be based in semiotic analysis.

Blumenberg proposes that the general "antinomy of technology" is a dialectic between "*performance* and *insight*" (Leistung *und* Einsicht), which the doorbell illustrates. The mechanical models, which one pulls or turns, intimate their function, whether to the eye or to the muscle. The mechanism may be hidden, but we know, even feel, its action. We have achieved a balance between mechanical performance and insight. This is different, Blumenberg tells us, in the case of the push-button doorbell: "The action of the hand is attributed to the effect heteromorphically and without any specificity—we no longer produce the effect, but only trigger it."[45] The disproportion between muscle and machine leaves the effect "available for us, as it were, within the design of the apparatus; indeed, it carefully hides its conditionality and the complexity of its realization from us in order to suggest itself to us as something effortlessly available. . . . Technization makes human actions increasingly unspecific" (PA, 385). When we push a button, it is as though we were using a sign; the

---

43. Kittler, *Eine Kulturgeschichte*, 207–27.
44. See also Oliver Müller's perspicacious essay "Natur und Technik als falsche Antithese."
45. Blumenberg, "Phenomenological Aspects," 385 (hereafter cited as PA).

action is a mere convention. Only once this has occurred can one "accidentally" ring the doorbell of an apartment when one means to turn on the light in the stairwell, a common occurrence in Germany, where the two push buttons are often similar enough to be confused in the dark. This heteromorphic effect continues the conventionalization of execution or function (*Leistung*) that technology introduces in the first place. The apparently innocent electric doorbell has introduced semantic error into the physical world.

Digital technology takes this conventionalization to the semantic extreme. Think of the ability to touch a screen to complete a purchase, or to set off a chain of material events that lead to your being driven to the airport, or to change the temperature in your house from hundreds of miles away. Contrast that type of ability with the use of a pulley. The pulley defers the work of the arm but retains the insight into the work. When you pull the rope, you see the bucket emerge from the well. The pulley illuminates relations of force while producing the result with no adjustment of muscle effort (so long as the pulley works). It thus also *obscures* the relations of force. The electrical machine, on the other hand, presents the action that it really will perform (ringing the bell inside the apartment) as a sign standing in an arbitrary relation to the performance. The button is a convention; the pulley *pulls*. In both of these guises, technization offers undigested performance capacity to the understanding, stripping it of insight and increasing its power. The last vestiges of the technical object's illustration of the physical operation so easily made commensurate with the lifeworld disappears into the electrical wire.

The continuity between mechanical and digital technologies allows Blumenberg to retain the crucial insight of Husserl's account of technology while denying the theoretical distinction between technology and the lifeworld. *The Crisis of European Sciences* had shown that the technology question was an epistemological one, that "technization is a process that takes place in the *theoretical* substrate itself" (PA, 381). Blumenberg sees in Husserl the possibility of this epistemological understanding of technology. But he also sees the distinction between the technical and the lifeworld as too rigid,[46] writing that "technization is the 'transformation of a formation of meaning which was originally vital' into method, which then can be passed on without carrying along the 'meaning of its primal establishment' [*Urstiftungssinn*]" (PA, 381). The self-satisfying intuitive wisdom that subtends the lifeworld is no longer visible in the development of a "mere function." This allows Blumenberg to argue that

---

46. Here I diverge from Hubig, "Es fehlt der letzte Schritt," who depicts a Blumenberg in agreement with Husserl.

"primarily, technology is not a sphere of certain objects resulting from human activity. In its primordiality [*Ursprünglichkeit*], it is a state of human world relation itself" (PA, 381; cf. 399). Husserl's understanding of Galileo both points to the larger problem of technology and—although Blumenberg emphasizes that Husserl tries to avoid it—runs the risk of a theoretical complacency that "demonizes" the technical and allows it to wallow below the level of the concept in philosophy (PA, 382–83). Husserl has a way to prevent this, but does not see it, and so cannot counter the fetishistic popular discourse on technology, which construes it as nothing more than the "constant multiplication and condensation of this thing-world" of technical objects (PA, 361). Technology is not in dialectical tension with nature or spirit but harbors the conflict between performance and insight. The origin of the technical cannot, in this sense, be the phenomenal world of machines (PA, 399), nor can it be some supervening factor that arrives from outside the lifeworld.[47] The lifeworld itself must split from within, "already at the level of intuiting what is given, the relationship between modern man and the world is differentiated" (PA, 359; translation modified). This presents itself neither as pure lifeworld nor as pure technology but instead as rhetoric, as the outgrowth and proliferation of signs, which dialectically combine performance and insight in a process not rooted in any "being," or phenomenological neutrality, to which we could appeal. Blumenberg, in finding this pressure point in Husserl's theory, avoids the type of distinction that guides Weizenbaum and, as I have argued, Dreyfus as well. The technical comes to regulate ("control") the lifeworld (PA, 386–87), reintegrating itself as an "authentic" part of the semantic, embodied situation in which humans find themselves.

Where Dreyfus decried formalization, Blumenberg recognizes it as an integral part of the technical-lifeworld complex. Formalization's roots run deep: it is "nothing but the most handy, most serviceable type of *functionalization* of what has already been achieved once [or performed, *des einmal Geleisteten*]" (PA, 390), providing the basis for the "storage" and "regulated association" of real mechanisms that otherwise operate solely according to the laws of physics (PA, 390; translation modified). Formalization is "what gains its applicability independently of any insight into its actual execution" (PA, 390–91). The formal and the mechanical thus make up a single paradigm, two sides of the insight/performance coin. Any doctrine of method "seeks to create *unreflected repeatability*, a growing foundation of presuppositions that may always be involved but is not always actualized" (PA, 391). But where Husserl sees

47. Blumenberg, *Schriften zur Technik*, 398–99.

loss, Blumenberg sees conversion. The lifeworld, once technicized, becomes a world of conventionally designated meanings, or signs. Where Husserl looks for a "fulfilled intentionality," the complete possession of the object in all its aspects and "keeping-oneself-open for this abundance" (PA, 384), Blumenberg sees the partial possession of effective operational names as itself legitimate. The "inner disposition" of consciousness is to offer these operational results to reason, trading in the "treasury bonds for the assets that they cover" (PA, 384). But as in the autonomous and highly complex financial sphere of this metaphor, there is no final trade-in—value floats in the web of its own complexity. Technization "constantly increase[es] the 'sign values,' the nominal representations, the uncovered bonds" providing a sort of unwarranted ownership (PA, 384). What is "owned" in this metaphor is the performance of ringing the bell (for it is here that Blumenberg introduces this example). The difference between the bell and the hall light is obscured. The world is filled with transparent signs standing for ungrounded processes. The world of the machine is the world of rhetoric.

Rhetoric is, for Blumenberg, the systematization of an "anthropological 'radical'": "Substituting verbal accomplishments for physical ones."[48] The transparency that technization forces on the world—and which also obscures that world—is continuous with the basic semantic operation of communication in general. To indicate to another human, to impress on her or convince her, of anything at all, is to replace physical action with verbal stuff.

Technization is a shortcut from speech or idea to action, crystallizing or setting grooves in the world along which we appear to move with a speed that resists "reflection" (AA, 193–96). The human relation to reality is "indirect, circuitous, delayed, selective, and above all 'metaphorical,'" Blumenberg tells us. Predicates are "institutions," conventions used to fend off the overwhelming demands that reality would place on us if we did not prevent it. But we do not assign predicates to *objects*, grasping something *as* something. Instead we grasp things *through* other things, making up a metaphorical "detour" away from the "object in question" toward some other (AA, 189). In this way we make the object available to ourselves—to see and to use, for insight and manipulation. To judge is to identify; to metaphorize is to make a symbol, something to *replace* something else both semantically and operationally. In this replacement, reality as "nature" gains "rhetorical tincture" (AA, 205). Blumenberg concedes that this tincture may be present in varying amounts—some cultural milieus may make the difference more visible—but

48. Blumenberg, "Anthropological Approach," 187 (hereafter cited as AA).

he insists that in our "highly artificial reality-environment [*Umweltswirklich-keit*]," the drops of rhetoric in our very conception of nature are hard to see precisely because they are ubiquitous. When we say *res, non verba*, we mean "things" that are already free of any purely "natural" sanction. This is why Rüdiger Campe can say that "the question concerning technology for Blumenberg is from now on articulated only through the practice of metaphorology."[49] Metaphor, as the vehicle of rhetoric, illustrates the opacity that remains in every act of consciousness, including the invention and use of consciousness-imitating technologies. Philosophy can only incorporate technology at the appropriate level if it admits, with Kant, who was the "first to deny that inner experience has any priority over external experience," that the human has "no immediate, no purely 'internal' relation" to herself. We are only ever an "appearance" to ourselves (AA, 207).

Consciousness itself contains the tincture of the dialectic between insight and performance, which it shares with rhetoric and technology. Semantic space was always artificial. But if AI can easily slip into the stream of rhetoric, become relational, and even locate itself in a meaningful "situation," then where is the dividing line between artificial and human intelligence? And lacking that division, how can there be a critical standpoint from which to see the rapid development of AI systems?

Blumenberg's Second-Wave Critique of AI

It is not enough to say that AI has entered semantic space today. Deep learning systems permeate visual, economic, and organizational spaces of all kinds. They have become increasingly common, as vast amounts of data are generated both by sensors and by natively digital processes globally.[50] But while these systems are engaged in meaningful interaction and distribution of resources, philosophical critique remains in a highly abstract mode, often limited to considerations of whether and in what sense these algorithms can be said to be "intelligent."[51] Where AI discourse is not hampered by the metaphysics of intelligence, it tends to rely on first-wave critique, elaborating or doubling down on Dreyfus's framework. Blumenberg's short fragment finds some daylight between these positions.

Phenomenology and AI each grasp one side of the split in Copernican consciousness, experience and quantification in their purest forms. And while

---

49. Campe, "From the Theory of Technology," 121.
50. See the wide-ranging account in Bratton, *Stack*.
51. Such critique includes even the most technical philosophical account to date, Buckner, "Empiricism without Magic."

both are resolutely antimetaphysical, both allow the fantasy of absolutely grounded knowledge through a side door, in the "presumptive" unity of the subject in the phenomenological reduction, and in the authentic participation in dialogue in the case of the machine. But legitimacy cannot be grounded, for Blumenberg. Our ability to make the results of reflection into an ongoing factor in experience cannot justify the search for pure objectivity. Likewise, no set of protocols can account for what results when those protocols are set into action. Theory cannot afford to maintain too bright a line between symbol system and application, between reflection and perception. Second-wave AI critique must start from the fact of artificial yet authentic semantic space. The critical judgment, if we follow Blumenberg, cannot be a rear-guard action against algorithms already coconstituting meaning and distributing value and labor, but instead must seek to construct, both practically and theoretically, the world of those artificial semantics. Many routes are available for such a construction—one of them is intermittency.

ELIZA is downstream from the unity of the "consciousness-analog machine" on which it runs. Its tree structure, its visitation of lists from keyword inputs, relies on the homogenization of data and program by means of the switch, on the one hand, and its significance as numbers, on the other. Von Neumann's architecture created this homogenization, running data and program from one bus to the active memory of the machine, where computations occurred. A single medium homogenizes two disparate streams, making each element (data point) both data and (potential) manipulation by program. To know which is which, you need to check, which is exactly what the operating system does to run programs as programs and treat data as data. The same holds true of LISP statements, which consist of s-expressions made up of atomic elements and other s-expressions, homogenized into lists. ELIZA presents, in good grammatical form, the results of computation of symbols in a medium (in two layers, although this picture is obviously simplified). The returned symbols are a symbolic expression that we cannot disaggregate. When the program says "can you think of anybody in particular?" in response to "everybody hates me," the statement may not trigger a scan of people we know to produce a list, but instead a reflection on the assumed hyperbole (or ellipsis: "I feel that" is usually implied in the statement "everybody hates me"). ELIZA has not "grasped" this hyperbole but remains "generically rhetorical" by virtue of the association of symbols. That association is an intermittent process triggered by our speech but presenting itself as symbolic expression. We may suspect that ELIZA does not "understand," but that is not the point. By revealing rather than concealing a lack of linguistic understanding,

ELIZA forces the analysand to confront the nature of rhetoric itself, which in turn pushes us into reflection, itself split between insight and performance. The artifact is "relational" because it presents this dialectic of transparency and obscurity in the medium of symbols.

Intermittency, says Blumenberg, is not a "mechanical interjection" but "genuinely something like the 'testing' [checking] of impressions for their commensurability among each other, the homogenization of the 'stream of consciousness'" (DP, 43). Whatever comes in as input, it must be checked for internal consistency, but this cannot be done according to a single program, "mechanically." We cannot simply "check" our own symbolic expressions— even putatively private ones—either, separating facts from memories, analytic truth from synthetic effects, concepts from contents. If we could, all knowledge would be potentially certain. Artificial intelligence, so far from "achieving" consciousness, apes its lack of transparency. The true analogy of the computer and the mind lies in their mutual limitations, and their reliance on signs as medium.

The intermittency of semantic production, whether organic or technological, must be taken as fundamental to any future critique of AI. The lesson from Blumenberg would be that *correction*, while useful in individual instances, cannot be the ethos of such a critique. True, learning systems often learn the "wrong" thing—but in doing so, they make more semantic stuff, increasing the autonomy of the sphere of signs from whatever they are supposed to refer to. By thickening meaning without securing its referent, they thus do exactly what Blumenberg saw machines in general doing since the early modern period—demonstrating the disproportion between convention and action, performance and insight. Blumenberg himself hewed to a Kantian thought in the face of this most modern problem, arguing for a regulative commitment to the procedural results of science and an orientational tack in the space of reason. But AI undermines this two-track picture, since it uses scientific protocols to intervene in the public process of reasoning itself (rhetoric). But here, too, Blumenberg has given us a clue. Rhetoric, after all, is constituted by those conventional marks that cannot be traded in for their putative underlying values: signs. Blumenberg's achievement is to show us out of the impasse of a transcendental critique that can only ever protest the rapid advance of AI technologies. To go beyond a mere suggestion of what our attitude toward that advance should be, we must follow the line Blumenberg pointed us to but did not himself pursue, that of an account of the semiotics of artificial intelligence. The "veil of symbols" is not a garment that can be removed but the location where action and consciousness, performance and insight, matter and idea, fail to merge, yet constitute legitimacy.

Leif Weatherby teaches at New York University.

References

Agre, Philip. *Computation and Human Experience*. Cambridge: Cambridge University Press, 1997.

Arendt, Hannah. *Crises of the Republic*. New York: Harcourt Brace, 1972.

Arendt, Hannah. "The Modern Concept of History." *Review of Politics* 20, no. 4 (1958): 570–90.

Bajohr, Hannes. "Hans Blumenberg's Early Theory of Technology and History." *Graduate Faculty Philosophy Journal* 40, no. 1 (2019): 3–15.

Blumenberg, Hans. "An Anthropological Approach to the Contemporary Significance of Rhetoric." In Blumenberg, *History, Metaphors, Fables*, 177–208.

Blumenberg, Hans. *Beschreibung des Menschen*. Frankfurt am Main: Suhrkamp, 2006.

Blumenberg, Hans. "Der Phänomenologe kann sich nur selbst berichtigen." In *Zu den Sachen und Zurück*, edited by Manfred Sommer, 19–44. Frankfurt am Main: Suhrkamp, 2002.

Blumenberg, Hans. *Geistesgeschichte der Technik*, edited by Alexander Schmitz and Bernd Stiegler. Frankfurt am Main: Suhrkamp, 2009.

Blumenberg, Hans. *The Genesis of the Copernican World*, translated by Robert M. Wallace. Cambridge, MA: MIT Press, 1987.

Blumenberg, Hans. *History, Metaphors, Fables: A Hans Blumenberg Reader*, edited by Hannes Bajohr, Florian Fuchs, and Joe Paul Kroll. Ithaca, NY: Cornell University Press, 2020.

Blumenberg, Hans. *The Legitimacy of the Modern Age*, translated by Robert M. Wallace. Cambridge, MA: MIT Press, 1999.

Blumenberg, Hans. "Phenomenological Aspects on Life-World and Technization." In Blumenberg, *History, Metaphors, Fables*, 358–99.

Blumenberg, Hans. *Schriften zur Technik*, edited by Alexander Schmitz and Bernd Stiegler. Berlin: Suhrkamp, 2015.

Blumenberg, Hans. "Theory of Nonconceptuality." In Blumenberg, *History, Metaphors, Fables*, 259–97.

Bratton, Benjamin H. *The Stack: On Software and Sovereignty*. Cambridge, MA: MIT Press, 2015.

Buckner, Cameron. "Empiricism without Magic: Transformational Abstraction in Deep Convolutional Neural Networks." *Synthese*, no. 195 (2018): 5339–72.

Campbell-Kelly, Martin, William Aspray, Nathan Ensmenger, and Jeffrey R. Yost. *Computer: A History of the Information Machine*. Boulder, CO: Westview, 2014.

Campbell-Kelly, Martin, and Daniel D. Garcia-Swartz. *From Mainframes to Smartphones: A History of the International Computer Industry*. Cambridge, MA: Harvard University Press, 2015.

Campe, Rüdiger. "From the Theory of Technology to the Technique of Metaphor: Hans Blumenberg's Opening Move." *Qui Parle* 12, no. 1 (2000): 105–26.

Cantwell Smith, Brian. *The Promise of Artificial Intelligence: Reckoning and Judgment.* Cambridge, MA: MIT Press, 2019.

Cardon, Dominique, Jean-Philippe Cointet, and Antoine Mazières. "Neurons Spike Back: The Invention of Inductive Machines and the Artificial Intelligence Controversy." *Réseaux*, no. 211 (2018): 173–220.

Dreyfus, Hubert L. *What Computers Can't Do: The Limits of Artificial Intelligence.* Rev. ed. New York: HarperCollins, 1978.

Dyer-Witheford, Nick, Atle Kjosen, and James Steinhoff. *Inhuman Power: Artificial Intelligence and the Future of Capitalism.* London: Pluto, 2019.

Dyson, George. *Turing's Cathedral: The Origins of the Digital Universe.* New York: Pantheon, 2012.

Erickson, Paul, Judy L. Klein, Lorraine Daston, Rebecca Lemov, Thomas Sturm, and Michael D. Gordin. "Enlightenment Reason, Cold War Rationality, and the Rule of Rules." In *How Reason Almost Lost Its Mind: The Strange Career of Cold War Rationality*, 27–50. Chicago: University of Chicago Press, 2013.

Flasch, Kurt. *Hans Blumenberg, Philosoph in Deutschland: Die Jahre 1945 bis 1966.* Frankfurt am Main: Klostermann, 2017.

Fleming, Paul. "The Perfect Story: Anecdote and Exemplarity in Linnaeus and Blumenberg." *Thesis Eleven*, no. 104 (2011): 72–86.

Gill, Karamjit S. "From Judgment to Calculation: The Phenomenology of Embodied Skill; Celebrating Memories of Hubert Dreyfus and Joseph Weizenbaum." *AI and Society* 34, no. 2 (2019): 165–75.

Haugeland, John. *Artificial Intelligence: The Very Idea.* Cambridge, MA: MIT Press, 1989.

Haverkamp, Anselm. "Die Technik der Rhetorik: Hans Blumenbergs Projekt." In *Ästhetische und metaphorologische Schriften*, by Hans Blumenberg, edited by Anselm Haverkamp, 433–54. Frankfurt am Main: Suhrkamp, 2001.

Heidegger, Martin. "Die Herkunft der Kunst und die Bestimmung des Denkens." In *Denkerfahrungen 1910–1976*, 135–49. Frankfurt am Main: Klostermann, 1985.

High-Speed Computing Devices. 1950. New York: McGraw-Hill.

Hörl, Erich. "Die offene Maschine: Heidegger, Günther und Simondon über die technologische Bedingung." *MLN* 123, no. 3 (2008): 632–55.

Hubig, Christoph. "Es fehlt der letzte Schritt: Lebenswelt, Natur und Technik im Ausgang von Blumenbergs Husserl-Rezeption." *Journal Phänomenologie* 35 (2011): 25–36.

Husserl, Edmund. *Die Krisis der europäischen Wissenschaften und die transzendentale Phänomenologie.* Hamburg: Meiner, 1996.

Kelleher, John H. *Deep Learning.* Cambridge, MA: MIT Press, 2019.

Kittler, Friedrich. *Eine Kulturgeschichte der Kulturwissenschaft.* Munich: Fink, 2001.

Kittler, Friedrich. *Gramophone Film Typewriter*, translated by Geoffrey Winthrop-Young and Michael Wutz. Stanford, CA: Stanford University Press, 1999.

LeCun, Yann, Yoshua Bengio, and Geoffrey Hinton. "Deep Learning." *Nature*, no. 521 (2015): 436–44.

McCarthy, John. "The LISP Programming System." August 13, 2006. www-formal .stanford.edu/jmc/recursive/node4.html#tex2html.

McCarthy, John. "LISP Session." In *History of Programming Languages*, edited by Richard Wexelblat, 173–97. New York: Academic, 1981.

McCarthy, John, M. L. Minsky, N. Rochester, and C. E. Shannon. "A Proposal for the Dartmouth Summer Research Project on Artificial Intelligence." August 31, 1955. jmc.stanford.edu/articles/dartmouth/dartmouth.pdf.

Medina, Eden. *Cybernetic Revolutionaries: Technology and Politics in Allende's Chile.* Cambridge, MA: MIT Press, 2011.

Mende, Dirk. "Histories of Technicization: On the Relation of Conceptual History and Metaphorology in Hans Blumenberg." *Telos*, no. 158 (2012): 159–79.

Mirowski, Philip. *Machine Dreams: Economics Becomes a Cyborg Science.* Cambridge: Cambridge University Press, 2002.

Mirowski, Philip, and Edward Nik-Kah. *The Knowledge We Have Lost in Information: The History of Information in Modern Economics.* Oxford: Oxford University Press, 2017.

Müller, Oliver. "Natur und Technik als falsche Antithese: Die Technikphilosophie Hans Blumenbergs und die Struktur der Technisierung." *Philosophisches Jahrbuch* 115 (2008): 99–124.

Müller-Sievers, Helmut. "Kyklophorology: Hans Blumenberg and the Intellectual History of Technics." *Telos*, no. 158 (2012): 155–70.

Peters, Benjamin. *How Not to Network a Nation: The Uneasy History of the Soviet Internet.* Cambridge, MA: MIT Press, 2016.

Recki, Birgit. "Auch eine Rehabilitierung der instrumentellen Vernunft: Blumenberg über Technik und die kulturelle Natur des Menschen." In *Erinnerung an das Humane: Beiträge zur phänomenologischen Anthropologie Hans Blumenbergs,* edited by Michael Moxter, 39–61. Tübingen: Siebeck, 2011.

Schumm, Marion. "Blumenberg und die Intermittenz des Bewusstseins." In *Permanentes Provisorium: Hans Blumenbergs Umwege,* edited by Michael Heidgen, Matthias Koch, and Christian Köhler, 189–205. Munich: Fink, 2015.

Suchman, Lucy. *Human-Machine Reconfigurations: Plans and Situated Actions.* Cambridge: Cambridge University Press, 2007.

Turing, Alan. "Computing Machinery and Intelligence." *Mind*, no. 236 (1950): 433–60.

Turkle, Sherry. "Authenticity in the Age of Digital Companions." *Interaction Studies: Social Behaviour and Communication in Biological and Artificial Systems* 8, no. 3 (2007): 501–17.

Turkle, Sherry. *The Second Self: Computers and the Human Spirit.* Cambridge, MA: MIT Press, 2004.

Weizenbaum, Joseph. *Computer Power and Human Reason: From Judgment to Calculation.* New York: Freeman, 1976.

Weizenbaum, Joseph. "ELIZA: A Computer Program for the Study of Natural Language Communication between Man and Machine." *Communications of the ACM* 9, no. 1 (1966): 36–45.

Wetters, Kirk. "Working Over Philosophy: Hans Blumenberg's Reformulations of the Absolute." *Telos*, no. 158 (2012): 100–118.

Zill, Rüdiger. "Von der Atommoral zum Zeitgewinn: Transformationen eines Lebensthemas; Hans Blumenbergs Projekt einer Geistesgeschichte der Technik." *Jahrbuch Technikphilosophie* 3 (2017): 291–314.

A Well-Tempered Modernist

Colin Lang

In the Akademie der Künste in West Berlin on April 21, 1966, Hans Blumenberg delivered a lecture on Paul Valéry and his appreciation for the unique intelligence of Leonardo da Vinci and his work: "Paul Valérys möglicher Leonardo da Vinci."[1] The lecture formed part of a series of texts that the philosopher was to devote to the French poet, whom he cites with great frequency in many of his other works. The first Valéry text appears just two years before the Akademie lecture, and it is a characteristically long and difficult read on the idea of the "*objet ambigu*" in Valéry's fictitious Socrates in his dialogue "Eupalinos."[2] In the same year as the delivery of the lecture, 1966, Blumenberg published two more texts in which Valéry and the figure of ambiguity play a critical role: "Speech Situation and Immanent Poetics" and "The Essential Ambiguity of the Aesthetic Object." Together these texts form a concentrated attempt by Blumenberg to address the character and rhetorical complexity of aesthetic

This article, in a very shortened form, was first delivered at the conference "New Approaches to Hans Blumenberg," organized by the Zentrum für Literaturforschung, on October 11, 2019, in Berlin. My thanks to Hannes Bajohr for the invitation and for all the respondents, especially Pini Ifergan, who articulated in his questions what I was at the time unaware of. All translations from the German are mine unless otherwise noted.

1. It is well known to Blumenberg philologists and experts that a different version of a similar text appears in the Blumenberg estate at the Deutsches Literaturarchiv (DLA). No further reference is made to this version, for it in no way represents a dramatic shift from the arguments of the published version of the lecture. My thanks to Dorit Krusche at the DLA for assistance.

2. See Blumenberg, "Socrates and the *Objet Ambigu*," where Blumenberg refers to Valéry's "Eupalinos ou l'architecte."

New German Critique 145, Vol. 49, No. 1, February 2022
DOI 10.1215/0094033X-9439615   © 2022 by New German Critique, Inc.

encounters—works of art in particular.[3] The year 1966 also saw the first edition of Blumenberg's massive study of modernity as an age defined by human self-assertion (*Selbstbehauptung*) and the appearance of productivity,[4] which should be viewed as a related intellectual occupation alongside the philosopher's meditations on modernist art.

The results of this period of activity are mostly without clear examples from the world of art, or the sense that Blumenberg is comfortable in a terrain of the visually, and not linguistically, oriented art forms.[5] Valéry at times feels like a crutch, an interlocutor whom Blumenberg trusts to take him through the unchartered waters of art—his Virgil, so to speak.

Blumenberg states at the outset of his lecture that it is concerned with "a theory of the possibility of understanding [*eine Theorie der möglichkeit des Verstehens*] in history and across the centuries."[6] Blumenberg continues by instructing his listeners that this is precisely what Valéry was on the path to recovering in his many treatises on the Renaissance polymath, which began with "Note et digression" in 1919 and continued until 1933. There Blumenberg points to the French poet's own formulation of "Le Possible d'un Léonard," which then serves as the titular point of entry for Blumenberg's talk. This possibility is what occasions Valéry's analysis of an artist who constructs out of history, not returning to it as origin or merely imitating it as nature. Blumenberg identifies Valéry's exemplary treatment of Leonardo in the broader context of attempts to establish history as such at a crucial moment that was for both the French poet and Blumenberg "the transformation of historical understanding in an aesthetic process"[7]—illustrative of a new conception of history

---

3. For useful discussions of Blumenberg's work on Valéry, see Krauthausen, "Hans Blumenbergs präparierter Valéry"; Krauthausen, "Hans Blumenbergs möglicher Valéry"; Koch, "Valéry, Blumenberg und die Phänomenologie der Geschichte"; and Ralf Konersmann, "Stoff für Zweifel." See also the reflections of Blumenberg's colleague, Hans Robert Jauss, in "Eine doppelte Konjunktur."

4. Blumenberg, *Die Legitimität der Neuzeit*. This is of course confounded with the fact that in German the adjective *modern* refers to both modernity and modernism.

5. For a stimulating and very different discussion of Blumenberg's relationship to images, see Heidenreich, "Porträtsammlung und Bilderverbot," esp. 24–27. Heidenreich's focus, as the volume in which his text appears attests, is *Bildwissenschaft*, which maintains an ambiguous position on works of art. Whether Blumenberg shared this ambivalence is another question, though, given his few references to the work of Aby Warburg, the terms of these art-historical investigations could not have been completely unknown to the philosopher. From Blumenberg's reticence when it came to the history of art, one can point to at least one further point of reference (other than Warburg): the work of the pre-Columbian art historian George Kubler, whose most methodologically searching work, *The Shape of Time*, was translated into German by Blumenberg's daughter, the art historian Bettina Blumenberg, as *Die Form der Zeit*. Unfortunately, there are no references to Kubler's work in the Blumenberg estate. My thanks to Dorit Krusche for assistance.

6. Blumenberg, "Paul Valérys möglicher Leonardo," 194.

7. Blumenberg, "Paul Valérys möglicher Leonardo," 197.

in the modern era. In the most simplistic terms, this is the deepest connection to Blumenberg's work in the sprawling *Legitimacy* volume published in the same year as the Akademie lecture. The context—in an art school, in the lecture series "Boundaries and Convergences of the Arts" ("Grenzen und Konvergenzen der Künste")—is key, and the language, rhetorical figures, and descriptions that Blumenberg chooses offer another "possibility" here: that of comparison to other texts around 1966.

For Blumenberg, the historical distance between Valéry and Leonardo opens this space of "the possible," one actualized in the experience of the Renaissance master's work in the context of nineteenth-century Paris. Distance is foundational: when we see a work of art, it is almost always the result of a production that predates the viewing of that individual piece, though this does not mean that we are discovering some essential quality of the work that it originally intended. This would be to ignore the constructedness of the work in question, which must be preserved and left open for the experience of this work at another point, often far removed from when it was originally conceived. This may sound like a hinderance to interpretation, but Blumenberg finds two aspects simultaneously exemplary in Valéry's work on Leonardo: Leonardo was a model modern artist, and Valéry was a model modern interpreter. Blumenberg says of Valéry's characterizations of Leonardo that "he describes a modern experience of the work of art and discovers its *possibility* at a stage of aesthetic reflection that permits this experience but does not intend it."[8] This is what Blumenberg set out to prove in his lecture—the paragon of the possible, in both Valéry and Leonardo—to pick up the strand in Valéry that seemed to "permit" his reading of the poet's work in 1966.

What is present in the Akademie lecture is the figure of the possible, which courses through Leonardo and the epochal shift to modernity as an age of self-determination, discovered in the work of a modern poet—a field of resonances that connects these otherwise historically disparate figures (Leonardo, Valéry, Blumenberg). What can be gleaned are two fundamental preoccupations that Blumenberg returns to throughout his career: the figure of distance and the concept of self-assertion.[9] The latter is harder to determine or make

8. Blumenberg, "Paul Valérys möglicher Leonardo," 220. The original reads: "Er beschreibt eine moderne Erfahrung des Kunstwerkes und entdeckt ihre Möglichkeit auf einer Stufe der ästhetischen Reflexion, die diese Erfahrung zwar zulässt, aber nicht intendiert." My emphasis.

9. One need merely consider the language used in what is likely Blumenberg's most-cited book, whose second part is titled "Theological Absolutism and Human Self-Assertion" ("Theologischer Absolutismus und humane Selbstbehauptung"). See Robert M. Wallace's splendid translation, *The Legitimacy of the Modern Age.*

clear in its connection to Blumenberg's contemporaneous work on modernity. For self-assertion is not exactly self-awareness, which forms part of the focus of the scattered musings on art and the aesthetic in these texts. Distance, on the other hand, was a leitmotif in much of what Blumenberg wrote and seemed to believe in. Beginning with his professorial dissertation in 1950 until the publication of *Lebenszeit und Weltzeit* in 1986 (basically, the philosopher's entire intellectual career), distance in this cluster of writings should be understood both phenomenologically *and* historically—at times, one through the other. That is, phenomenologically speaking, distance is the prerequisite for the aesthetic encounter—that whatever we see is not coextensive with us—and thereby creates the foundational conditions under which we see or experience, tout court. According to Blumenberg, this distance can be one of space or of time.[10]

Two points are worth noting in Blumenberg's reading. One, Valéry's experience is unquestionably a modern one. The French modernist never pretends or "intends" to close the distance between himself and the Renaissance polymath, nor does the work that Valéry sees "intend" to be read by someone else, at another time. Second, a distinction is hinted at, but never explicitly made by Blumenberg, between the work of art and the experience of that work. Without assuming too much about Blumenberg's theory of the artwork (as far as I know, no such definition is ever concretely formulated), it is clear that the experiential as such plays a less important role than the possibility that such works of art allow or occasion. Blumenberg, in other words, does not dive head first into a theory of reception, as does his colleague Hans Robert Jauss, who shared a similar fascination with Valéry and even cotaught a seminar with Blumenberg on the poet in 1962, which Jauss credited for having spawned his research on reception.[11] If aesthetics in this limited case of Valéry and Leonardo names the experience in conjunction with a specific work—what that work in question elicits or engenders—then what Blumenberg offers is a theory of the artwork in which the said work "permits" an "experience but does not intend it," creating at least the mental "distance" between experience and thing/object/artwork. The clear distinction between what a work of art allows (occasions to be experienced) and what it intends is undertheorized in the limited glosses on this text.[12] Often, aesthetics and art are elided, even though this sentence makes clear that Blumenberg is all too aware that they are not one and the same.

10. Blumenberg, *Care Crosses the River*, 11.
11. Krauthausen, "Hans Blumenbergs möglicher Valéry," 42–43.
12. See n. 3.

In what follows, I attempt to characterize Blumenberg's theory of the artwork in these unique years of activity on the subject as "modernist," both for the reliance of those years on Valéry and for their resonances with contemporaneous formulations of modernism in the United States in art criticism. The connection becomes even clearer by putting Blumenberg's Valéry lecture alongside comments he offered about artworks as the respondent to two papers delivered at a meeting of the Poetik und Hermeneutik research group that he cofounded. There as well, also in 1966, we witness a direct encounter with modernism whose terms and judgments are nearly identical to those of Clement Greenberg, and Michael Fried, in particular, at a moment that, for many, signaled not the height of the modernist project but its decadent decline into dogma.[13] Nevertheless, the literature in both English and German on this moment is vast, and it is not my concern to take issue with, or defend, the conclusions that were critical of Greenberg and Fried, including those made by artists and their works around 1966. Rather, I offer a glimpse of how such a reading of Blumenberg is made "possible" by a deviation[14] into contemporaneous thinking on modernism that is occasioned by Blumenberg's lecture delivered on another writer's excursus on the example of Leonardo, a figure of singular artistic merit. The mere existence of Fried's and Greenberg's modernisms (to be fair, they have their differences) is my focus, not a historical meditation on the failures or potential problems of these leading voices of American art criticism around 1966, who subsequently served as a critical catalyst for much different, more nuanced, takes on the art of the present in the United States. As I hope to show, the very notion of Blumenberg's modernism is

13. The literature here is indeed cumbersome and, one could argue, fundamental for the discipline of art history in the United States and Germany. *October*, the highly influential American journal for art, criticism, and theory, was founded out of this debate. The weight of this criticism of Greenberg and Fried is not evidence of its success or need for improvement; that is a matter of interpretation. Suffice it to say that 1966 was an important year for American art criticism and for its verdict on the continued merits of the project of modernist painting and sculpture outlined by Greenberg, Fried, and its most significant critic, Rosalind Krauss (cofounder of *October*).

14. The German term is *Abweichung*, a reference to Adorno's "Valérys Abweichungen" (1960), the second of two texts on Valéry in the years predating Blumenberg's lecture; the other is "Valéry Proust Museum" (1953, trans. 1981). Both deal with a comparison between the French poet and Marcel Proust. That Blumenberg was aware of these texts is a fair assumption, given Adorno's reputation, though these texts are never cited in Blumenberg's Valéry lecture. Adorno's own temperament is certainly one that Blumenberg did not share, as evidenced by his near total omission of the language of political economy through his oeuvre. For Blumenberg's odd fit within the landscape of postwar German theory, see Fleming, *"Verfehlungen,"* and Jay, "Against Rigor," which address Blumenberg specifically, though their approaches are less speculative than the present article. I am indebted to the work of many who have opened up the possibilities of reading Blumenberg in this way.

more specific than the recourse to this term might lead some to believe, and borrows much of what Theodor W. Adorno called the conservativism in Valéry's thinking on art. The term *well-tempered modernist* is a quotation from Valéry's *Pièces sur l'art* (1934), where he describes "un modernisme bien tempéré"[15] to disparage the Salon painters of the 1880s, whose historicist tableaux he saw as reactionary to the achievements of Manet and his generation. The difference in my use is that it is meant to describe a latent, even ambivalent, modernism for a philosopher (Blumenberg) who was concerned more with medieval philosophy than with contemporary art.

––––––––

What informs Blumenberg's encounter with the aesthetic, and with Valéry more closely, is anathema to much of what one might call the aesthetic today. For in distance, Blumenberg privileges the rhetorical separation that is a prerequisite—a foundational condition—for any encounter with the work of art or other "aesthetic" object. In other words, the shudder of the experiential, the close encounter with the artwork, is not high on the list. Not by a long shot. The investigation and articulation of distance go all the way back to Blumenberg's habilitation, "The Ontological Distance: An Investigation into the Crisis of Husserl's Phenomenology," accepted in 1950.[16] And while distance courses through Blumenberg's corpus, I contend that what informs the earliest work on distance in the late 1940s returns with typical acumen and investigative depth in the much-overlooked volume *Lebenszeit und Weltzeit*.[17] In that work it is clear that the historical distance that seems a perquisite for the modern, or *modernist*, nature of Valéry's encounter takes giant steps into a fundamental temporal structure of the world, one in which world-time (*Weltzeit*) and the lived time of one's experience (*Lebenszeit*) are forever separated, distanced. Though it is never referenced by Blumenberg explicitly, there is a tacit agree-

15. Valéry, "More Obiter Dicta."
16. See n. 3. The literature on distance is vast, and the term appears with such frequency in Blumenberg's oeuvre that it would take many pages to cite the relevant references. The first serious study and engagement with distance occurs in Blumenberg's *Habilitationsschrift*, "Die ontologische Distanz." The crux of Blumenberg's investigation of distance is here more phenomenologically determined, while a later version of distance as *actio per distans* reflects a greater engagement with distance as anthropological. See the posthumously assembled volume Blumenberg, *Beschreibung des Menschen*, esp. 508, 632.
17. Blumenberg, *Lebenszeit und Weltzeit*. One argument, which has seemed to go unnoticed or, at the very least, undertheorized, is that the work in this book continues a line of thinking first opened in the professorial dissertation over three decades earlier.

ment with Adorno's comparison of Valéry and Marcel Proust in his "Valéry Proust Museum" from 1953, where Adorno detects a current of Henri Bergson in Proust's acceptance of the museal condition of artworks and the experiences they engender: "The primacy Proust assigns the flux of experience and his refusal to tolerate anything fixed or determinate have a sinister aspect— conformity, the ready adjustment to changing situations he shares with Bergson."[18] Blumenberg's 1966 lecture on Valéry took place in front of dignitaries from the arts and politics—not in a museum—a more suitable environment for a discussion of the French poet, who was no fan of the modern cult of the museum.

Though Adorno opposes the sensibility of Valéry and Proust, the specter of Bergson and vitalism plays a pivotal role in both, and despite Valéry's work devoted to the French philosopher, Adorno finds more of the "sinister" elements hinted at in Proust's openness to experiential fluidity. Without delving too deeply into Adorno's model, I would argue that both he and Blumenberg shared a similar postwar distrust of the outcomes of *Lebensphilosophie*, specifically its fascist realities in the 1930s and 1940s. Blumenberg's phenomenological privileging of distance is set directly against what Adorno had termed "sinister" in Bergson. Adorno anticipates Blumenberg when he concludes in his "Valéry Proust Museum" that "it is only when the distance is established between the observer and works of art that the question of their continuing vitality can arise."[19]

To say this more explicitly, I propose that the crux of *Lebenszeit und Weltzeit* makes the case against Bergson even more damning, without putting the blame solely on vitalism. In one section of the book, Blumenberg argues that at the core of the National Socialist ideology was a "madness" (*Wahn*) that attempted a congruency between lived time and world-time.[20] Blumenberg's crucial theorization of distance is hinted at in the Akademie lecture and then made more explicit without reference to art in the 1986 volume.

———

For many familiar with Blumenberg, the aesthetic in the context of artworks is a rare find, and the theories, when disclosed, are significantly less convincing and worked out than other areas of the philosopher's works. This makes the

18. Adorno, "Valéry Proust Museum," 183.
19. Adorno, "Valéry Proust Museum," 179.
20. Blumenberg, "Die Kongruenz von Lebenszeit und Weltzeit als Wahn."

constellation of texts in question such an aberrant but nevertheless meaningful blip in Blumenberg's corpus, and one wonders what it was between 1964 and 1966 that caused such a flurry of activity on a discipline that does not occur with the same breadth and erudition as, say, myth or metaphor in the philosopher's better-known output. One feels Blumenberg wrestling with the demands of his subject—art—which is rerouted time and again through the figure of Valéry in these years.[21] Blumenberg is clearly at pains in his lecture to describe how Valéry, in his appreciation of Leonardo, could actualize the Renaissance figure, make him "contemporary" or, at the very least, modern. Blumenberg is fully aware that, if Valéry is to be taken as a model in his lecture, it is partly based on the "possible" or possibility of Leonardo in the present—hence the *möglicher* in the lecture's title—as well as the desire and phenomenological drive to put Leonardo in dialogue with the French poet at the time of his reading.

In his lecture Blumenberg offers a close reading of Valéry's essays on Leonardo. He is mainly preoccupied with reconstructing the method Valéry employs in his approach to the historical figure as part of a "theory of the possibility of historical understanding." This method consists in forgoing any recourse to actual historical or biographical data and instead aims at finding "the inner law" of Leonardo, that is, to reconstruct the conditions of the possibility of Leonardo to appear historically. Blumenberg turning to Valéry's wish for a "possible Leonardo" is thus thoroughly modern in at least two senses. First, Leonardo is, for Blumenberg, the epitome of the self-asserting modern championed as "exemplary" in the *Legitimacy* volume,[22] and so Valéry turns out to be not just a crutch but also a confirmation of the modernness of the Renaissance figure. Second, Blumenberg highlights the historical constructedness of Leonardo for Valéry, which itself also turns out to be exemplary, for it relies on a connection founded on the possibility of such a figure, as opposed to

---

21. The anecdotal evidence suggests a more sustained interest in art, exhibitions, and so on. See the reflections of Blumenberg's daughter about having made a few treks in the summer of 1962 to a Paul Klee exhibition in Baden-Baden, and a Francis Bacon retrospective at the Kunsthalle Mannheim as well, in Blumenberg, "Eine Frage der Belichtung."

22. "On the threshold of this century, an exemplary figure of the daring interest in what is remote, out of the way, unexamined, or traditionally prohibited was Leonardo da Vinci (1452–1519). His interest in the playfully varying nature that neither commits itself to its forms nor exhausts them, an interest in what had hitherto remained invisible to the onlooker at the world spectacle, in what was hidden deep in the sea and distant in time in a world that was growing older, and in the realm of the unrealized possibilities of nature and of human invention—all this is pure, as though crystallized, *curiositas*, which enjoys itself even when it stops short of its object at the last moment and leaves it alone" (Blumenberg, *Legitimacy of the Modern Age*, 363).

an open-ended experiential, empathic relationship to the artist. This is where an overtly aesthetic approach to Blumenberg's preoccupation with Valéry in these years would necessarily fall short of seeing the concentration on possibility not as an effect of the artwork but as its motivational force. There is nothing in the Blumenberg literature from the mid-1960s that would suggest anything less than an attempt to wrestle with the foundational questions driving an artist to make something whatsoever.

In other words, Blumenberg cannot, and certainly does not, pretend to erase his own position between Valéry and Leonardo, which leaves the question of Blumenberg's direct art context hanging as he delivers his lecture in the auditorium of an institution devoted to art. What works or theories of the art object were foundational, influential, for his philosophy, if any?[23] The historical distance that Blumenberg treats with such care is here a kind of lingering question, one that is not provided in the Blumenberg estate in Marbach but that I intend to make something *möglich* out of nonetheless.

I propose that Blumenberg supports his own view of modernism through his reading of Valéry. This might sit poorly both with those who reject a brief look at this short period of Blumenberg's activity and with those who have a more troubled relationship with the term *modernism*, especially as it pertains to the visual arts in the mid-1960s. For many, 1966 was already a twilight of those ambitions gathered under the label of high modernism, at least as far as the narrative is concerned in the US context, though there have been considerable afterlives of that narrative in the German one as well.[24] There is no real

23. The references to art history are scant, though that does not necessarily entail that Blumenberg was not thinking about the complex structure of modernist practice, even if it was more textual than visual for the philosopher. At the risk of assuming a hesitation or resistance to engage with the contemporary discourse on modernism in the visual arts, a lecture at an art academy was certainly occasion to do so. The fact that Blumenberg's rhetorical move is to make something modern out of the modernist Valéry is telling. For Valéry's importance to both Blumenberg and the early formation of Poetik und Hermeneutik, see Amslinger, *Eine neue Form von Akademie*, esp. chap. 6, "Valéry und die Vieldeutigkeiten." Amslinger references a text by a former student of Blumenberg who describes Valéry as "an exemplary author" for Blumenberg (173).

24. Clement Greenberg and his "formalist" criticism were a lightning rod in Germany, as elsewhere, well into the ensuing decades. In the western European context, both the French journal *Macula* (1976–79) and the German magazine *Texte zur Kunst* (1990 to the present) featured Greenberg as a model of art criticism, whether that was to be rejected, embraced, or something in between. According to Isabelle Graw: "The modernist aesthetic judgment is based solely on 'immanent' features of the work, and pays the price for this with a high amount of arbitrariness, subjectivity, and violence. And it leaves out other factors, like concrete historical conditions or unwritten laws of the art world that help explain the gestalt or materiality of an artwork. In fact, a similar type of aesthetic judgment was widespread among German critics at the end of the '80s; the magazine *Texte zur Kunst* (which I founded with Stefan Germer in 1990) was directed against this. We wanted an art criticism that didn't take the

evidence to suggest, in the archive or elsewhere, that Blumenberg was aware of the modernist debates raging in New York during the mid-1960s. The names Clement Greenberg, Rosalind Krauss, Michael Fried, and others tied to this moment are never mentioned. I would propose, therefore, that this does not deny a potential historical conjuncture between Blumenberg's lecture and the terms of modernist art criticism in the United States; on the contrary, such a conjuncture is made "possible" by Blumenberg's reading of Valéry's modern Leonardo, in the context of a lecture in an art academy in West Berlin in 1966, by implying that Blumenberg should be understood in dialogue with a discourse in art criticism that produced powerful, if highly contested, definitions of modernism in the visual arts in the United States.

The year 1966 was a watershed for serious artistic practice in New York, which saw the emergence of movements and forms that strove to displace modernism as championed by critics like Greenberg and Fried. Whether climax or apogee, Fried specifically made a stand against some of the newer artistic developments that challenged the tenets of modernist painting and sculpture. Fried and Blumenberg were unaware of each other, but the affinities are nevertheless clear on the terms of Fried's critique of minimalism and its challenge to modernist principles, founded largely on the question of time, and the anxiety that the divide between the time in which a work existed and the time in which it was experienced was blurring and threatened to descend into what Fried referred to as "theatricality."

A second, if related, claim is that the period of activity under investigation here did not end because the subject of art and aesthetics was not highlighted explicitly by Blumenberg. What I mean by a modernist sensibility is the recognition of the irrevocable, ineliminable divide between the time in which one experiences something like a work of art and the time in which that work of art first came into being and continues to exist in the present: in other words, its self-assertiveness.

––––––––

What I want to turn to first is the second thread in Blumenberg's 1966 lecture that I highlighted above: the investigation of modes of self-consciousness, self-

aesthetic experience for granted, which reflected its preconditions and renegotiated the borders between the work and its context. Nevertheless, we put a portrait of Clement Greenberg on the first cover, because we still considered him (and especially his early texts) a valuable starting point for rigorous analysis" (Bois et al., "Mourning After," 70).

reflexivity, as a way to describe formal integrity in these earliest Valéry texts. What one hears in much of this writing is a typical vexation with the forces of history, a paragon of modernism. Here is Blumenberg, again from the Akademie lecture: "History no longer nourishes the spirit as a reliable substance, but it irritates it, frightens it, unsettles it precisely as the past."[25]

Indeed, the tone here is also striking for the antagonism it shows toward history as inheritance or mere "substance." Perhaps Blumenberg is thinking of Ernst Cassirer's work *Substanzbegriff und Funktionsbegriff*,[26] but the notion of history as an active, "unsettling" force also underlies much thinking about "how modernism works," as Fried once put it.[27] In a published text for Poetik und Hermeneutik that appeared in the same year as the Akademie lecture, "Speech Situation and Immanent Poetics"—a text whose very title is a German translation of Valéry's *condition verbale* quoted in the text's epigraph— Blumenberg similarly asserts that "history as an ominous, oppressive experience is a modern phenomenon."[28] The entire volume in which "Speech Situation" appears is devoted to poetry as the paradigm of modernity. Of course, the German adjective *modern* is used to denote something both modern *and* modernist; which one is meant depends on the context. Blumenberg was concentrated on a question of modernist form—a *condition verbale*—as he tackled the French poet's modernist encounter with the artist Leonardo, which is something quite other than, or more than, linguistic form.

Later in the lecture, as his thinking on Valéry's thoroughly modern Leonardo becomes clearer, Blumenberg stunningly claims that what the poet is doing, writing about Leonardo, is not just exemplary for the dialogue between poet and artist, at some great historical remove. Blumenberg actually uses this historical encounter between Valéry and Leonardo to make more sweeping conclusions about the very nature of modern perspective—not the perspective represented in a work of art but the one in the work of interpretation vis-à-vis history more generally. Blumenberg calls it *Kritik*, a term that carries less weight in his larger projects. Here is Blumenberg as he moves into more wholesale conclusions about the value of Valéry's untimely appreciation of the old

25. Blumenberg, "Paul Valérys möglicher Leonardo," 198. The original reads: "Die Geschichte nährt den Geist nicht mehr als verlässliche Substanz, sondern sie reizt ihn, schreckt ihn auf, verunsichert ihn gerade als Vergangenheit."

26. Additionally, Blumenberg mentions Cassirer's volume explicitly in the lecture that he delivered on being awarded the Kuno Fischer Prize in 1974 (in the present issue). For the relevance of Cassirer's work to Blumenberg, see Pavesich, "Hans Blumenberg's Philosophical Anthropology."

27. Fried, "How Modernism Works."

28. Blumenberg, "Speech Situation and Immanent Poetics," 497.

master: "Only historical self-awareness [*Selbsterfahrung*] leads to that stage of critique [*Kritik*], the perception of perspectival conditionality and presumption, where the process toward the purity of the aesthetic work can first take place."[29] This is nearly a paraphrase of Adorno's earlier reflections on distance in the "Valéry Proust Museum" essay. Distance is now elaborated by Blumenberg as "the perception of perspectival conditionality and presumption," one associated with critique.

There is quite a bit to unpack here. First, we have the appearance of *Selbsterfahrung*, a sign that Blumenberg is retreating from the ambiguity of the artwork into more familiar territory to ground the significance of Leonardo for his own epochal conception of modernity's legitimacy, published in the same year.[30] The existence of self-awareness belongs as much to the development of an artwork out of the images of the Middle Ages, according to Hans Belting,[31] but it equally belongs to a more claustrophobic experience of modernity and its "forced inwardness" in Valéry's epoch, that of modernism. It matters little if one considers the poet a conservative or reactionary modernist, as Adorno in many respects does, but Blumenberg, strikingly, puts himself into dialogue with yet another dialogue between two artistic figures, and his perspective (Blumenberg's)—that of someone in the mid-1960s in western Europe—is writ large, even if that seems to play little role outside the context of a mostly hermetic intellectual trajectory.

The recourse to critique is simultaneously exhilarating and confusing. Whatever the lecture entails, it is not a treatise on Immanuel Kant, and the critique that Blumenberg mentions here is connected to self-awareness or self-perception.[32] Wherever that notion of critique is heading, the very least that can be made of its appearance is that it references a system, a method, a logic, in which historical self-awareness is channeled through perspectivism.[33] This

29. Blumenberg, "Paul Valérys möglicher Leonardo," 216. The original reads: "Erst geschichtliche Selbsterfahrung führt auf jene Stufe der Kritik, der Wahrnehmung perspektivischer Bedingtheit und Präsumtion, auf der Prozess zur Reinheit des ästhetischen Werkes hin überhaupt einsetzen kann."

30. See n. 15.

31. See Belting, *Bild und Kult*. The argument is well rehearsed, but the basic teleology is clear: Belting argues that the work of art first comes into being with the self-awareness that one is creating a work of art and not an image that is to function within a particular religious context. The German field of *Bildwissenschaft* has been heavily influenced by such thinking, but Blumenberg's investigations of self-assertion are quite different, and I would hesitate to put him into an image-oriented area of inquiry.

32. *Kritik* in German means both "critique" and "criticism." It is not clear whether Blumenberg intends the former or the latter, but in most of his corpus he makes reference to critique more often than not. In the quotation mentioned in n. 29, it could be either.

33. The investigation of perspectivism returns with greater concentration in the later work on the Copernican revolution, Blumenberg, *Genesis*. Blumenberg wrote an early précis of this research

quote has to be put back into conversation with the earlier mention of "history as a force that unsettles and irritates." This is eerily close to a kind of sensibility—*Stimmung*, really—of the modern subject seen from the inside out. Blumenberg moves back to Valéry, reminding us that he is talking about Valéry's dialogue with Leonardo, and not just his own semiprivate conversation with the poet.[34] Blumenberg returns to Valéry's words to offer yet another agonistic move, one befitting the context of mid-1960s Germany (East and West). Blumenberg summarizes, using the poet's words, that "the way space is thematized in Leonardo means, of course, not that it [space] is turned into an object but that it becomes resistance [*Widerstand*]."[35]

This is a concept of reality as resistance that Blumenberg attributes to the poet but that he had expanded on in this period of activity in his "Concept of Reality and the Possibility of the Novel" (1964),[36] which from the title alone signals the connection to the 1966 lecture and the debt to Valéry. Eight years after the lecture, Blumenberg expanded on questions of "aesthetic interest," with less direct connection to the novel as such, and instead with a greater political concentration on what he calls an "aesthetic sensibility" in his "Preliminary Remarks on the Concept of Reality":

> Against this realism, there is another that breaks open the immunization of consciousness through consistency by means of paradox, contradiction, and the absurd. "Real reality is always unrealistic," as Kafka put it; and this conception is directed against the disappointment that finds in successful consistency only the dull "and so on" of the always already given. From this perspective, the aesthetic sensibility does not tolerate the successful performance of the theoretical attitude. To the pragmatic concept of reality as an actuality in consciousness, only that is valid which cannot be rejected, suppressed, and leveled to the status of a theoretical object. The quotidian—which cannot be of interest to the theoretician, because it is already incorporated into the consistency of the ordinary—must seem like the enormity that does not require any distracting events to be restored to that kind of reality with which man is engaged in such a way that he has always already retracted his attention from

---

project in 1964: Blumenberg, *Kopernikus im Selbstverständnis der Neuzeit* (*Copernicus in the Self-Understanding of the Modern Age*). See also the contribution of Johannes Endres in the present issue.

34. According to Krauthausen's research, the lecture was planned as part of a four-part Valéry study ("Blumenberg's möglicher Valéry," 39). The Akademie lecture appears to be a preliminary draft of the chapter devoted to Valéry's appraisal of Leonardo.

35. Blumenberg, "Paul Valérys möglicher Leonardo," 219. The original reads: "Die Art, wie der Raum bei Leonardo thematisch wird, bedeutet freilich nicht, dass er zum Gegenstand, sondern dass er zum Widerstand wird."

36. Blumenberg, "Concept of Reality."

it. This turn of the aesthetic interest can only be understood if one conceives of it as running counter to the capacity of theory, which long ago successfully took on what is out of the ordinary.[37]

This more general resistance outlined here takes on a direct connection to the visual arts in Blumenberg's reply to the conditions of pop and op art in 1966 as respondent to the art historians Jürgen Wissmann and Max Imdahl during the third meeting of Poetik und Hermeneutik, titled "The No Longer Beautiful Arts" ("Die nicht mehr schönen Künste").[38] Blumenberg contends that art of the period in question (op and pop) was no longer geared to aesthetic pleasure, what many at that time and later would call an "anti-aesthetic" impulse. The volume features a range of topics devoted to histories of ugliness, as well as aesthetics generally. The two art-historical texts, however, deal more with the crossover of art into everyday life in pop and op art. Imdahl's short text ends with a discussion of what he dubs "Optical Art," whereas Wissmann's essay focuses exclusively on the question of "pop." Blumenberg's response to Imdahl and Wissmann takes aim at the attempt in both contributions to ground pop and op in the context of art-historical precedents, accounting for their relevance in 1966.

For those familiar with the early years of Poetik und Hermeneutik, flipping through the massive volume (over seven hundred pages) and seeing images by Andy Warhol and Roy Lichtenstein is extraordinary. While Imdahl discusses early European avant-garde traditions to the present, Wissmann's is a more horizontal approach. The response that follows is called "'Op,' 'Pop,' or the Endless Ending of the History of Art" ("'Op,' 'Pop,' oder die immer zu Ende gehende Geschichte der Kunst").[39] In his response Blumenberg has much to say about the terms of pop's embrace of representational language. While there is no mention of Greenberg anywhere in the volume, the critic's absence is conspicuous indeed, since Wissmann, in his treatment of pop, cites Leo Steinberg,[40] a figure whose championing of pop precedents like Robert Rauschenberg and Jasper Johns was premised on a direct opposition to Greenberg. In fact, Greenberg's judgment on pop (and he mentions op as well) was

37. Blumenberg, "Preliminary Remarks on the Concept of Reality," 136.

38. Jauss, *Die nicht mehr schönen Künste*. Imdahl's contribution is titled "Vier Aspekte der ästhetischen Grenzüberschreitung in der bildenen Kunst" ("Four Aspects of Aesthetic Boundary Breaches in the Fine Arts"); Wissmann's is "Pop Art oder die Realität als Kunstwerk" ("Pop Art or Reality as Artwork").

39. Blumenberg et al., "Zehnte Diskussion." The meetings took place September 4–10, 1966, in Lindau, on Lake Constance in West Germany.

40. Wissmann, "Pop Art oder die Realität als Kunstwerk," 515.

available through the archive of the Greenberg papers at the Getty in Los Angeles only after the critic's death in 1994. According to the art historian James Meyer, an expert on the period in question, Greenberg delivered two lectures on pop in the early 1960s.[41] The most sustained engagement and critique of the movement occurred in an undated manuscript that was later published in *Artforum* in a 2004 special issue titled "Pop after Pop."[42] The lecture is mostly predictable and glosses over much in the history of art, unlike the Imdahl or Wissmann essays, but the similarity on the terms and judgment between the critic and Blumenberg is striking nonetheless.

Neither Greenberg nor Blumenberg, it turns out, seems to have anything flattering to say about the reemergence of figurative, or representational, painting after modernist forms of abstraction in the earlier decades of the century. In his lecture Greenberg contends, "From the later 1940s to the early 1960s there was hardly any question in the minds of most interested people but that avant-garde painting par excellence, advanced, ambitious, momentously original painting and sculpture, were abstract—abstract almost by definition." A few lines later he drops the hammer: "Pop art has drawn, to good effect, on the acquisitions of pure and abstract painting but it has not, so far, contributed anything to it in return."[43] Blumenberg is of course more grounded in the theoretical question of subjectivity and aesthetic experience as it concerns other modernist forms, like the novel in this volume, but his verdict on the attempts by the two art historians to ground the history of pop in an evolution of the avant-garde similarly refers to the reappearance of representational art. The German term that Blumenberg uses is *Gegenständlichkeit*, which means "objectivity" or "objecthood" as well as "the representational." In his response to the historicization of pop (then apparently still in question for those at the Poetik und Hermeneutik meeting), Blumenberg suggests:

> In this respect, the supposed representational nature [*Gegenständlichkeit*] of "pop art" is only possible and understandable after the completely played out de-objectification [*Entgegenständlichung*] of the abstract phase; the object can be brought out again in its most ostentatiously "ordinary" form and brutally displayed and exhibited without mediation, because a mutated way of seeing can be assumed which is no longer in danger of allowing the factually displayed "object" to be regarded and to act as a carrier of the quality to be experienced aesthetically.[44]

41. Meyer, "Introduction."
42. Greenberg, "Pop Art."
43. Greenberg, "Pop Art," 52.
44. Blumenberg et al., "Zehnte Diskussion," 691.

The German play between objectivity or objecthood (*Gegenständlichkeit*) and de-objectification (*Entgegenständlichung*) allows for a more elastic dance with the root of the word, *Gegenstand* (object), crucial to the argument, as Blumenberg then speaks at the end of the citation of "the object . . . as a carrier," which in the German is described as "Objekt" (quotation marks in the original). *Object* here seems to hold a lower place within the hierarchy of artistic forms than *Gegenstand*, which makes the translation to Greenberg's terms more challenging. Again, to be clear, I am not arguing that either figure shared common intellectual ground on the subject. Greenberg, the critic, was much more concerned with judgments of taste than Blumenberg, the philosopher, but the determinations fall on similar terms, with nearly equivalent verdicts: representational art in pop does not belong to an evolution of modernist nonobjectivity; rather, it leaves those debates and its structures of self-investigation behind even as it profits from them.

Additionally, I propose that one see Blumenberg's recourse to the term *quality* in his response as a critical move, one befitting a critic and not merely a philosopher. The presence of Siegfried Kracauer at the meeting of Poetik und Hermeneutik is more than slightly conspicuous, and the New York émigré contributes to the discussion that Blumenberg chairs. The entire volume was subsequently dedicated to Kracauer, who died just two months after the group convened. The constellation of contemporary art forms, modernist critics (Valéry and Kracauer), and their structural correspondences with concurrent debates in art criticism in New York (of which Kracauer was no doubt aware) create the ground on which a meditation on Blumenberg's modernist and critical tendencies between 1964 and 1966 is possible. I would go so far as to say that by failing to hear the concatenation of voices around this moment, ignoring their likely overlaps and intellectual affinities, would miss the very essence of Blumenberg's Akademie lecture to discover something possible (*möglich*) for the present.

———————

Taking stock of the inventory of terms in the Akademie lecture and the Poetik und Hermeneutik text, and the response to Imdahl and Wissmann (all 1966), reveals the following: the modern experience of history as frightening, oppressive, and unsettling; historical self-awareness within the umbrella of critique or criticism; and resistance as the principal determinant of this historical consciousness. All of this, of course, is couched in an attempt to wrestle with the conditions of possibility that allow for modern experiences of artworks. Blumenberg announces such an approach two years earlier in the first meeting of Poetik und Hermeneutik, in "The Concept of Reality and the Possibility of the Novel,"[45] where it could be said that the possibility of the novel that is argued there is one and the same as that of Valéry's Leonardo.[46] But what about the works themselves? As mentioned, Blumenberg hesitates to name much other than Paul Klee on occasion,[47] but rarely, if ever, does he attempt to offer the interpretive gambits that he associates with Valéry. The closest one can find to such discussions occurs in the context of "creativity" or the "creative being," as in the 1957 essay "'Imitation of Nature': Toward a Prehistory of the Idea of the Creative Being,"[48] where creation in the modern sense is something more *and* less than the mimetic drive to imitate nature. The creative drive in modernity divorced from the mimetic picks up steam in the analysis of Nicolas of Cusa's *idiota* in *The Legitimacy of the Modern Age*.[49] What is key for Blumenberg here is the idea of modern modes of image and object making that are constructed, much like the modern subject's need to construct a self through assertion. It is no surprise that when Blumenberg turns to Valéry in the later 1966 texts—"Speech Situation" and "The Essential Ambiguity of the Aesthetic Object"—he does so with respect to linguistic form, poetry, more precisely. However, there are some startling verdicts offered on the visual arts as well, for example, when Blumenberg declares that "modern painting and modern sculpture do not wish to be instruction manuals for illusions, making something else visible; they want to be that, and nothing but that, which they present themselves to be."[50] Given Blumenberg's discussion in this passage of Pablo Picasso, Alexander Archipenko, and Henry Moore, the translation could just as well be "the modernist image and modernist sculpture [*das moderne Bild, die moderne Plastik*]."

This is so close to Greenberg's thinking about self-reference and abstraction around the same year that it feels as if Blumenberg is practically ventriloquizing the modernist drive toward self-sufficiency and autonomy that the New York critic would identify and champion in his later essays around the time of Blumenberg's text, but of course Blumenberg seemed unaware of those debates around modernism in the United States, least of all in the context of art. However, compare his proclamation with Greenberg's formalist defense

---

45. See n. 29.
46. My thanks to Hannes Bajohr for pointing out this connection.
47. Blumenberg, "Speech Situation and Immanent Poetics," 454.
48. Blumenberg, "'Imitation of Nature.'"
49. Blumenberg, *Legitimacy of the Modern Age*, 534.
50. Blumenberg, "Essential Ambiguity of the Aesthetic Object," 446.

in "Modernist Painting" from a few years earlier: "The essence of Modernism, as I see it, lies in the use of characteristic methods of a discipline to criticize the discipline itself, not in order to subvert it but to entrench it more firmly in its area of competence."[51]

The conjunction of contemporaneous concerns with self-awareness as well as distance (to follow) is signaled rather conspicuously by the appearance of an exhibition that opened in New York just six days after Blumenberg delivered his lecture: "Primary Structures: Younger American and British Sculptors," curated by the late Kynaston McShine at the Jewish Museum. "Primary Structures" has since been canonized in art history, seen by many as a turning point in the history of modernist sculptural practice, effectively challenging modernism as what is investigated only within the boundaries of a specific medium (painting and sculpture, chiefly).[52] As Greenberg argues: "It quickly emerged that the unique and proper idea of competence of each art coincided with all that was unique in the nature of its medium. The task of self-criticism became to eliminate from the specific effects of each art any and every effect that might conceivably be borrowed from or by the medium of any other art."[53]

"Primary Structures" instead celebrated hybrid versions of more traditional medium-specific practices, like painting and sculpture, to the point of the dissolution of those definitions entirely, according to some—sculpture that hung on the wall like painting, large volumetric forms that were anchored neither to a pedestal nor to a specific site. For those who viewed the decomposition favorably, the show marked the emergence of a rising tide now dubbed minimalism, pitted in many ways as the terminus ad quem of modernist ideology, then already on the wane in New York. For others, "Primary Structures" marked a renunciation of the project of self-criticism—not a continuation—that had underpinned the discourse surrounding much of the painting and sculpture in the previous decades. The first and most trenchant critique of this new hybrid evolution of non-medium-specific art was leveled by Fried, a close colleague to and younger critic of Greenberg,[54] who just one year after the

51. Greenberg, "Modernist Painting," 100. Although the text was first published as a pamphlet in 1960, a revised version appeared in 1965, and an important edition of the essay (cited here) was anthologized in 1966.

52. In his authoritative book on this period, James Meyer writes, "The Primary Structures replaced the traditional, pedestal scale of sculpture with architectural scale" (*Minimalism*, 24).

53. Meyer, *Minimalism*, 24.

54. Fried himself acknowledges the connection in the preface to his later collection of art criticism: "The deepest, though also the most difficult, acknowledgment I have saved for last. No one familiar with the pieces gathered in this book will need to be told how indebted they are to the writings of the late Clement Greenberg, whom I am not alone in regarding as the foremost art critic of the twentieth century. As I explain in the introduction, I knew Greenberg personally and on more than a few occa-

exhibition at the Jewish Museum published his now-infamous attack on the aesthetic terms championed by the so-called minimalists: "Art and Objecthood."[55] A central argument of Fried's critique is that the minimalists, whom Fried disparages as "literalists," abandoned the modernist project of self-criticism by making work whose criteria were nebulous at best.

The question of medium and its relation to definitions of modernism is of less interest and intellectual overlap with Blumenberg than the temporal implications spelled out in Fried's reproach, as well as the question of objecthood, which, for Fried, had to be overcome in serious art. The German translation of "Art and Objecthood" is "Kunst und Objekthaftigkeit,"[56] though in the context of their use, *Objekthaftigkeit* and *Gegenständlichkeit* are functionally equivalent in Blumenberg's use of the latter in his response to pop art. Fried's argument hinges on two things: the modernist's defeat of objecthood as well as the "literalist" (read: minimalist) embrace of it; and the issue of time, a rather compelling if sketchy phenomenological account of how time—the work of art's resistance to, or embrace of, temporality—is configured by the experience of a minimalist work.[57] First, the question of objecthood and its suspension or sublation in modernist painting and sculpture is characterized in "Art and Objecthood" as follows:

> What has compelled modernist painting to defeat or suspend its own objecthood is not just developments internal to itself, but the same general, enveloping, infectious theatricality that corrupted literalist sensibility in the first place and in the grip of which the developments in question—and modernist painting in general—are seen as nothing more than an uncompelling and presenceless kind of theater. It was the need to break the fingers of this grip that made objecthood an issue for modernist painting.[58]

For Fried, even more than for Greenberg and Blumenberg, objecthood posed a specific obstacle to modernist painting that it had to overcome. Fried charged that the "literalists" had given in, accepted defeat before ever really putting up

---

sions visited studios and warehouses to look at recent painting and sculpture with him, and for several years I enjoyed not his friendship (the difference between our ages alone might have precluded that) but at least his qualified approval" (*Art and Objecthood*, xvii).

55. Fried, "Art and Objecthood."

56. Fried, "Kunst und Objekthaftigkeit."

57. This is spelled out in Pamela M. Lee's excellent analysis of Fried's essay and the issue of time: *Chronophobia*, 37–81. While Lee accuses Fried of what she calls "chronophia," she ignores the essential divide that Blumenberg discusses in *Lebenszeit und Weltzeit*. Fear of mediatized time is not quite the same as awareness of the ineradicable divide between one's life-time and world-time.

58. Fried, "Art and Objecthood," 20.

a fight. Take one of Donald Judd's wall-mounted *Untitled (Stack)* objects from 1967, which exemplifies that inbetweenness of its formal approach, hanging on a wall like painting but in fact being a series of identical metal and glass shelves that look more like sculpture than any flat surface. The way in which this occurs in the art that Fried bemoans falls precisely on the issue of the *experience* of that artwork, where objecthood is inherently tied to the conditions of experience. Fried declares, "The concepts of quality and value—and to the extent that these are central to art, the concept of art itself—are meaningful, or wholly meaningful, only within the individual arts. What lies between the arts is theater."[59] The "theater" reference has little to do with the dramatic art, at least as a discipline. It is rather about the way in which the art that Fried criticizes operates as a kind of open solicitation to viewers, without ever being self-reliant (or self-assertive) as works, needing the public like a showman needs spectators.

What is worth noting here, as if hardly any stone had not already been turned by Fried's many interlocutors,[60] is not only that the theatrical is linked to the hazy gray zone between mediums (painting and sculpture) but that the theatrical per se revolves again around a temporal axis: the experience of a minimalist work is unending; one does not know when things begin and where they end. Toward the conclusion of his critique, Fried summarizes, "Here finally I want to emphasize something that may already have become clear: the experience in question [of the minimalist work par excellence, according to Fried] *persists in time*, and the presentment of endlessness which, I have been claiming, is central to literalist art and theory is essentially a presentment of endless, or indefinite, *duration*."[61] This is tied to a particular stress on the nature not just of the experience of the work under scrutiny—its endlessness—but of experience as a value, or criterion, for the work of this group of artists. As Fried suggests, for them "experience alone is what matters."[62]

———

Whether the attention around 1966 to modernism is well deserved is something that art historians have been debating since "Art and Objecthood" first

59. Fried, "Art and Objecthood," 21.

60. In addition to Lee's *Chronophobia*, there are a few reliable summaries of the arguments and limits of "Art and Objecthood": Meyer, "Writing of 'Art and Objecthood'"; Foster, "Crux of Minimalism"; and Fried's own reflections, "Introduction to My Art Criticism," esp. 40–47.

61. Fried, "Art and Objecthood," 22.

62. Fried, "Art and Objecthood," 19.

appeared in the pages of *Artforum* in 1967. The mention of theater here has also had its fair share of commentators, but the question that resonates with Blumenberg has more to do with the uncomfortable unknowing of where the work ends and the viewer begins, the endless experience, the endlessness of experience itself. In modernist art, Fried will tell us, the work is self-sufficient and present whether we are there to see it or not: it does not depend on us. This idea of self-sufficiency is hard to distinguish from that offered by Valéry in his *Pièces sur l'art* as a rebuke against reductivism: "The will to simplicity in art is fatal every time it becomes self-sufficient and deludes us into saving ourselves some trouble."[63]

In contrast, the assertion that Fried makes hangs not on the irreducibility of an artwork and the experience of it but on its "instantaneousness,"[64] a point that falls short of grounding the distinction between modernist art and theater on the temporality in which artwork and viewer exist. In short, the modernist work does not need or require a viewer for its activation or intelligence of form, a kind of vengeance the artwork enacts on itself, lest it fall into a "theater" of insecurity. The question is whether this kind of self-criticism is analogous to Blumenberg's concept of modernity as self-assertion (*Selbstbehauptung*).

In lieu of trying to answer that question, I would compare the terms of Fried's critique—the literalists' embrace of objecthood, and the endless duration of experience that embrace engenders—with what Blumenberg has to say about the work of art vis-à-vis Valéry in his 1964 text on the figure of the *objet ambigu*:

> Unlike the scientist's hypothesis, the work of art seeks not to dissolve the riddle of the given, but to substitute the own and human for the foreign indissolubility, to put the pleasing, enjoyable indissolubility of the human work—whose character of reality as resistance is thus equivalent to the given but lacks the sting of theoretical unrest—in the place of the agonizing indeterminacy of what is encountered from an inscrutable source. The interpretation of the work of art will therefore always be satisfied with a solution that is not the dissolution of the given but may leave conscious the indeterminacy of other possibilities, while the theoretical hypothesis of the scientist is burdened with the possibility of other, surpassing solutions, of which none can, however, definitively rule out that their verification may fail.[65]

63. Valéry, "About Corot," 138.
64. Fried, "Art and Objecthood," 22.
65. Blumenberg, "Socrates and the *Objet Ambigu*," 435.

Again, the reference to resistance is remarkable, though the sting in this instance is not history but "theoretical unrest," an indeterminacy that may well lead to a kind of temporal endlessness à la Fried or, worse yet, a merger between lived time and world-time. What can joust against this endlessness is a work that is self-referential, constantly safeguarding the temporal (historical and phenomenological) distance that is a prerequisite of the experience. Much of the thinking with Valéry does not really stay within the realm of the aesthetic. Art was indeed a brief flirtation but one that Blumenberg was clearly searching for, attempting to investigate it with the same level of erudition and theoretical complexity as other phenomena, which is why the background of the lecture, and a potential correspondence—unaware of one another (Greenberg, Fried, Blumenberg)—is all the more compelling. Even in the later work, Blumenberg returns again and again to distance as separation, but not as an amateur aesthetician hanging on to a dead French poet who decided to not write poetry.

Time, it seems, is a driving force behind the encounter with Valéry. It is historical time, both contingent and configurable within a certain constellation: Blumenberg and Valéry, Valéry and Leonardo, and so forth. Perhaps Fried's remonstrance needed its own interlocutor, not an artist, maybe, but a "possible" philosopher, a Blumenberg. The terms of the critique of this stepping out of modernist self-awareness that minimalism supposedly enacted may well have been more adequately defined in the terms offered by Blumenberg's contemporaneous essays, lectures, and response to other essays and lectures.

In a late passage in the penetrative and difficult *Lebenszeit und Weltzeit*, Blumenberg's concluding remark might have more eloquently adjudicated between modernism and its post-afterlives. "The mundane subject completes itself by making the most difficult of all concessions that can be expected of it; to let *its* world become *the* world, to witness the transformation of its lifetime as only one of many life-times into world-time and as such alienated from itself."[66] Adorno suggests that Valéry's allegiance to Bergson's ideas is what actually unites the poet with Proust, and Adorno even mentions that Valéry delivered the eulogy for Bergson's funeral. Adorno's conclusion is puzzling. Blumenberg pays little or no attention to Adorno's characterization of Valéry, his favorite aesthetic interlocutor. Blumenberg, like Fried, is no fan of the vitalist fantasy of immanence, either in the realm of experience or in the work of art itself. What separates Blumenberg's modernism from Valéry's is the experience of the war and Blumenberg's mistrust, most explicitly argued,

66. Blumenberg, *Lebenszeit und Weltzeit*, 306.

in *Lebenszeit und Weltzeit*, that it was impossible to differentiate the project of making life the one and only horizon of the world from the Nazi ideology that saw death and destruction as a way to dominate and control the present. Modernist form is forged in the spaces of this distance, vitalist or otherwise, and Blumenberg, as a well-tempered modernist, is all too aware of the need to maintain and guard this separation. The distance occasioned the reflections on Valéry and art during this brief but fecund period of activity. This was not a distance that Blumenberg would collapse or ignore; rather, he took its possibility back into the hermetic world of phenomenological inquiry, where time as such could be posited without recourse to poetry, painting, or sculpture. For those drawn to Blumenberg's work, the curious flurry of activity on art is not as haphazard as its brief existence might lead us to believe. Art was not an object of lasting inquiry for the philosopher, but its forms and modes of presentation provided the necessary deviation (*Abweichung*) to establish distance as a prerequisite for both art and history.

Colin Lang is an independent scholar and critic living in Berlin.

References

Adorno, Theodor W. "Valéry Proust Museum." In *Prisms*, translated by Samuel Weber and Shierry Weber, 173–85. Cambridge, MA: MIT Press, 1981.

Adorno, Theodor W. "Valérys Abweichungen." *Neue Rundschau* 71, no. 1 (1960): 1–34.

Amslinger, Julia. *Eine neue Form von Akademie: Poetik und Hermeneutik—die Anfänge*. Paderborn: Fink, 2017.

Belting, Hans. *Bild und Kult: Eine Geschichte des Bildes vor dem Zeitalter der Kunst*. Munich: Beck, 1990.

Blumenberg, Bettina. "Eine Frage der Belichtung: Über den Philosophen Hans Blumenberg." *Neue Zürcher Zeitung*, July 13, 2015.

Blumenberg, Hans. *Beschreibung des Menschen*, edited by Manfred Sommer. Frankfurt am Main: Suhrkamp, 2006.

Blumenberg, Hans. *Care Crosses the River*, translated by Paul Fleming. Stanford, CA: Stanford University Press, 2010.

Blumenberg, Hans. "The Concept of Reality and the Possibility of the Novel." In *History, Metaphors, Fables: A Hans Blumenberg Reader*, edited by Hannes Bajohr, Florian Fuchs, and Joe Paul Kroll, 499–524. Ithaca, NY: Cornell University Press, 2020.

Blumenberg, Hans. "Die Kongruenz von Lebenszeit und Weltzeit als Wahn." In Blumenberg, *Lebenszeit und Weltzeit*, 80–85.

Blumenberg, Hans. *Die Legitimität der Neuzeit*. Frankfurt am Main: Suhrkamp, 1966.

Blumenberg, Hans. "Die ontologische Distanz: Eine Untersuchung über die Krisis der Phänomenologie Husserls." Habilitation diss., University of Kiel, 1950.

Blumenberg, Hans. "The Essential Ambiguity of the Aesthetic Object." In *History, Metaphors, Fables: A Hans Blumenberg Reader*, edited by Hannes Bajohr, Florian Fuchs, and Joe Paul Kroll, 441–48. Ithaca, NY: Cornell University Press, 2020.

Blumenberg, Hans. *The Genesis of the Copernican World*, translated by Robert M. Wallace. Cambridge, MA: MIT Press, 1987.

Blumenberg, Hans. "'Imitation of Nature': Toward a Prehistory of the Idea of the Creative Being." In *History, Metaphors, Fables: A Hans Blumenberg Reader*, edited by Hannes Bajohr, Florian Fuchs, and Joe Paul Kroll, 316–57. Ithaca, NY: Cornell University Press, 2020.

Blumenberg, Hans. *Kopernikus im Selbstverständnis der Neuzeit*. Mainz: Verlag der Akademie der Wissenschaften und der Literatur Wiesbaden, 1965.

Blumenberg, Hans. *Lebenszeit und Weltzeit*. Frankfurt am Main: Suhrkamp, 1986.

Blumenberg, Hans. *The Legitimacy of the Modern Age*, translated by Robert M. Wallace. Cambridge, MA: MIT Press, 1983.

Blumenberg, Hans. "Paul Valérys möglicher Leonardo da Vinci: Vortrag in der Akademie der Künste in Berlin am 21. 4. 1966." *Forschungen zu Paul Valéry / Recherches Valéryennes* 25 (2012): 193–227.

Blumenberg, Hans. "Preliminary Remarks on the Concept of Reality." In *History, Metaphors, Fables: A Hans Blumenberg Reader*, edited by Hannes Bajohr, Florian Fuchs, and Joe Paul Kroll, 117–26. Ithaca, NY: Cornell University Press, 2020.

Blumenberg, Hans. "Socrates and the *Objet Ambigu*: Paul Valéry's Discussion of the Ontology of the Aesthetic Object and Its Tradition." In *History, Metaphors, Fables: A Hans Blumenberg Reader*, edited by Hannes Bajohr, Florian Fuchs, and Joe Paul Kroll, 400–440. Ithaca, NY: Cornell University Press, 2020.

Blumenberg, Hans. "Speech Situation and Immanent Poetics." In *History, Metaphors, Fables: A Hans Blumenberg Reader*, edited by Hannes Bajohr, Florian Fuchs, and Joe Paul Kroll, 449–65. Ithaca, NY: Cornell University Press, 2020.

Blumenberg, Hans, Max Imdahl, Clemens Heselhaus, Jürgen Wissmann, Siegfried Kracauer, Karl-Heinz Stierle, and Wolfgang Preisendanz. "Zehnte Diskussion: 'Op,' 'Pop,' oder die immer zu Ende gehende Geschichte der Kunst." In Jauss, *Die nicht mehr schönen Künste*, 691–705.

Bois, Yve-Alain, Thierry de Duve, Isabelle Graw, Arthur C. Danto, David Reed, Elisabeth Sussman, and David Joselit. "The Mourning After: A Roundtable." *Artforum* 41, no. 7 (2003): 66–71.

Cassirer, Ernst. *Substanzbegriff und Funktionsbegriff: Untersuchungen über die Grundfragen der Erkenntniskritik*. Berlin: Cassirer, 1910.

Fleming, Paul, "*Verfehlungen*: Hans Blumenberg and the United States." *New German Critique*, no. 132 (2017): 105–21.

Foster, Hal. "The Crux of Minimalism." In *Minimalism*, edited by James Meyer, 271–75. New York: Phaidon, 2000.

Fried, Michael. "Art and Objecthood." *Artforum* 5, no. 10 (1967): 12–23.

Fried, Michael. *Art and Objecthood: Essays and Reviews*. Chicago: University of Chicago Press, 1998.

Fried, Michael. "How Modernism Works: A Response to T. J. Clark." *Critical Inquiry* 9, no. 1 (1982): 217–34.

Fried, Michael. "An Introduction to My Art Criticism." In *Art and Objecthood: Essays and Reviews*, 1–74. Chicago: University of Chicago Press, 1998.

Fried, Michael. "Kunst und Objekthaftigkeit." In *Minimal Art: Eine kritische Retrospektive*, edited by Gregor Stemmrich, 334–74. Dresden: Verlag der Kunst, 1995.

Greenberg, Clement. "Modernist Painting." In *The New Art: A Critical Anthology*, edited by Gregory Battcock, 100–110. New York: Hutton, 1966.

Greenberg, Clement. "Pop Art." *Artforum* 43, no. 2 (2004): 51–53.

Heidenreich, Felix. "Porträtsammlung und Bilderverbot: Hans Blumenberg (1920–1996)." In *Ideengeschichte und Bildwissenschaft: Siebzehn Porträts*, edited by Jörg Probst and Jost Philipp Klenner, 10–32. Frankfurt am Main: Suhrkamp, 2009.

Imdahl, Max. "Vier Aspekte der ästhetischen Grenzüberschreitung in der bildenen Kunst." In Jauss, *Die nicht mehr schönen Künste*, 493–505.

Jauss, Hans Robert, ed. *Die nicht mehr schönen Künste: Grenzphänomene des Ästhetischen*. Munich: Fink, 1968.

Jauss, Hans Robert. "Eine doppelte Konjunktur: Goethe und Napoleon—Valéry und Blumenberg." *Akzente* 37, no. 3 (1990): 216–19.

Jay, Martin. "Against Rigor: Hans Blumenberg on Freud and Arendt." *New German Critique*, no. 132 (2017): 123–44.

Koch, Matthias. "Valéry, Blumenberg und die Phänomenologie der Geschichte." In *Alles Mögliche: Sprechen, Denken und Schreiben des (Un)möglichen*, edited by Reinhard Babel, 37–52. Würzburg: Königshausen und Neumann, 2015.

Konersmann, Ralf. "Stoff für Zweifel: Blumenberg liest Valéry." *Internationale Zeitschrift für Philosophie*, no. 1 (1995): 46–66.

Krauthausen, Karin. "Hans Blumenbergs möglicher Valéry." *Zeitschrift für Kulturphilosophie* 6, no. 1 (2012): 39–63.

Krauthausen, Karin. "Hans Blumenbergs präparierter Valéry." *Zeitschrift für Kulturphilosophie* 6, no. 1 (2012): 211–24.

Kubler, George. *Die Form der Zeit*, translated by Bettina Blumenberg. Frankfurt am Main: Suhrkamp, 1982.

Kubler, George. *The Shape of Time: Remarks on the History of Things*. New Haven, CT: Yale University Press, 1962.

Lee, Pamela M. *Chronophobia: On Time in the Art of the 1960s*. Cambridge, MA: MIT Press, 2004.

Meyer, James. "Introduction." *Artforum* 43, no. 2 (2004): 51–53.

Meyer, James. *Minimalism: Art and Polemics in the Sixties*. New Haven, CT: Yale University Press, 2001.

Meyer, James. "The Writing of 'Art and Objecthood.'" In *Refracting Vision: Essays on the Writings of Michael Fried*, edited by Jill Beaulieu, Mary Roberts, and Toni Ross, 61–96. Sydney: Power Institute Foundation for Art and Visual Culture.

Pavesich, Vida. "Hans Blumenberg's Philosophical Anthropology: After Heidegger and Cassirer." *Journal of the History of Philosophy* 46, no. 3 (2008): 421–48.

Valéry, Paul. "About Corot." In *Degas, Manet, Morisot*, edited by Jackson Mathews, 134–54. New York: Pantheon, 1960.

Valéry, Paul. "Eupalinos ou l'architecte." In vol. 2 of *Oeuvres*, edited by Jean Hytier, 79–147. Paris: Gallimard, 1960.

Valéry, Paul. "More Obiter Dicta." In *Degas, Manet, Morisot*, edited by Jackson Mathews, 73. New York: Pantheon, 1960.

Wissmann, Jürgen. "Pop Art oder die Realität als Kunstwerk." In Jauss, *Die nicht mehr schönen Künste*, 507–30.

Hans Blumenberg and Leonardo

Johannes Endres

The Prehistoric Ground of the Image and Blumenberg's Image Theory

Considerations of art, and art-theoretical concerns, run through Hans Blumenberg's work from beginning to end. They are embedded in a complex network of philosophical, anthropological, and epistemological meditations, which lead back only indirectly to the objects to which they pertain. They are, moreover, filtered through multiple layers of references, presented as second-order observations of observations of others. What complicates the matter even further is that the subjects of Blumenberg's aesthetic thoughts, such as ancient philosophical theories of imitation, the reality concept of the eighteenth- and nineteenth-century European novel, Paul Valéry's poetry and twentieth-century abstract art, tend to carry complexities of their own. Blumenberg's views can therefore not simply be stripped from the historical and conceptual baggage with which they come.

On the other hand, the engagement with Blumenberg's ideas is clearly worth the effort. The depth and richness of his knowledge and the acuity of his reflections make him one of the most distinguished philosophers of art of the second half of the twentieth century in Germany and beyond—next to (much better-known) poststructuralist thinkers in the wider context of which he found himself placed when his earlier metaphorological writings were rediscovered in the 1980s. What makes his contribution stand out, however, also in contrast to the former, is not least the framing of his views in a historical as well as prehistorical deep time.

New German Critique 145, Vol. 49, No. 1, February 2022
DOI 10.1215/0094033X-9439629   © 2022 by New German Critique, Inc.

Especially Blumenberg's accounts of the history of evolution inform his reflections on art throughout, accounts broadly developed in his *Beschreibung des Menschen* (2006).[1] The following attempt to shed light on Blumenberg's theories of visual art and the image thus traces his related thoughts all the way back to the historical origin of the human ability to create images and to perceive them as windows into the real world. But it also must interrogate later scenarios in which the modern perception of the artistic image as a quasi window to an objective world was once again reinforced. The latter occurred, most notably, during the Renaissance and the discovery of linear perspective as a representational technique. The following investigations therefore focus on Blumenberg's reflections on Leonardo's art and aesthetics on which he frequently commented, first and foremost in the context of his reception of Valéry's essays on Leonardo.[2] Equally relevant to an understanding of Blumenberg's aesthetics are Leonardo's views on the relationship of the image to other media such as language and text. In fact, Blumenberg's reception of Leonardo continues the so-called *paragone* discourse of the Renaissance, that is, the famous historical debate of whether painting is inferior to its "sister arts," poesy, music, and sculpture.[3]

But Blumenberg is not only continuing such a conversation. He is also questioning and inverting its historically established outcome. Despite the seemingly favorable tone of his remarks on Leonardo, Blumenberg's understanding of Leonardo's art and science is rooted in criticism. In that, it deviates from the most important source of his Leonardo reception, Valéry's essays on Leonardo, published between 1895 and 1928, including annotations added in 1931, that frame Blumenberg's references to Leonardo on many levels.[4] My considerations therefore start out more generally, by reconstructing what can be called Blumenberg's "image theory" and how it is related to language- and word-based forms of representation. I then turn to his critical comments on Leonardo and on Valéry's readings of Leonardo. As I show, Blumenberg deeply distrusts images in general and representational art in particular, for the same

1. For Blumenberg's evolutionary history of art, see Endres, "Hans Blumenbergs paläolithische Weltkunstgeschichte."

2. Paul Valéry served not only as a "stylite" for the research group Poetik und Hermeneutik (Müller, "Subtile Stiche," 250), especially through Blumenberg's essay "Socrates and the *Objet Ambigu*," first published in 1964, but also as a lifelong reference point to Blumenberg himself, ever since a joint seminar with Hans Robert Jauss in Giessen in 1962.

3. Leonardo, *Treatise*; Leonardo, *Leonardo on Painting*; Farago, *Leonardo da Vinci's "Paragone."*

4. On Valéry's Leonardo, see esp. Huyghe, "Leonardo"; Jallat, *Figure*; Blüher, "Leonardo da Vincis *Quaderni*"; Kemp, "'Hostinato Rigore'"; and Schmidt-Radefeldt, "Randnotizen." Besides Valéry's extensive comments on Leonardo and Joseph Gantner's book on Leonardo, Blumenberg used at least two other sources of Leonardo's work: Leonardo, *Tagebücher und Aufzeichnungen*; Leonardo, *Literary Works*.

reason that he thinks highly of the capacities of language and literature to conceptualize its subject in a contrary and nonmimetic way. Thus the prominence of the "metaphor" in his philosophy negatively affects his views on a visual imagery proper, which appears to lack the level of complexity and indirectness attributed to the former. His obvious inclination toward "modern" art—art since the late nineteenth century, in particular impressionist art and abstract art of the twentieth century—follows from an epistemological bias that is grounded in a critical analysis of the Copernicanism of Leonardo's science and the world picture of his age—a Copernicanism eventually overruled by a multiplicity of contesting viewpoints in the periods following it. By recontextualizing Leonardo within the framework of his time, rather than modernizing him as Valéry had done, Blumenberg achieves a paradoxical outcome: he accounts for Leonardo's historical position to the same extent that he underrates the achievements of his art.

The principles of Blumenberg's image theory can be extrapolated from a centerpiece of his analysis of Plato's cave allegory in his *Höhlenausgänge* from 1989. Here Blumenberg discusses the painterly activities of early humans as he deduces them from Plato's philosophical allegory. In doing so, the reading of Plato's text supersedes an archaeological account of cave painting to which the author only points in passing. It is therefore a philosophical model that stands in for a historical reality that cannot but abide by the conceptual confines put in place by that model. Consequently, Plato's cave turns into an allegory of a "Gesamtkunstwerk" (total artwork) that comments on the image-producing practices intrinsic to human nature and culture alike.[5]

Set against the overwhelming "absolutism" of a perilous world outside, which it both reenacts and copes with, the primal image is meant to please through its counterfactual beauty. Replacing the sight of the outside world, of which Plato's cave dwellers remain deprived, its artificiality successively fades away. It takes on the substance of the things it depicts while hiding its status as a human-made image under the guise of a natural object.[6] Eventually, to the self-deceiving people in Plato's cave, all images appear as "Acheiropoieta," icons made without human hands.[7] Blumenberg therefore compares them to totemistic objects, which are not recognized as images either.[8] Like totemistic

5. Blumenberg, *Höhlenausgänge*, 167.
6. Blumenberg, *Höhlenausgänge*, 31.
7. Blumenberg, *Höhlenausgänge*.
8. Blumenberg, "Wirkungspotential," 331; see also Blumenberg, "Das dritte Höhlengleichnis," 715: "One should not forget that the artificial objects in those caves [the 'classical' caves of Plato and Aristotle], following the principle of *ars imitator naturam* [art imitates nature], could only be understood as depictions of natural objects, and rightly so" (my translation).

objects, they are experienced only through their sanctioning quality, as an "expression of the passiveness of a demonic spell *or* as imaginative excess of an anthropomorphic appropriation of the world and a theomorphic enhancement of man."[9] Plato's allegorical caveman thus takes the place of another, utterly Western fantasy, the primitive mind ascribed to the earliest people. Blumenberg arrives at such a conclusion by conceiving of both Plato's cave people and the people from a prehistoric age as instances of an erstwhile "mythical consciousness."[10] The anthropological turn to which Blumenberg's *Beschreibung des Menschen* testifies both extensively and critically is therefore at work in his theory of the primordial man and his art already.[11]

Central Perspective; or, A Case against the Window Image

What is more, Blumenberg's aesthetics carry forward an anthropological and paleontological presumption in their very design. It is encapsulated in Blumenberg's image theory, which is inscribed into a larger theory of the beginnings of the human mind.[12] Thus Blumenberg's speculations about the origin of human creativity turn into a founding myth of his philosophical theory as a whole, a myth to which his comments on art-historical images in the proper sense will be returning. At the same time, this foundational myth is responsible for the fact that images and image descriptions are basically absent from his work, because they would only prolong the shortcomings inherent in images since their earliest appearance. But the primal scene of the painting caveman also indicates that Blumenberg's iconic skepticism might not be directed at images in general but is restricted to images that, knowingly or not, imitate and re-create the nature of their subject. His image theory thus lends itself to a criticism of representational images and the so-called window image, a historical image concept commonly associated with Alberti and the Renaissance that renders the image surface transparent to a reality apparently extending behind it.[13]

9. Blumenberg, "Wirklichkeitsbegriff und Wirkungspotential," 331. In an image-related context, "theomorphization" (the rendering of an object as something divine) is also prominent in Worringer, "Kritische Gedanken."

10. Blumenberg, "Wirklichkeitsbegriff und Wirkungspotential," 331. See also Blumenberg, *Höhlenausgänge*, 57.

11. Blumenberg, *Beschreibung*. Blumenberg seems to sympathize with a view of historical and anthropological developments in line with Ernst Haeckel's so-called biogenetic law and its assumed parallelism between phylogenesis and ontogenesis (see Blumenberg, "Socrates," 430; and Blumenberg, *Beschreibung*, 541, 567, 572).

12. For the following, see also Endres, "*Ekphrasis*"; and Endres, "Hans Blumenbergs paläolithische Weltkunstgeschichte."

13. Alberti, *On Painting*, 19 ("On Painting"); Krüger, *Das Bild als Schleier*. To be clear, it is not the Renaissance concept of perspective itself that is at stake in the following but Blumenberg's and Valéry's recourses to the former.

Valéry has characterized and criticized such an image concept and the attitude it imposes on its beholder in *Introduction à la méthode de Léonard de Vinci*, from 1894, on which Blumenberg comments at great length: "What the spectator sees is only a less or more faithful representation of bodies, gestures, and landscapes, as though he were looking out through a window of the museum. The picture is judged by the same spirit as reality. . . . The fact is that the picture, in accordance with unconscious demands, is supposed to represent the physical and natural conditions of our own environment."[14] Valéry chastises such a view as foolish and contrasts it with a proper understanding of images and their pictorial surfaces as "obstacles" or objects of "resistance"— a term used by Blumenberg to designate Valéry's image concept in line with Blumenberg's own idea of a concept of reality adequate for the modern age.[15] Understood as obstacles, images resist the attempt to look through them at some alleged reality underneath:

> I believe, on the contrary, that the surest method of judging a picture is to identify nothing at first, but step by step, to make the series of deductions demanded by the simultaneous presence of colored masses in a definite area; then one can rise from metaphor to metaphor, from supposition to supposition, and so attain, in the end, to knowledge of the subject—or sometimes to sheer consciousness of pleasure, which we did not always feel in the beginning.[16]

14. Valéry, *Leonardo, Poe, Mallarme*, 46–47; Blumenberg, "Valérys möglicher Leonardo," 221. As the two volumes of Valéry's *Oeuvres* and the copy of the German translation of Valéry's Leonardo essays by Karl August Horst (Valéry, *Leonardo*) from Blumenberg's estate at the Deutsche Literaturarchiv, Marbach (DLA), reveal, Blumenberg studied, underlined, and annotated Valéry's essays in the French original and the German translation interchangeably. See also Krauthausen, "Hans Blumenbergs präparierter Valéry"; Krauthausen did not yet have access to Horst's translation in Blumenberg's library (for more on Blumenberg's annotations in his copy of Valéry, *Oeuvres*, see below). Besides Valéry's *Oeuvres* and his *Cahiers*, both in the Pléiade edition, there is a volume of essays on Valéry from the Wege der Forschung series (Schmidt-Radefeldt, *Paul Valéry*) in Blumenberg's library that shows underlining as well.

15. Blumenberg, "Paul Valérys möglicher Leonardo," 219; Blumenberg, "Socrates," 434. On "resistance" as a fourth (and final) concept in Blumenberg's taxonomy of concepts of reality, see Blumenberg, "Concept of Reality and the Possibility of the Novel," 505. As I demonstrate elsewhere, the relevance of *Widerstand* in Blumenberg's revised image theory closely resembles the relevance of *Widerstreit* (conflict) in Husserl's image theory (*Phantasie*, §§22–25).

16. Valéry, *Leonardo, Poe, Mallarme*, 47. See Blumenberg's somewhat meandering paraphrase of Valéry's position: "Valéry's idea of painting, which he develops by the example of Leonardo, is certainly bound up with the object-like figurativeness of the painting, but this figurativeness is secondary and instrumental in relation to a non-figurativeness, which in the artist is primarily present as the colors' disposition on the surface" ("Socrates," 433).

Reading Valéry, Blumenberg understands quite well that such a way of seeing a two-dimensional image not only goes against the suppositions of the Renaissance image concept but challenges Plato's image concept as well. In response to such a double challenge, Valéry attempts to transcend the representational qualities of images through a literary paradigm ("metaphor").[17] Blumenberg, on the other hand, restores a Platonic image concept, at least for the image's primeval beginnings, a concept that his own aesthetic preferences will eventually leave behind.[18] For the time being, however, images comply with an age-old "curse of aesthetics" that expresses itself in their tendency to paint over reality's "original terrors" instead of bringing them to mind.[19] In doing so, they fall prey to a "thematically fixed objecthood" that constitutes their basic "weakness."[20] In short, while agreeing with Valéry that images should overcome their inherent realism and should cease to be "instruction manuals for illusions,"[21] Blumenberg disagrees with Valéry's notion that the window image of the Renaissance already steps in such a direction. What prevents it from doing so is its reliance on linear perspective, a technique famously associated with Leonardo's name and work: "The conflict, which ensues here with the technique of central perspective, is palpable, and the reader [Valéry] and his hero [Leonardo] are nowhere farther apart from each other than here."[22] Despite his protestations to the contrary, Blumenberg suspects Valéry of modernizing his subject by suggesting an image concept to Leonardo and the Renaissance that is in fact his own.[23] Conflating the boundaries between himself and his protagonist, Valéry's exegesis of Leonardo ends up in an act of *"uncritical diffusion."*[24] It is this that Blumenberg cannot let pass.

17. Blumenberg, "Paul Valérys möglicher Leonardo," 203, 205. On Plato's image theory, in contrast to Leonardo's, see Welsch, "Das Zeichen des Spiegels."

18. Blumenberg can therefore also suggest that the "confinement [*Verklammerung*] between the original and the copy" is an "inescapable" legacy of the *"concept of the image"* ("Concept of Reality and the Possibility of the Novel," 515).

19. Blumenberg, *Lions*, 18; Blumenberg, *Work*, 15. Hence the following dictum from Blumenberg's estate (DLA), indexed as HGL, underlines both the pleasingness of images and their questionability in an intellectual respect (I am grateful to Bettina Blumenberg for her permission to quote, here and below, from Blumenberg's papers at the DLA): "To study 'images' with any other intent than an aesthetic one would be ridiculous" ("Bilder" ernsthaft und in anderer Absicht als einer ästh[etischen] zu studieren, wäre lächerlich) (my translation). As his estate documents as well, Blumenberg collected countless clippings of photographs of artworks from newspapers and magazines. The vast majority were impressionistic paintings; almost all the clippings represent panel paintings.

20. Blumenberg, "Socrates," 435.

21. Blumenberg, "Essential Ambiguity," 446.

22. Blumenberg, "Paul Valérys möglicher Leonardo," 215 (my translation). See also Valéry's brief discussion of the effects of central perspective in Leonardo's *Last Supper* (*Leonardo, Poe, Mallarme*, 48).

23. Blumenberg, "Paul Valérys möglicher Leonardo," 219.

24. Blumenberg, "Paul Valérys möglicher Leonardo," 222 (my translation).

Paragons and **Paragone***: Leonardo and Valéry*

Valéry's rereading of the window image also evokes the historical context of the Renaissance *paragone*. In the question of which of the arts, painting, sculpture, literature, or music, deserves the highest praise, Valéry's own preference in the matter is obvious. By treating the panel painting as a nonmimetic and basically aniconic entity, Valéry transforms it into a textlike artifice that can be read by piecing its "metaphors" together. He thus contradicts Leonardo's verdict in *Trattato della pittura*, which is in favor of the pictorial arts while downgrading their literary counterparts:

> The eye, which is called the window of the soul, is the principal way through which the mind can most copiously and magnificently consider the infinite works of nature, and the ear is second to it, becoming noble through hearing about things that the eye has beheld. If you historians, poets, or mathematicians had not seen these things with the eye, you would hardly be able to report them in writing. And if you, poet, represent a narrative with a painting of the pen, the painter with a brush will more easily make it satisfying and less tedious to comprehend.[25]

Leonardo thus prioritizes painting above all other arts due to its capacity to create a "real likeness" that is nearer to a man than his "name," which "changes in various countries."[26] Conversely, in the face of seeing, the worthiest of all senses, poetry pales to "blind painting." Knowing of Leonardo's prejudice against writing and text, Valéry summarizes his position almost haltingly: "But for Leonardo, language is not all."[27] In return, he works Leonardo's praise for painting into an ambitious theory in which painting takes the place of philosophy, a discipline that tries "to express in speech or writing the results of [its] meditations."[28] Invoking Leonardo himself, Valéry declares: "*I mean that painting was his* [Leonardo's] *philosophy.*"[29] Valéry thus directly embarks on Leonardo's eulogy on painting. That seems to go against his above-cited reading of the window image along the lines of a literary artifact whose metaphors and abstract formulas are to be decoded. Yet, at a second glance, it becomes apparent that Valéry's understanding of Leonardo's images is no longer geared to features typically associated with visual images. For Valéry, images, including Leonardo's, are not vivid expressions of a tangible

25. Leonardo, *Treatise*, 1:18, §30.
26. Leonardo, *Treatise*, 1:18, §30.
27. Valéry, *Leonardo, Poe, Mallarme*, 134.
28. Valéry, *Leonardo, Poe, Mallarme*.
29. Valéry, *Leonardo, Poe, Mallarme*, 143; see Leonardo, *Treatise*, 1:5, §8: "Painting is therefore philosophy . . . "

reality by way of resemblance but a partly linguistic, partly mathematical "continuity" extended "with the help of metaphors, abstractions, and special languages."[30] Valéry's commendation of painting therefore follows Leonardo's and goes against it at the same time.

For Valéry, Leonardo's images are images and texts at once. They represent a system of "analogies" that does not reference its subject directly but is connected to it through a complicated "calculation of successive phases."[31] To such an analogical figure, which Valéry also relates to the "infinitesimal calculus" of mathematics, rather than representationality, intuition and contiguity are critical.[32] The paragon of such an artwork is obviously not the pictorial image but the literary text and the syntagmatic connections that organize it. Language, on the other hand, is nonrepresentational in Valéry's view, which brings it close to music and the kind of self-referentiality that is typical for Western music since the arrival of the classical symphony in the late eighteenth century.[33] Text and music thus both differ from the pictorial image in that they replace the idea of an assimilation of the represented to its representation by an artistic concept that autonomously generates its subject. Consequently, an overall notion of "construction" orchestrates Valéry's Leonardo interpretation throughout, culminating in the idea of an "intellectual parthenogenesis" according to which the work of art brings forth its topic without fertilization by the object itself.[34] Hence Valéry can declare that the subjects of art—no matter whether visual art, writing, or music—"are never to be found except in oneself."[35] As I show, to Blumenberg such a description of the cultural achievement embodied in the Renaissance concept of linear perspective seems hardly accurate.

30. Valéry, *Leonardo, Poe, Mallarme*, 31.

31. Valéry, *Leonardo, Poe, Mallarme*, 41.

32. Valéry, *Leonardo, Poe, Mallarme*, 79. Valéry derives the idea of a mathematical calculus from Henri Poincaré and his method of "reasoning by recurrence" (*Science*, 11–21). On Valéry's use of the concept of analogy and its relevance to Leonardo's own thinking, see Kemp, "'Hostinato Rigore'"; and Kemp, "Analogy."

33. Valéry, *Leonardo, Poe, Mallarme*, 154; Blumenberg, "Paul Valérys möglicher Leonardo," 222.

34. See, e.g., Valéry, *Leonardo, Poe, Mallarme*, 49 (on "the word *construction*"); and Blumenberg, "Paul Valérys möglicher Leonardo," 199, 204, 207. On the "problems of intellectual parthenogenesis," see Valéry, *Leonardo, Poe, Mallarme*, 106.

35. Valéry, *Leonardo, Poe, Mallarme*, 108. This is being said about the subject of Valéry's essay, Leonardo himself—a fact that indicates the constant self-reflectivity of Valéry's discourse. It has been often observed that Valéry mirrors himself in his "possible" Leonardo (Blumenberg, "Paul Valérys möglicher Leonardo," 195, 203, 216). Not least has Valéry's fragmentary writing style, especially in his *Cahiers*, been traced back to Leonardo's literary notes (Blüher, "Leonardo da Vincis *Quaderni*"). On the impact that Leonardo's studies on the flight of birds had on Valéry, see Krauthausen, "Zwischen Aufzeichnung."

Valéry and Blumenberg on Leonardo's Architectural Sketches and Scientific Drawings

But Valéry appears to have anticipated such a concern already. This is one reason he touches on Leonardo's painterly work—or any of his works—just in passing. The *Mona Lisa* and *The Last Supper* are at least mentioned briefly, while the artist Leonardo at large is notably absent from Valéry's deliberations:[36] "The artists and art-lovers who have turned these pages in the hope of renewing some of the impressions to be obtained at the Louvre, or in Florence and Milan, must excuse me for disappointing them."[37] Valéry's Leonardo essays lack images and image descriptions to the same extent that his rereading of the window image puts a decidedly literary symbol system in its place. The only works that get some more attention are, not surprisingly, Leonardo's so-called deluge drawings and architectural sketches.[38] They stand out among his creations to the extent that they no longer adhere to the visual regime of central perspective. Following Valéry, Blumenberg has expressed this by saying that Leonardo's architectural sketches launch a new "interpretation of space . . . , one that finally breaks with the concept of the architectural theatre setting, that is a reality only for one privileged point of view."[39] Obviously, Leonardo's art appeals all the more to Valéry *and* Blumenberg the more it abandons perspectival techniques. In fact, Leonardo's drawings and sketches announce themselves as harbingers of a modern art that eventually leaves behind artistic concerns still vital to the Renaissance.[40] The form of art that in Valéry's and Blumenberg's eyes becomes exemplary for a postmimetic and postperspectival

36. Valéry, *Leonardo, Poe, Mallarme*, 47–48. Further—equally brief—mentions of Leonardo's artistic works can be found in his *Cahiers*, 1:1067 (*Vitruvian Man*), 2:692 (*Annunciata*). The sources of Valéry's readings of Leonardo, basically all dating from the late nineteenth century, have been documented by Kemp, "'Hostinato Rigore.'" See also Krauthausen, "Hans Blumenbergs möglicher Valéry," 51.

37. Valéry, *Leonardo*, 60. See also Blumenberg, "Valérys möglicher Leonardo," 194, 197 (on Valéry's failure to comment on *sfumato* and *impeto* in Leonardo). In a 1939 essay on Leonardo, usually not considered an integral part of his Leonardo essays and thus missing from the Pléiade edition of his works, Valéry conceded: "Maybe . . . I sometimes find his writings so much more to my taste than his paintings" (*Zur Ästhetik und Philosophie der Künste*, 146; my translation).

38. Valéry, *Leonardo, Poe, Mallarme*, 33, 51–52; Blumenberg, "Paul Valérys möglicher Leonardo," 216, 222.

39. Blumenberg, "Paul Valérys möglicher Leonardo," 222 (my translation). Valéry and Blumenberg both identify these sketches of concentric buildings erroneously as possible sketches for *Saint Peter* in Rome.

40. On Leonardo's varying views on linear perspective, see Leonardo, *Notebooks*, §§40–109. After 1500 the concept of linear perspective becomes less relevant for Leonardo, who begins to favor perspectival techniques such as *sfumato* (see, e.g., Fehrenbach, "Der oszillierende Blick").

image concept is therefore the "ornament," right next to architecture and music, which are "per se ruled out from the ideal of an imitation of nature":[41] "They [architecture and music] *produce* realities, which are meant to *signify only themselves.* Yet such a principle is disobeyed where the constructional idea speculates for a definite and privileged perspective, where it is, so to speak, geared to a definite view and does not allow for a full freedom of space as arbitrariness of potential experiences."[42]

Valéry and Blumenberg thus sympathize with an image concept that eventually moves beyond the mimetic and representational window image and substitutes it with what Blumenberg considers the ambivalent aesthetic object, a concept modeled on Valéry's famous "objet ambigu." Different from Valéry, though, Blumenberg finds its prototype *not* in the art of Leonardo, whom Valéry reads against the grain, but in modern art and its nonfigurative aesthetics:

> One could argue that such a notion [of the "ambiguity of the aesthetic object"] is contradicted by the phenomenon that linear perspective has been neutralized in modern painting. Quite the contrary: this process confirms precisely that the technical determination of the spectator's point of view, chosen by the artist, is a nuisance to be eliminated. The inclusion of a plurality as the simultaneity of aspects into the picture itself (Picasso), and likewise the ruptured structure of anticipation in sculpture (Archipenko, Moore), confirm that the aesthetic object should no longer force the viewer's choice of interpretive standpoint, but should rather leave it open, and that it, exactly because of this, condenses into a new degree of reality. The disdain for generating illusion, which was connected to the technique of linear perspective and with satisfying typical anticipations of space, rests on a dismissal of the sacrifice made when the aesthetic work becomes the terminus, the absolute point of reference of the aesthetic relation. Modern painting and modern sculpture do not wish to be instruction manuals for illusions, making something else visible; they want to be that, and nothing but that, as which they present themselves to be.[43]

Hence the dismissal of a privileged viewpoint as favored by central perspective goes hand in hand with a dismissal of the traditional prerogative of the visual arts to mimetically and realistically picture its objects. That way, Blumenberg arrives at his image theory through a critical reception of Valéry's

41. Valéry, *Leonardo, Poe, Mallarme,* 49; Blumenberg, "Socrates," 412–13.
42. Blumenberg, "Paul Valérys möglicher Leonardo," 222 (my translation).
43. Blumenberg, "Essential Ambiguity," 446.

essays on Leonardo whose anachronistic account he undoes without dissolving his aesthetic bias that favors an image concept that negates a representational paradigm.[44]

From the "Possible" to the Historical Leonardo: Blumenberg against Valéry

Blumenberg's rehistoricization of Leonardo unfolds in various steps and on various levels.[45] First, he disagrees with Valéry's ideal of a "Poésie pure" that aims to extract "a given, rare substance from language" and pursues an "inherent quality, as the result of a possible selection."[46] Instead, Blumenberg suggests that poeticity is the result of a "process of dismantling common language's obviousness,"[47] that is, a literary strategy of defamiliarization and deconventionalization that replaces a substantial definition of poetry with a functional one. Second, he disagrees with Valéry's settlement of the image-text *paragone*. The kind of modern poetry and art that Valéry privileges makes for an unfair measure by which to judge Leonardo and the art of the early modern period. Like the "no-longer-beautiful arts,"[48] they are, instead, the product of a historical evolution in which different artistic media came to serve different concepts of reality and different expressive needs in a variety of ways. Valéry thus misses an important opportunity, a critique of Leonardo's art that follows from a critique of the episteme of his time. Blumenberg's *paragone*, on the other hand, remains faithful to an almost religious belief in epochs by arranging historical art forms in an ascending line, from pictorial to literary and from more to less mimetic.[49] Thus what lyric poetry and nonfigurative art

44. In Blumenberg's estate at the DLA one finds another version of his essay "Paul Valérys möglicher Leonardo," abbreviated PVY, in which Blumenberg clearly expresses the differences he sees between Valéry's Leonardo and the historical figure (about whom little might be known but who did exist): "He [Valéry] concerned himself as little with Goethe as he did with Leonardo or Socrates; he fabricated all three almost completely" (Er hat sich mit Goethe so wenig beschäftigt wie mit Leonardo oder mit Sokrates; er hat alle drei nahezu frei erfunden) (my translation). Research on the subject has frequently overlooked Blumenberg's disagreement with Valéry, let alone his criticism of Leonardo himself (see, e.g., Krauthausen, "Hans Blumenbergs möglicher Valéry"). For less affirmative readings of Blumenberg's writings on Valéry, see Konersmann, "Stoff"; Koch, "Valéry"; and Flasch, *Hans Blumenberg*, 224–31, 456–70.

45. Blumenberg's historical approach also manifests itself in the extensive underlining he adds to the *Introduction biographique* of his copy of Valéry, *Oeuvres*, 1:11–72—as if he wanted to prove Valéry wrong also in the case of the latter's own life.

46. Blumenberg, "Speech Situation," 457; Flasch, *Hans Blumenberg*, 457.

47. Blumenberg, "Speech Situation," 458.

48. Jauss, *Die nicht mehr schönen Künste.*

49. For a critical account of Blumenberg's allegiance to thinking in epochs, see Flasch, *Hans Blumenberg*, 452. Blumenberg himself emphasizes the heuristic function of the concept of epochs, for instance, in his introduction to Cues, *Die Kunst der Vermutung*, 10–11.

are to the modern age is the novel to the seventeenth and eighteenth centuries and the pictorial image to the Renaissance: art forms that represent, first and foremost, their respective age.[50] In such a view, however, the Renaissance comes to occupy an ambivalent position. It both promotes a mimetic art concept and begins to question it. Such questioning can be seen, according to Blumenberg, in mannerism and painters like Parmigianino, who experiment with a "deformation" of central perspective.[51] It then continues, since Gottfried Wilhelm Leibniz and the "Genieästhetik" (aesthetics of genius), with a general paradigm shift from other art forms to writing and text.[52] And it finally concludes with the poetry of T. S. Eliot, Ezra Pound, and Valéry himself,[53] as well as with the pictorial abstractions of Paul Klee,[54] Henri Matisse,[55] and others. In the wake of such a process, the principle of an imitation of nature is being pushed back constantly, following a tendency that Leonardo prepares for but is not yet a part of himself:

> Without being aware of the metaphysical background, Oskar Walzel traces the mid-eighteenth-century idea of the creative genius back to Leibniz. Walzel makes it especially clear how the comparison of God to the creative artist already contained within it the artist's comparison of himself to God. In terms of *logic*, there will be nothing added here between the Renaissance and the *Sturm und Drang*. It is nonetheless decisively important that *poetry* comes to achieve a particular significance in this comparison. While the comparison of God to the master craftsman and the painter go back to antiquity, now the poet becomes the preeminent "creator," and not coincidentally, but rather—as is now simply obvious—because of the destruction of the mimesis idea. In his *Treatise on Painting*, Leonardo da Vinci established the similarity of the painter to God: by imitating nature, the painter imitates its creator. And the rebellion of Mannerism against mimesis had de facto only managed an ostentatious deformation of nature.[56]

Looking back from such a historical vantage point at Valéry's ideal of aesthetic "purity," Blumenberg finds it to be a "final and late product of aes-

---

50. Blumenberg, "Imitation," 353.
51. Blumenberg, "Imitation," 317–18, 353.
52. Blumenberg, "Imitation," 353.
53. Blumenberg, "Essential Ambiguity," 444; Blumenberg, "Speech Situation," 464.
54. Blumenberg, "Imitation," 356–57; Blumenberg, "Speech Situation," 454.
55. Blumenberg, "Imitation," 319n8.
56. Blumenberg, "Imitation," 353. The reference is to Walzel, *Prometheussymbol*, and to Walzel's history of the idea of the artist as a genius. Blumenberg develops a critique of the mimesis principle in reference to Cusa's nonrepresentational concept of the "vestige" or "trace" in *Legitimacy*, 497.

thetic reflection" rather than an artistic option available at all times.[57] Most notably, it cannot be projected backward onto Leonardo and the image concept of the Renaissance: on the contrary, the latter keeps pointing to "another, exemplary being" instead of becoming "this exemplary being" itself.[58] Leonardo's Renaissance art "means" more than it "is."

Leonardo and Copernicus: Perspective Reevaluated

In the end, the reason Blumenberg disagrees with Valéry's reading of Leonardo lies in his analysis of the Renaissance invention of central perspective. For Blumenberg, central perspective is a pictorial device that originated from the epochal threshold between the late Middle Ages and the early modern period.[59] As such, it responds to a secular shift that was initiated by thinkers such as Augustine, Thomas Aquinas, and Nicholas of Cusa, who realized that a world created through an act of divine arbitrariness could hardly be a world created for humankind's sake: if God had autocratically opted for this world instead of any other, then the Aristotelian idea that nature and humankind were embedded in a meaningful whole was no longer viable. As a result, the world as creation found itself at odds with the world as cosmos. The only remaining stratum, though, in which the teleological belief in a world revolving around the sphere of human needs could be retained was the self-made universe of human products and artistry: "There was no mention at all any more of a telos directed at man, and made *for* man in a strict sense is only what is brought forth by the *artes* of man. Man is the being that can bring forth a region of reality teleologically assigned to him, and in that region he is the point of reference [*Sinnbezug*] of all things."[60]

Consequently, the Aristotelian art principle of an imitation of nature was no longer defensible either. Why imitate a nature that had lost its philosophical and theological reputation? Yet due to the authority of the Aristotelian principle that had outlived its demise, any new principle still had to follow its model. This is where Blumenberg's interpretation of Cusa's famous episode of the spoon carver from his *Idiota de mente* (1450) comes into play in which the old doctrine of the mimetic arts is salvaged by transposing it to an imitation of the "*ars infinita* [infinite art] of God himself."[61] As an imitation of God's creativity, the mimesis principle stays alive and, applied to a human-made cre-

---

57. Blumenberg, "Paul Valérys möglicher Leonardo," 216–17.
58. Blumenberg, "Imitation," 356.
59. Blumenberg, "Paul Valérys möglicher Leonardo," 218.
60. Blumenberg, "Kosmos," 71 (my translation). See also Blumenberg, *Legitimacy*, 457–596.
61. Blumenberg, "Imitation," 320.

ation of the world, helps bridge the abyss between a previously teleological universe and its post-teleological redesign. Such a redesign occurs at first in the technological realm, as with Cusa's spoon-carving craftsman, and is adopted by the fine arts thereafter:

> It is of immeasurable significance that here the entire pathos of creative, originary human beings breaking with the principle of imitation is expressed by a *technician*—not by an *artist*. This distinction is probably *positively* accentuated here for the first time, and therein lies the value of the testimony, when one looks ahead and sees how almost immediately creative testimonials center on pictorial art and poetry. Part of the development of art from the end of the Middle Ages on is precisely that it becomes the place where the artist begins to discuss himself and his creative spontaneity.[62]

In Blumenberg's considerations it will be Leonardo's privilege to unite both—a post-teleological redesign of a no-longer-teleological nature and the idea of a godlike artist—in the same person: "That a key figure of nascent modernity such as Leonardo da Vinci should have been both an artist and a technician is no coincidence but rather confirms the unity of origin."[63] But even Leonardo cannot divest himself of the venerable doctrine according to which art has to imitate nature. While he shifts the scope of what is imitated from the *natura naturata* to the *natura naturans* (just like Cusa did), that is, to nature's own creativity, and thus alleviates the comparison of the artist to a godlike figure, Leonardo still seems to prolong an art-theoretical terminology that is actually outdated.[64] Such an anachronism, it turns out, is due to a dilemma Leonardo and his contemporaries find themselves in:

> The creative self-consciousness that emerged at the border between the Middle Ages and the modern period found itself ontologically inarticulable. As painters began to search for a "theory," they assimilated Aristotelian poetics: the creative "notion" [*Einfall*] was referred to with the metaphor of *enthusiasmo* [enthusiasm] and by using expressions of a secularized *illuminatio* [enlightenment]. The difficulty of articulation in the face of the overemphasis

---

62. Blumenberg, "Imitation," 321. See also Blumenberg, "Relationship," 312, where it seems to be the artist who claims the idea of *inventio* prior to the technician.

63. Blumenberg, "Relationship," 312. See introduction to Cues, *Die Kunst der Vermutung*, 58.

64. See also Fehrenbach's critical discussion of Blumenberg's verdict about Leonardo's alleged attachment to the mimesis principle (Fehrenbach, *Licht und Wasser*, 62–64). Krauthausen's suggestion that Blumenberg does not even mention Leonardo in "Nachahmung der Natur" is incorrect ("Hans Blumenbergs möglicher Valéry," 46).

of the *imitatio* [imitation] tradition *and* the Renaissance gesture of rebellion are all of a piece. The appearance of something that had become ontologically unquestionable constituted a zone of legitimacy in which new ways of understanding could only succeed with force.[65]

A similar ambivalence, between a breakthrough of the new and a preservation of the old, also characterizes Leonardo's scientific and technological endeavors. According to Blumenberg, Leonardo's attempts to build an "airplane" ("Flugmaschine") attest to an exemplariness of the flight of birds that remains to serve as a model for an otherwise mechanical enterprise. Leonardo's related experiments thus drag along the Aristotelian imitation principle in a realm where the problem's solution lies in its abandonment: "The airplane was an actual *invention* in that it freed itself from the old dream of imitating the flight of birds and solved the problem using a new principle."[66] While this might not be an accurate statement on behalf of Leonardo's studies, which around 1505 took a different direction, leaving behind the idea that the wing beat of birds could be considered a model for a flying machine,[67] it underlines the core of Blumenberg's argument. It seems as if the revolutionary curiosity and inventiveness of the Renaissance had been in need of a fig leaf that could hide its metaphysical impertinence behind a seemingly conventional thought. Leonardo's situation thus closely resembles the situation of his famous contemporary, Copernicus, whom Blumenberg mentions regularly in the context of Leonardo: both had to reconcile the revolutionary appeal of their discoveries with recourse to older ideas and convictions, which they did not want to fully dismiss yet.[68]

In Copernicus's case, such reconciliation was one between the lately gained realization of humanity's physical location in the margins of the universe and the simultaneous anthropocentrism of a world revolving around humanity's curious gaze. It was therefore Copernicus's impetus to bring the newly discovered "astronomical world model" in line with the older "metaphysical world conviction," according to which the cosmos was centered in humankind.[69] To do so, he had to establish an "inner foundational connection

65. Blumenberg, "Imitation," 323–24.

66. Blumenberg, "Imitation," 323. See also Blumenberg, *Paradigms*, 68. For Valéry's comments on Leonardo's studies on flying, see Valéry, *Leonardo, Poe, Mallarme*, 24, 36, 63; and Valéry, *Cahiers*, 1:336–37, 853.

67. Fehrenbach, "Taking Flight," 277; Laurana, *Leonardo on Flight*.

68. Blumenberg, "Kopernikus," 461. Pierre Duhem's famous thesis about the medieval roots of Leonardo's worldview is discussed by Blumenberg on the occasion of his review of Anneliese Maier's research on the natural philosophy of the fourteenth century ("Die Vorbereitung der Neuzeit").

69. Blumenberg, "Kosmos," 65 (my translation). See also Wetz, *Hans Blumenberg*, 68–91.

between a humanist world view and the new world model."[70] The only way he could relate again what was no longer related was through a perspectival technique that allowed him to "renounce the cosmological center position of humankind . . . because through such a renouncement he could maintain and confirm the center position of human rationality."[71] Copernicus's technique thus closely resembles the one that in Leonardo's oeuvre figures as central perspective: a view of the visible world suggestively geared to the human eye that contemplates it. Because of its conciliatory nature, central perspective not only brings to mind but also needs to conceal the ambivalence on which it is built: between a world made in favor of humankind, on the one hand, and the relativity and subjectivity of such a view, on the other. Nevertheless, the sights that central perspective engenders cannot but betray their dependence on an enabling yet contingent standpoint that could as well be different:[72]

> Discovery of *perspective* and discovery of *prejudice* are equally founding events of the early modern period; what comes from it is "standpoint awareness" as the all-pervasive reflection or reflective maxim, but also eventually awareness of the limitations of a possible self-localization, of the possibility to ideologically functionalize even this seemingly ultimate endeavor of self-understanding. Leonardo's genealogy from the *scientia della pittura* to perspective and from there to astronomy is not that mythical and its extension from astronomy to monadology and from there to historicism wouldn't be that mythical either.[73]

In other words, the resemblance the window image creates between the object and its representation is one that is conscious of the contingency on which it rests, while it also hides such a fact behind an imitation principle that

70. Blumenberg, "Kosmos," 64 (my translation).

71. Blumenberg, *Kopernikus im Selbstverständnis*, 30 (my translation).

72. Panofsky refers to this double-sidedness of central perspective as the togetherness of a "subjective visual impression" and the "objectification of the subjective" (*Perspective*, 66). Although Blumenberg nowhere refers to Panofsky's famous essay, he was certainly aware of it, as he made a note of it on one of his index cards. Instead, he keeps referencing the works of Dagobert Frey ("Kunst und Weltbild"; *Gotik und Renaissance*), an Austrian art historian infamous for his involvement with German Nazism, whenever an art-historical account of central perspective is in demand. On the history of central perspective and its demise, from a perspective independent of Blumenberg's yet with similar results, see Boehm, *Studien zur Perspektivität*; Giesecke, "Der Verlust der zentralen Perspektive"; and Borchmeyer, "Aufstieg und Fall."

73. Blumenberg, *Kopernikus im Selbstverständnis*, 17n1 (my translation). See also introduction to Cues, *Die Kunst der Vermutung*, 27.

lends said resemblance an objective status.[74] But the visual image cannot but fall behind the complexities and differentiation that language-based representation is capable of: it cannot present a perfectly illusionary image and revoke such a view at once. The visual image of the window type thus must appear more realistic and less ambiguous than it actually is. Hence what Leonardo himself knows, his works cannot put on display: the worlds he creates are as real as they are fictive.

Central perspective therefore is, and has to be, nontransparent in regard to its own principles. This idea Blumenberg seems to have developed directly from one of Valéry's Leonardo essays. There Valéry comments on the necessary obfuscation, which the standpoint of the spectator has to undergo in order to render the viewed image visible in the first place: "The image it [Leonardo's 'perfected consciousness'] brings to mind spontaneously is that of an invisible audience seated in a darkened theater—a presence that cannot observe itself and is condemned to watch the scene confronting it, yet can feel nevertheless how it creates all that breathless and irresistibly directed darkness."[75] Central perspective thus prioritizes "seeing" over "being-seen," reverting, as it were, the anthropological and paleontological primal scene in which the visibility of the human race was its greatest threat, causing its retreat to the secluded, cave-like comfort zone of seeing without being seen.[76] But while Valéry links such a state of splendid isolation to his concept of the "pure I" ("le moi pure"), a "theoretical being" devoid of any name and history, which he identifies with Leonardo and his science,[77] Blumenberg stops short of such a cathartic conclusion. Instead, his Leonardo finds himself projected at the historical backdrop of the Renaissance and the age's ambivalence between old and new.

As a matter of fact, Blumenberg can therefore associate Leonardo's world picture with a pre-Copernican as well as a post-Copernican view, insofar as his work still knows of "a privileged standpoint of man as its chosen spectator" and, at the same time, is "without regard to man and a specific observational standpoint."[78] Analogously, Blumenberg's 1965 essay *Kopernikus im*

74. Blumenberg expresses this same idea in regard to Cusa's reading of the all-seeing image of God in *De vision dei*, an image whose gaze is "always only a gaze 'for me,'" not an objectifiable property of the image itself (Cues, *Die Kunst der Vermutung*, 310; my translation). Ironically, the icon discussed in Cusa's essay is a medieval *vera icon* and not a perspectival Renaissance-type image—a fact Blumenberg does not reflect.

75. Valéry, *Leonardo, Poe, Mallarme*, 96–97. Obviously, the situation of the witness of the perspectival image closely resembles that of Plato's caveman in Blumenberg's account.

76. Blumenberg, "Paul Valérys möglicher Leonardo," 215.

77. Valéry, *Leonardo, Poe, Mallarme*, 102, 106.

78. Blumenberg, "Paul Valérys möglicher Leonardo," 223 (my translation). On the "anti-medieval trait" of central perspective that, by privileging "seeing" over "being seen," provides human consciousness with a "new tenure," see 215 (my translation).

Selbstverständnis der Neuzeit references Leonardo as an example of Copernican standpoint consciousness, while his 1966 essay "Paul Valérys möglicher
Leonardo" denies his physics any "Copernican forebodings."[79] Such inconsis-
tency is not least owed to Leonardo's (and his time's) ambivalence in the matter.[80] Blumenberg's frequent observation that Leonardo "should have been
both an artist and a technician is no coincidence" therefore needs to be understood properly.[81] It is not the case that the painter just executed what the technician had contrived already. The "unity" of the two, technician and painter,
points at their respective "origin," the rebelliousness of the Renaissance's scientific discoveries, on the one hand, and the lack of a similarly complex theory
of art, on the other.[82] Hence the traditional mimesis principle has to cover for a
pictorial aesthetics that, in the name of central perspective, speaks to its scientific genesis while also making it invisible through the naturalistic appeal of the
very images that it prompts. The "unity of theoretical curiosity and aesthetic
firstness of sight, which manifests itself so uniquely in any and every of Leonardo's sketches," hence has to be taken as that:[83] the aesthetic equivalent of a
world that seems to reveal itself as a sheer given to the exploring eye.[84]

Blumenberg on Leonardo's Science: Cave Exits and the Deluge
Blumenberg barely talks about Leonardo's artistic work—like Valéry he
mostly mentions the sketches and drawings as instances of a postperspectival
and post-teleological art. Despite that, he holds Leonardo's studies on nature in
high esteem,[85] most prominently his so-called "Fragment einer Höhlenfor-

79. Blumenberg, *Kopernikus im Selbstverständnis*, 17n1 (my translation); Blumenberg, "Paul
Valérys möglicher Leonardo," 223. Valéry's own aesthetics Blumenberg considers "Copernican in a
decidedly catching-up sense" (nachholenden Sinne) ("Die Selbsterfindung," 57; my translation).
80. On one of his index cards (now at the DLA), Blumenberg states: "The overcoming of perspective in modern painting is tantamount to the elimination of the point of view of the spectator in science"
(Die Überwindung der Perspektive in der modernen Malerei entspricht der Ausschaltung des Betrach-
terstandpunktes in der Wissenschaft) (my translation). The ambiguities of such statements also follow
from a nonlinear conception of history typical for Blumenberg that not only permits but invites leaps
and nonsimultaneities (see Bajohr, "Hans Blumenberg's History").
81. Blumenberg, "Relationship," 312. See Blumenberg, "Paul Valérys möglicher Leonardo," 211,
213; and Valéry, *Leonardo, Poe, Mallarme*, 205.
82. Blumenberg, "Imitation," 324. Contrary to Freud, who in Leonardo's persona perceives a
dichotomy of artist and scientist (*A Fantasy*), Blumenberg sees the two as necessarily correlated ("Neugierde," 36). On the history of the idea of a scientist/artist dichotomy in Leonardo scholarship, see Fehrenbach, "Leonardos Vermächtnis?"
83. Blumenberg, "Paul Valérys möglicher Leonardo," 213 (my translation).
84. That such an account, despite its ambiguities and reservations, underestimates the complexities
of Leonardo's optical theory and aesthetics will be taken up below.
85. See Blumenberg, "Paul Valérys möglicher Leonardo," 215, 223; Blumenberg, *Legitimacy*,
636n29, 363–64; Blumenberg, *Höhlenausgänge*, 261, 273–74n58, 629; Blumenberg, *Genesis*, 334;

schung" (fragment of a cave exploration), which Blumenberg treats as a ground-breaking document of the scientific turn of the early modern period:

> On the threshold of this century, an exemplary figure of the daring interest in what is remote, out of the way, unexamined, or traditionally prohibited was Leonardo da Vinci (1452–1519). His interest in the playfully varying nature that neither commits itself to its forms nor exhausts them, an interest in what had hitherto remained invisible to the onlooker at the world spectacle, in what was hidden deep in the sea and distant in time in a world that was growing older, and in the realm of the unrealized possibilities of nature and of human invention—all this is pure, as though crystallized, *curiositas*, which enjoys itself even when it stops short of its object at the last moment and leaves it alone. A characteristic example is given by the fragment on the investigation of a cave, which remained fragmentary not only by accident—in its form—but also by virtue of its outcome.[86]

Leonardo's science and his antiteleological agenda force him to look behind the scenes of a world whose veneer his paintings still uphold (according to Blumenberg). In doing so, Leonardo's studies set foot into a creation that no longer seems to care about humanity but extends its realm beyond the visible and the lifespan of the human race. Hence his speleology introduces an idea that will be carried to an extreme in the apocalyptic visions of his visual and textual deluge fantasies. They seem to go as far as to deny humankind "a livability on earth" and thus serve as the "epitome of an a-teleology" that Leonardo's thinking appears to be aimed at after all.[87] Copernicus, for his part, had responded to such an intellectual threat by reinstating a humanist and "platonic eschatology," the idea of human rationality as bringing the centrifugal tendencies of a radically unhinged universe back into line.[88] Leonardo does much the

---

Blumenberg, "Imitation," 322–23; and Blumenberg, *Paradigms*, 68. Even when mentioning Leonardo's remarks on Botticelli and the latter's deliberations on how to discover images in stains on walls, Blumenberg refrains from discussing Leonardo's aesthetics. Instead, he takes the quote as an example of Leonardo's "universality" ("Paul Valérys möglicher Leonardo," 209–11). For Leonardo's note, see Leonardo, *Treatise*, 1:59, §93. See also 1:50–51, §76; 1:108–9, §261.

86. Blumenberg, *Legitimacy*, 363. For the passage in question, see Leonardo, *Notebooks*, §1339. According to Pedretti, Leonardo's account carries at least "poetic" traits (*Literary Works*, 2:294). Blumenberg's reference to Leonardo's *Madonna on the Rocks* as "Höhlenmadonna" also reveals the formative role of Joseph Gantner's book on Leonardo as well as the prevalence that Leonardo's science takes in Blumenberg's views even where his artistic work is at stake (Blumenberg, *Legitimacy*, 639n3; Gantner, *Leonardos Visionen*, 102).

87. Blumenberg, *Genesis*, 334, 498; Blumenberg, "Paul Valérys möglicher Leonardo," 206, 224; Blumenberg, "Teleologie," 676.

88. Blumenberg, *Genesis*, 334.

same, namely, through the aesthetics of the window image that recenters a lost perspective on the picture plane.[89] Following Blumenberg, his images therefore preserve what Leonardo's scientific and technological investigations have long dissolved: a world based on and centered on a human viewpoint. To that effect, his study of birds and their flight expresses this symptomatic conflict as well, at least in Blumenberg's perception: it experiments with a "view from above," traditionally reserved for the gods, and simultaneously alleviates the sinfulness of such a thought by couching it in the aesthetic terms of an imitation of nature.[90] Only in the duality of *"imitatio"* and *"inventio"* can Leonardo's method thus come to itself.[91]

But the anxiety that determined the medieval mind whenever boundaries were at stake is still at work also in Leonardo's thought experiments. That is at least what Blumenberg argues in his response to Valéry's aphorism about Leonardo's and Pascal's "abyss"—a passage from Valéry's work that, according to its many reflections in his estate at the DLA, Blumenberg must have been obsessed with.[92] In it, Valéry suggested that the rationality of Leonardo's science did not allow for a metaphysical terror of the kind Pascal, the Catholic theologian, had felt:[93] "No revelations for Leonardo. No abyss opening on his right. An abyss would make him think of a bridge. An abyss might serve for his trial flights of some great mechanical bird."[94] Valéry thus sees his Leonardo

---

89. Introduction to Cues, *Die Kunst der Vermutung*, 27.

90. Blumenberg, *Legitimacy*, 636n247. Again, Blumenberg is following a suggestion by Gantner, *Leonardos Visionen*, 138, 143, 148–49 (once more, Leonardo's art, in this case the *Mona Lisa*, comes into view solely as a testimony of his scientific ideas).

91. Blumenberg, "Relationship," 313. On the relationship of imitation and invention in Renaissance art theory, including Leonardo, see Kemp, "From Mimesis."

92. See, e.g., the following note from Blumenberg's estate (with the index UNF 925): "The other aspect is that abysses don't belong to the orderly world. This great idea of Leonardo's, Valéry, coming across his antipode Pascal at the end of his century, did not dare to use. Leonardo went by a Neptunian eschatology: a world ruled by weathering and erosion, the ablation of mountains and even continents, the replenishment of the depths of the sea. The world would be in the end what could only qualify her as a heavenly body: a perfect sphere whose entire surface is completely covered by the sea. Abysses would then have been an episode" (Das andere Moment ist, daß Abgründe nicht in eine ordnungsgemäße Welt gehören. Diesen großen Gedanken Leonardos hat Valéry, am Ende seines Jahrhunderts auf seinen Antipoden Pascal stoßend, nicht zu verwenden gewagt. Leonardo hatte eine neptunische Eschatologie: eine Welt, beherrscht von Verwitterung und Erosion, von der Abtragung der Gebirge und sogar der Kontinente, der Auffüllung der Meerestiefen. Sie würde am Ende sein, was sie als Weltkörper erst qualifizieren könnte: durch vollkommene Bedeckung ihrer gesamten Oberfläche mit dem Ozean die vollkommene Kugel. Abgründe wären dann eine Episode gewesen) (my translation).

93. For more context, see the explanations given by the editor in Valéry, *Leonardo, Poe, Mallarme*, 437.

94. Valéry, *Leonardo, Poe, Mallarme*, 79.

removed from any religious unrest typical for the past or a figure like Pascal. Blumenberg, on the other hand, wonders whether Leonardo's science had put such older concerns at rest or whether the problem of modern technology had to be reconceived in the very face of it:

> If the Leonardo of Valéry's dictum had really thought of a bridge in the face of the abyss, then he, too, would have merely leapt over the stage of feeling horror, but he would not have omitted it. The act of self-assertion, which avoids exposure to the chasm's pull in the first place, does not make it disappear. Thinking from one fixed point to another—which includes the leap as much as giving oneself up to transcendence—receives its necessity and energy precisely from the anxiety about its ineliminable discontinuities.[95]

To Blumenberg, especially Leonardo's so-called deluge drawings underscore such an inner conflict between self-assertion and anxiety. The deluge drawings belong to a body of drawings, nowadays held at Windsor Castle, that first enjoyed popularity after the 1920s. As Frank Fehrenbach has shown, their existence was not even known prior to the 1830s and gained attention only in the 1880s, due to Jean Paul Richter's standard edition of Leonardo's *Literary Works,* which reprinted the artist's thematically related notes.[96] Still, from biographies and monographs on Leonardo the deluge drawings remained largely absent until Anny E. Popp's 1928 book *Leonardo da Vinci: Zeichnungen.* Only through Kenneth Clark's highly influential 1939 study *Leonardo da Vinci: An Account of his Development as an Artist* did they receive their still-common, almost mythical nimbus as the logical end point of a genius's work that was presumably directed at its final dissolution in despair and ruin. While such a view of the deluge drawings has been rejected in current research, it was still in full flower when Blumenberg encountered Leonardo.[97] It was not least propagated by Joseph Gantner's *Leonardos Visionen von der Sintflut und vom*

---

95. Blumenberg, "Phenomenological Aspects," 359–60. See also the following note from Blumenberg's estate at the DLA (indexed as UNF 1002): "For he who in the face of an abyss devises a bridge may himself be its bold designer and builder—the people he imagines to cross that abyss, thanks to such unique bridging, need no longer look into the abyss. . . . The inventors may be as unfrightened as they please, they have a world of the opposite, of timidity, safeties and walkability, to back their designs" (Denn wer angesichts des Abgrundes auf eine Brücke sinnt, mag zwar selbst ihr kühner Konstrukteur und Erbauer werden—die Menschen, die er als den Abgrund überschreitende im Auge hat, sollen gerade durch den einmaligen Brückenschlag den Blick in den Abgrund nicht mehr nötig haben. . . . Die Erfinder mögen unerschrocken sein, wie sie wollen, sie haben zum Hintergrund ihres Entwerfens eine Welt ihres Gegenteils, des Kleinmuts, der Sicherungen und Begehbarkeiten) (my translation).

96. Fehrenbach, "Leonardos Vermächtnis?," 11–12; Leonardo, *Notebooks,* 607–9.

97. Fehrenbach, "Leonardos Vermächtnis?"; Welsch, "Water or Wind?"

Untergang der Welt (1958), to which Blumenberg refers whenever the artist's deluge drawings and writings come into view. Gantner argued that Leonardo, when nearing his end, felt committed to again destroy a universe that he himself had helped build.[98] The destructive urge that supposedly expresses itself in the deluge drawings thus serves as a flip side of Leonardo's drive for knowledge, so that the artist Leonardo appears to be fighting the scientist.[99] However, Blumenberg follows less Gantner's proposition of a dilemma of art and science than his hint at the pivotal role of the deluge drawings for an understanding of Leonardo as a whole.[100] For Blumenberg, science and art formed a "unity" in Leonardo, a necessary alliance between the systematically contradicting yet historically complementing principles of imitation and invention. Thus Leonardo was neither a nihilist in disguise (Gantner's view) nor a psychopath (Sigmund Freud's portrayal) but the exponent of an epochal shift that took him all the way from the Middle Ages to modernity and back again to the humanistic convictions of the classical age.[101] As such, he had to reintegrate the idea of a posthuman, eccentric universe, as envisioned by early modern science and philosophy, into a system that held on to the consolations of a world "*propter nos conditus*" (founded for us).[102]

The Nonrepresentational Image and the "Essentially Ambivalent Aesthetic Object"

At the same time, Blumenberg seems to have been impressed by Gantner's characterization of Leonardo's deluge drawings as nonperspectival images presaging the abstractions of the visual arts of Blumenberg's own age.[103] Such an idea echoes from the comments that at least indirectly concern Leonardo's art. It also brings us back to Blumenberg's image theory as well as to what may be seen as its counterpart, the "essentially ambivalent aesthetic object" that leaves perspectival techniques behind and opens itself up to a multiplicity of concurrent viewpoints. The latter ideal Blumenberg finds realized, above all else, in Valéry's poetics and in his commitment to an image concept that goes against

---

98. Gantner, *Leonardos Visionen*, 73.

99. Fehrenbach, "Leonardos Vermächtnis?," 9.

100. Another point of disagreement between Blumenberg and Gantner concerns their appreciation for Valéry's Leonardo, on whom Gantner comments rather critically (*Leonardos Visionen*, 39, 60).

101. On Blumenberg's critical reception of Freud's Leonardo, see Blumenberg, "Neugierde," 35–37; and Blumenberg, *Legitimacy*, 451. Zill does not mention this particular aspect of Blumenberg's Freud reception ("Zwischen Affinität und Kritik").

102. Blumenberg, "Kosmos," 64–65.

103. Gantner, *Leonardos Visionen*, 205; Fehrenbach, "Leonardos Vermächtnis?," 9.

the principles of imitation and vividness.[104] As an artistic ideal, it is clearly not—or only contrastingly—derived from examples of visual representation but from the indirectness, invisibility, and immateriality typical of verbal denomination. At the same time, it is aimed against linguistic instances such as the "classic allegory" that "always knows what it represents," whose "referential nexus claims to be univocal by way of this prior knowledge," and that is based on the idea that "the process of understanding may not rest until this univocal reference has been uncovered or apprehended."[105] Contemporary art, on the other hand, "neither presumes the abstract formulation of any specific content nor does it tend toward being comprehended in such a way. There must always remain the possibility of its being deciphered, but it cannot be realized; or rather, any interpretation may—indeed, must—allow for ambiguity, that is, the fact that it cannot be corrected through another, more self-evident one."[106]

With such a trajectory the traditional understanding of visual representation was at odds and hence had to be overcome: "The painterly technique of the central perspective, which assigns the observer his preferred and standardized place as a spectator, is an expression of this defense against the infinite variety of possible aspects."[107] A nonmimetic aesthetic in this sense has been adopted by the visual arts, too, to the extent that "modern painting and modern sculpture do not wish to be instruction manuals for illusions, making something else visible; they want to be that, and nothing but that, as which they present themselves to be."[108] The contrast to an image concept such as Leonardo's and his scientific worldview could hardly be more evident to Blumenberg:

> The aesthetic attitude lets the indeterminacy stand, it achieves the pleasure specific to it by relinquishing theoretical curiosity, which in the end demands and must demand univocity in the determination of its objects. The aesthetic attitude accomplishes less because it tolerates more and lets the object be strong on its own rather than letting it be absorbed by the questions posed to it in its objectivation.[109]

104. On Blumenberg's aesthetics of ambiguity (*Vieldeutigkeit*) and nonrepresentationality and their resonance in Valéry's art and art theory, see also Gamm, "Das Schönste," 101–8.

105. Blumenberg, "Essential Ambiguity," 443.

106. Blumenberg, "Essential Ambiguity," 443.

107. Blumenberg, "Socrates," 423. Here Blumenberg references Valéry, while the page that Blumenberg indicates (*Oeuvres*, 1:1167) does *not* contain any statement about central perspective. Nevertheless, Blumenberg made a note in the margins of his copy "Zentralpersp[ektive]."

108. Blumenberg, "Essential Ambiguity," 446.

109. Blumenberg, "Essential Ambiguity," 448. Compare the following passage from the manuscript indexed as PVY in Blumenberg's estate at the DLA (see n. 44) that also highlights the reciprocity of scientific curiosity and its linguistic means, on the one hand, and the ambiguity Blumenberg appre-

The window image and its visual regime, we are told one more time, have been equivalents of the theoretical curiosity of Leonardo's age and the epistemological agenda that underlies it. A truly modern art, be it visual or literary, however, has to leave both behind. While such insights might have been enabled by Blumenberg's study of Valéry's essays on Leonardo, they clearly disagree with Valéry's account of Leonardo as an antecedent of a modern, postperspectival image concept. Instead, they are consistent with Hans Robert Jauss's view of Leonardo and the art of the Renaissance. The joint seminar with his colleague in Giessen, in the summer of 1962, which Blumenberg mentions gratefully in connection with his studies of Valéry, seems to have fostered a shared view of the aesthetics of the Renaissance.[110] While speaking about Renaissance poetics in general, Jauss's verdict clearly replicates ideas that Blumenberg had entertained in his remarks on Leonardo all along: "Renaissance poetics did not take this final expectable step toward autonomous art which would have required a complete break with the *imitatio naturae*. The claim that poietic production can create more than just a second, more beautiful nature, i.e., a different, heretofore unrealized world, will not be made until the literary revolution of the eighteenth century."[111]

Such favoritism of nonrepresentational and nonperspectival art eventually prevents Blumenberg from acknowledging the complexities of Leonardo's image theory and art. Where he concedes complexity to Leonardo's work, Blumenberg speaks of the former's scientific ideas solely, compared to which the presumed mimetic aesthetics of the artistic work and the overwhelming evocativeness of Leonardo's Madonnas, portraits, and landscapes seem to form a pacifying contrast. What therefore cannot come into view are Leonardo's

---

ciates in artifacts, on the other: "The aesthetic use of language basically augments its ambiguity, as opposed to the tendency of scientific language, to enforce unambiguity all the way to the last corner of the medium" (Der ästhetische Gebrauch der Sprache ist wesentlich Steigerung ihrer Vieldeutigkeit, entgegen dem Trend der wissenschaftlichen Sprache, Eindeutigkeiten bis in den letzten Winkel des Mediums durchzusetzen; PVY, 11) (my translation). According to Gamm, Blumenberg's "epistemic universe" consists of "three principal perspectives or approaches to the world" ("Das Schönste," 101): the strive for unambiguousness of the sciences, the essential ambiguity of the aesthetic object, and the controlled polysemy of philosophy.

110. Blumenberg, "Socrates," 440. In the same footnote Blumenberg also mentions his plans for a "four-part study on Valéry," which he never completed (Krauthausen, "Hans Blumenbergs möglicher Valéry," 39; Flasch, *Blumenberg*, 465).

111. Jauss, *Aesthetic Experience*, 52. In turn, the idea that, in Leonardo's work, knowing is closely related to making and thus to power, Jauss adopted from Valéry (Jauss, *Kleine Apologie*, 26–28, 33; Valéry, *Leonardo, Poe, Mallarme*, 134–35; Krauthausen, "Hans Blumenbergs möglicher Valéry," 48; Flasch, *Hans Blumenberg*, 456).

images themselves as well as aspects of his theory of physics and perspective that pertain to problems far beyond those of linear perspective. Such aspects concern a temporalization of the artistic image, its restless negotiations between two- and three-dimensionality, the simultaneous presentation and withdrawal of its subject, its ambivalent movements from transparency to obfuscation, and even a veritable "crisis of perspective" that results from such constant notional and artistic interrogations.[112] Blumenberg's decision to see the "unity" of Leonardo's art and science in their shared *origin* allows him to perceive the two as related—and not just as opposites as Freud and others suggested—but it literally blinds him for the science *of* his art and the indirectness, circuitousness, and intellectual reservedness that it entails.[113]

While such an oversight might simply be due to a lack of knowledge at Blumenberg's end, there is also a systematic reason for it. The mimetic principle he sees at work, not only in Leonardo's art but in all images that adhere to a representational paradigm, preempts it from a kind of ambiguity that, in Blumenberg's textual universe, is the exclusive property of either language or visual abstraction. His theory of the primal image, which roots the imitationality of the image in its evolutionary genetics, thus precludes Blumenberg from any further-reaching discoveries. Even his outspoken sympathies for a progressive art that is nonrepresentational and postperspectival are therefore grounded in a primeval iconoclasm that precedes and underlies it. If Hans Belting was right to suggest that Germany, the proverbial land of poets and thinkers, has always had a "troublesome relationship" to the visual arts,[114] to which it also contributed little enough, then Blumenberg's work is a case in point. His theories, as well as the practice of his writings, are not least a warning of the many traps potentially encased in a visuality beyond control. On the other hand, the intellectuality that in turn congregates at the back of such an iconic skepticism misleads the author into overemphasizing the prognostic traits of Leonardo's science that supposedly anticipates a contemporary worldview and its problems, as if the backwardness of Leonardo's aesthetics would complement and instruct the modernity of his science. Despite its intellectual rigor, Blumenberg's study of Leonardo thus misses essential aspects of his work while diminishing its actual achievements.

112. For a detailed account of the intricacies of Leonardo's optical theories, see, e.g., Fehrenbach, *Licht und Wasser*, 158–69; Fehrenbach, *Leonardo da Vinci*, 17–27, 63–64; and Gombrich, "The 'What' and the 'How'" (especially on issues of standpoint determination and awareness).

113. For a critique of the either-or logic of Blumenberg's antithesis of imitation and invention in regard to Leonardo, see Fehrenbach, *Licht und Wasser*, 61–62.

114. Belting, *Germans and Their Art*.

Johannes Endres teaches comparative literature and art history at the University of California, Riverside.

References

Alberti, Leon Battista. *On Painting and on Sculpture: The Latin Texts of* De Pictura *and* De Statua, edited by Cecil Grayson. London: Phaidon, 1972.

Bajohr, Hannes. "Hans Blumenberg's History of Possibilities." *Journal of the History of Ideas* (blog), July 8, 2019. jhiblog.org/2019/07/08/hans-blumenbergs-history-of-possibilities.

Belting, Hans. *The Germans and Their Art: A Troublesome Relationship*. New Haven, CT: Yale University, 1998.

Blüher, Karl Alfred. "Leonardo da Vincis *Quaderni* und Valérys *Cahiers*: Zwei Diskurse der Diskontinuität." *Forschungen zu Paul Valéry / Recherches Valéryennes* 4 (1991): 89–102.

Blumenberg, Hans. *Beschreibung des Menschen*, edited by Manfred Sommer. Frankfurt am Main: Suhrkamp, 2014.

Blumenberg, Hans. "The Concept of Reality and the Possibility of the Novel." In Blumenberg, *History, Metaphors, Fables*, 499–524.

Blumenberg, Hans. "Das dritte Höhlengleichnis." *Filosofia* 11 (1960): 705–22.

Blumenberg, Hans. "Die Selbsterfindung des Unpoeten: Paul Valérys mögliche Welten." *Neue Zürcher Zeitung*, December 12, 1982, 57–58.

Blumenberg, Hans. "Die Vorbereitung der Neuzeit." *Philosophische Rundschau* 9, nos. 2–3 (1961): 81–133.

Blumenberg, Hans. "The Essential Ambiguity of the Aesthetic Object." In Blumenberg, *History, Metaphors, Fables*, 441–48.

Blumenberg, Hans. *The Genesis of the Copernican World*, translated by Robert M. Wallace. Cambridge, MA: MIT Press, 1987.

Blumenberg, Hans. *History, Metaphors, Fables: A Hans Blumenberg Reader*, edited and translated by Hannes Bajohr, Florian Fuchs, and Joe Paul Kroll. Ithaca, NY: Cornell University Press, 2020.

Blumenberg, Hans. *Höhlenausgänge*. 5th ed. Frankfurt am Main: Suhrkamp, 2016.

Blumenberg, Hans. "'Imitation of Nature': Toward a Prehistory of the Idea of the Creative Being." In Blumenberg, *History, Metaphors, Fables*, 316–57.

Blumenberg, Hans. *Kopernikus im Selbstverständnis der Neuzeit*. Mainz: Verlag der Akademie der Wissenschaften und der Literatur in Mainz, 1965.

Blumenberg, Hans. "Kopernikus und das Pathos der Vernunft: Das Denken der Neuzeit im Zeichen der kopernikanischen Wende." *Evangelische Kommentare* 6, no. 8 (1973): 460–65.

Blumenberg, Hans. "Kosmos und System: Aus der Genesis der kopernikanischen Welt." *Studium Generale* 10 (1957): 61–80.

Blumenberg, Hans. *The Legitimacy of the Modern Age*, translated by Robert M. Wallace. Cambridge, MA: MIT Press, 1983.

Blumenberg, Hans. *Lions*, translated by Kári Driscoll. London: Seagull, 2018.

Blumenberg, Hans. "Neugierde und Wissenstrieb: Supplemente zu 'Curiositas.' " *Archiv für Begriffsgeschichte* 14 (1970): 7–40.

Blumenberg, Hans. *Paradigms for a Metaphorology*, translated by Robert Savage. Ithaca, NY: Cornell University Press, 2010.

Blumenberg, Hans. "Paul Valérys möglicher Leonardo da Vinci: Vortrag in der Akademie der Künste in Berlin am 21. 4. 1966." *Forschungen zu Paul Valéry / Recherches Valéryennes* 25 (2013): 193–227.

Blumenberg, Hans. "Phenomenological Aspects on Life-World and Technization." In Blumenberg, *History, Metaphors, Fables*, 358–99.

Blumenberg, Hans. "The Relationship between Nature and Technology as a Philosophical Problem." In Blumenberg, *History, Metaphors, Fables*, 301–15.

Blumenberg, Hans. "Socrates and the *Objet Ambigu*: Paul Valéry's Discussion of the Ontology of the Aesthetic Object and Its Tradition." In Blumenberg, *History, Metaphors, Fables*, 400–440.

Blumenberg, Hans. "Speech Situation and Immanent Poetics." In Blumenberg, *History, Metaphors, Fables*, 449–65.

Blumenberg, Hans. "Teleologie." In vol. 6 of *Religion in Geschichte und Gegenwart*, edited by Kurt Galling, 674–77. 3rd ed. Tübingen: Mohr, 1962.

Blumenberg, Hans. "Wirklichkeitsbegriff und Wirkungspotential des Mythos." In *Ästhetische und metaphorologische Schriften*, edited by Anselm Haverkamp, 327–405. Frankfurt am Main: Suhrkamp, 2017.

Blumenberg, Hans. *Work on Myth*, translated by Robert M. Wallace. Cambridge, MA: MIT Press, 1985.

Boehm, Gottfried. *Studien zur Perspektivität: Philosophie und Kunst in der frühen Neuzeit*. Heidelberg: Winter, 1969.

Borchmeyer, Dieter. "Aufstieg und Fall der Zentralperspektive." In *Romantische Wissenspoetik: Die Künste und die Wissenschaften um 1800*, edited by Gabriele Brandstetter and Gerhard Neumann, 287–310. Würzburg: Königshausen und Neumann, 2004.

Cues, Nikolaus von. *Die Kunst der Vermutung: Auswahl aus den Schriften besorgt und eingeleitet von Hans Blumenberg*. Bremen: Schünemann, 1957.

Endres, Johannes. "*Ekphrasis*, Visual Description, and Iconic Skepticism in Hans Blumenberg's Writings." In *Leistungsbeschreibung: Literarische Strategien bei Hans Blumenberg / Describing Cultural Achievement: Hans Blumenberg's Literary Strategies*, edited by Ulrich Breuer and Tim Attanucci, 111–30. Heidelberg: Winter, 2020.

Endres, Johannes. "Hans Blumenbergs paläolithische Weltkunstgeschichte." In *Blumenbergs Verfahren*, edited by Hannes Bajohr and Eva Geulen. Göttingen: Wallstein, forthcoming.

Farago, Claire. *Leonardo da Vinci's "Paragone": A Critical Interpretation with a New Edition of the Text in the Codex Urbinas*. Leiden: Brill, 1992.

Fehrenbach, Frank. "Der oszillierende Blick: *Sfumato* und die Optik des späten Leonardo." *Zeitschrift für Kunstgeschichte* 65, no. 4 (2002): 522–44.

Fehrenbach, Frank. *Leonardo da Vinci: Der Impetus der Bilder*. Berlin: Matthes und Seitz, 2019.

Fehrenbach, Frank. "Leonardos Vermächtnis? Kenneth Clark und die Deutungsgeschichte der 'Sintflutzeichnungen.'" *Marburger Jahrbuch für Kunstwissenschaft* 28, no. 7 (2001): 7–51.

Fehrenbach, Frank. *Licht und Wasser: Zur Dynamik naturphilosophischer Leitbilder im Leonardo da Vincis.* Tübingen: Wasmuth, 1997.

Fehrenbach, Frank. "Taking Flight: Leonardo's Childhood Memories." In *Renaissance Studies in Honor of Joseph Connors,* edited by Machelet Israels and Louis A. Waldman, 274–87, 842–48. Florence: Villa i Tatti / Harvard University Center for Italian Studies, 2013.

Flasch, Kurt. *Hans Blumenberg, Philosoph in Deutschland: Die Jahre 1945 bis 1966.* Frankfurt am Main: Klostermann, 2017.

Freud, Sigmund. "A Fantasy of Leonardo da Vinci." In vol. 2 of *Minutes of the Vienna Psychoanalytic Society,* edited by Herman Nunberg and Ernst Federn, translated by Margarete Nunberg, 338–52. New York: International Universities Press, 1967.

Frey, Dagobert. *Gotik und Renaissance als Grundlagen der modernen Weltanschauung.* Augsburg: Filser, 1929.

Frey, Dagobert. "Kunst und Weltbild der Renaissance." *Studium Generale* 6 (1953): 416–23.

Gamm, Gerhard. "Das Schönste, was es gibt: Blumenberg und Valéry über ästhetische Effekte." *Zeitschrift für Kulturphilosophie* 2012, no. 1: 99–116.

Gantner, Joseph. *Leonardos Visionen von der Sintflut und vom Untergang der Welt: Geschichte einer künstlerischen Idee.* Bern: Francke, 1958.

Giesecke, Michael. "Der Verlust der zentralen Perspektive und die Renaissance der Multimedialität." In *Die Venus von Giorgione,* edited by Wolfgang Kemp et al., 85–116. Berlin: Akademie, 1998.

Gombrich, Ernst. "The 'What' and the 'How': Perspective Representation and the Phenomenal World." In *Logic and Art: Essay in Honor of Nelson Goodman,* edited by Richard S. Rudner and Israel Scheffler, 129–49. Indianapolis, IN: Bobbs-Merrill, 1972.

Husserl, Edmund. *Phantasie und Bildbewußtsein: Text nach Husserliana Band XXIII,* edited by Eduard Marbach. Hamburg: Meiner, 2006.

Huyghe, René. "Leonardo da Vinci und Paul Valéry." *Forschungen zu Paul Valéry / Recherches Valéryennes* 4 (1991): 4–21.

Jallat, Jeannine. *Figure de Léonard: Essai sur l'introduction à la méthode de Léonard de Vinci.* Service de réproduction des thèses, Université de Lille III, 1981.

Jauss, Hans Robert. *Aesthetic Experience and Literary Hermeneutics,* translated by Michael Shaw. 2nd ed. Minneapolis: University of Minnesota Press, 2008.

Jauss, Hans Robert, ed. *Die nicht mehr schönen Künste: Grenzphänomene des Ästhetischen.* Munich: Fink, 1968.

Jauss, Hans Robert. *Kleine Apologie der ästhetischen Erfahrung: Mit kunstgeschichtlichen Bemerkungen von Max Imdahl.* Konstanz: Universitätsverlag, 1972.

Kemp, Martin. "Analogy and Observation in the Codex Hammer." In *Studi vinciani in memoria di Nando de Toni,* 103–34. Brescia: Stamperia Fratelli Geroldi, 1986.

Kemp, Martin. "From Mimesis to Fantasia: The Quattrocento Vocabulary of Creation, Inspiration, and Genius in the Visual Arts." *Viator* 8 (1977): 347–98.

Kemp, Martin. "'Hostinato Rigore': Valéry's Leonardo from a Vincian Perspective." *Forschungen zu Paul Valéry / Recherches Valéryennes* 4 (1991): 25–46.

Koch, Matthias. "Valéry, Blumenberg und die Phänomenologie der Geschichte." In *Alles Mögliche: Sprechen, Denken und Schreiben des (Un)möglichen*, edited by Reinhard Babel, Nadine Feßler, Sandra Fluhrer, Sebastian Huber, and Sebastian Thede, 37–52. Würzburg: Königshausen und Neumann, 2014.

Konersmann, Ralf. "Stoff für Zweifel: Blumenberg liest Valéry." *Internationale Zeitschrift für Philosophie* 1 (1995): 46–66.

Krauthausen, Karin. "Hans Blumenbergs möglicher Valéry." *Zeitschrift für Kulturphilosophie* 6, no. 1 (2012): 39–63.

Krauthausen, Karin. "Hans Blumenbergs präparierter Valéry." *Zeitschrift für Kulturphilosophie* 6, no. 1 (2012): 211–24.

Krauthausen, Karin. "Zwischen Aufzeichnung und Konfiguration: Der Beginn von Paul Valérys *Cahiers*." In *Notieren, Skizzieren: Schreiben und Zeichnen als Verfahren des Entwurfs*, edited by Karin Krauthausen and Omar W. Nasim, 89–118. Zurich: Diaphanes, 2010.

Krüger, Klaus. *Das Bild als Schleier des Unsichtbaren: Ästhetische Illusion in der Kunst der frühen Neuzeit in Italien.* Munich: Fink, 2001.

Laurana, Domenico. *Leonardo on Flight.* Baltimore: Johns Hopkins University Press, 2004.

Leonardo da Vinci. *Leonardo on Painting: An Anthology of Writings by Leonardo da Vinci with a Selection of Documents Relating to His Career as an Artist*, edited by Martin Kemp. New Haven, CT: Yale University Press, 1989.

Leonardo da Vinci. *The Literary Works of Leonardo da Vinci*, compiled and edited Jean Paul Richter, enlarged and revised by Jean Paul Richter and Irma A. Richter. 3rd ed. 2 vols. New York: Phaidon, 1970.

Leonardo da Vinci. *The Notebooks of Leonardo da Vinci*, compiled and edited by Jean Paul Richter. 2 vols. New York: Dover, 1970.

Leonardo da Vinci. *Tagebücher und Aufzeichnungen: Nach den italienischen Handschriften übersetzt und herausgegeben von Theodor Lücke.* 2nd ed. Leipzig: List, 1952.

Leonardo da Vinci. *Treatise on Painting (Codex Urbinas Latinus 1270)*, translated and annotated by A. Philip McMahon. 2 vols. Princeton, NJ: Princeton University Press, 1956.

Müller, Oliver. "Subtile Stiche: Hans Blumenberg und die Forschungsgruppe 'Poetik und Hermeneutik.'" In *Kontroversen in der Literaturtheorie / Literaturtheorie in der Kontroverse*, edited by Ralf Klausnitzer and Carlos Spoerhase, 249–64. Bern: Lang, 2007.

Panofsky, Erwin. *Perspective as Symbolic Form*, translated by Christopher S. Wood. New York: Zone, 1991.

Pedretti, Carlo, ed. *The Literary Works of Leonardo da Vinci*, compiled and edited by Jean Paul Richter. 2 vols. Oxford: Phaidon, 1977.

Poincaré, Henri. *Science and Hypothesis.* London: Walter Scott, 1905.

Schmidt-Radefeldt, Jürgen, ed. *Paul Valéry (Wege der Forschung, 514)*. Darmstadt: Wissenschaftliche Buchgesellschaft, 1978.

Schmidt-Radefeldt, Jürgen. "Randnotizen zu Valérys 'Epoche des Leonardo.'" *Forschungen zu Paul Valéry / Recherches Valéryennes* 4 (1991): 79–88.

Valéry, Paul. *Cahiers*, edited by Judith Robinson. 2 vols. Paris: Gallimard, 1973–74.

Valéry, Paul. *Leonardo: Drei Essays*, translated by Karl August Horst. Frankfurt am Main: Insel, 1960.

Valéry, Paul. *Leonardo, Poe, Mallarme*, translated by Malcolm Cowley and James R. Lawler. Vol. 8 of *The Collected Works of Paul Valéry*, edited by Jackson Mathews. Princeton, NJ: Princeton University Press, 1972.

Valéry, Paul. *Oeuvres*, edited by Jean Hytier. 2 vols. Paris: Gallimard, 1957–60.

Valéry, Paul. *Zur Ästhetik und Philosophie der Künste*. Vol. 6 of *Werke*, edited by Jürgen Schmidt-Radefeldt. Frankfurt am Main: Insel, 1995.

Walzel, Oskar. *Das Prometheussymbol von Shaftesbury zu Goethe*. 2nd ed. Munich: Hueber, 1932.

Welsch, Wolfgang. "Das Zeichen des Spiegels: Platons philosophische Kritik der Kunst und Leonardo da Vincis künstlerische Überholung der Philosophie." *Philosophisches Jahrbuch* 90 (1983): 230–45.

Welsch, Wolfgang. "Water or Wind? Leonardo da Vinci's Drawings Windsor 12377–12386 Reinterpreted." *International Journal of Art and Art History* 6, no. 2 (2018): 51–65.

Wetz, Franz Josef. *Hans Blumenberg zur Einführung*. Hamburg: Junius, 2004.

Worringer, Wilhelm. "Kritische Gedanken." In *Fragen und Gegenfragen: Schriften zum Kunstproblem*, 86–105. Munich: Piper, 1956.

Zill, Rüdiger. "Zwischen Affinität und Kritik: Hans Blumenberg liest Sigmund Freud." In *Hans Blumenberg beobachtet: Wissenschaft, Technik und Philosophie*, edited by Cornelius Borck, 126–48. Freiburg im Breisgau: Alber, 2013.

Working on the Myth of the Anthropocene: Blumenberg and the Need for Philosophical Anthropology

Vida Pavesich

> The "naked truth" is not what life can live with.
> —Hans Blumenberg, *Work on Myth*

> A new word does not immediately gain acceptance,
> unless it is very apt.
> —Hans Blumenberg, *Work on Myth*

> Myth shows mankind engaged in working up and [mentally]
> digesting something that won't let it alone, that keeps it
> in a state of unease and agitation.
> —Hans Blumenberg, *Work on Myth*

If what Hans Blumenberg says about new words is true, then the term *Anthropocene* is apt indeed. Just now, no other word captures the urgency of the human predicament in relation to systems that reach far beyond us.[1] Initially, the word referred to a scientific debate about whether human impact on the

I am grateful to Hannes Bajohr for inviting me to contribute and an anonymous reviewer for helpful suggestions to this article.

1. Over the past forty years, many concepts and narratives that encapsulate the imprint of human societies on the global environment have emerged. Efforts to date the onset of an age called the Anthropocene vary widely. Some claim that we are still in the Holocene, and some reject the term entirely in

planet is so great that the Holocene has given way to a new geological age. The term migrated to the humanities, social sciences, and popular culture where it may designate an all-encompassing dystopian metanarrative,[2] a call for responsible stewardship, a Promethean planetary managerialism by experts, an ideology, or a "requiem for the species," among others.[3] What all Anthropocene narratives share, whether they stem from the humanities or the sciences, is an anxious preoccupation with our species' outsize influence on systems that support life on this planet. Neither antihumanism nor posthumanism has banished "man,"[4] who has returned with alarming stories about the dire straits in which we find ourselves, such as reduced biodiversity, depleted resources, acidified and plasticized oceans, and soaring rates of species extinction, including possibly our own. The Anthropocene is emphatically about humans, who are now center stage in an epic drama about both the aggregated effects of their own successes and unpredictable planetary processes that are "profoundly indifferent" to them.[5]

The Anthropocene has spawned a multidisciplinary and often fractious conversation. The geosciences program centers on identifying a new geological age in stratigraphic records, one in which humans have become "geological agents." Did it begin with the Industrial Revolution, or with the "Great Acceleration" since 1945?[6] Social scientists complain about a "unified and totalizing framing of the Anthropos,"[7] which obscures the diversity and differences in actual conditions and impacts of humankind across the planet. They also object

---

favor of, for example, the *Capitalocene*. Bonneuil examines and deflates many of the contenders in "Geological Turn."

2. Chernilo, who also argues in favor of philosophical anthropology in "Question of the Human," is responsible for this term.

3. See Baskin, "Ideology of the Anthropocene?" *Requiem for a species* is part of the title of Hamilton's book *Requiem for a Species: Why We Resist the Truth about Climate Change*. Biermann claims that "the Myth of Prometheus marks the beginning of the Anthropocene" (*Earth System Governance*, 47).

4. Bajohr presents a concise summary of the humanities' reception of "man's" return. See "Anthropocene and Negative Anthropology."

5. Chakrabarty, "Future of the Human Sciences," 42.

6. The Anthropocene Working Group, composed of twenty-nine scientists, aims to determine whether sufficient stratigraphic evidence exists to name a new geological age. They indicate that they will release a report in 2022 ("Anthropocene GSSP Project"). Zalasiewicz at first did not take this seriously, given that human existence on the planet is a mere blip on the radar of geological time. For a brief history of the group's discussion of the term (and the dissensions within the group), see Davison, "Anthropocene Epoch." See also Bauer and Ellis, "Anthropocene Divide," for how different scientific disciplines approach these problems.

7. Clark and Gunaratnam, "Earthing the Anthropos?," 148.

to inflated rhetoric that promotes technocratic planetary managerialism without attending to the social, political, cultural, and power relations that have contributed to environmental instability.[8] Others claim that capitalism is the main driver of accelerating disasters.[9] The humanities understandably raise questions about *Anthropos*. According to Christophe Bonneuil, the biological category of species has been elevated to a "causal explanatory" power that oversimplifies and overdetermines the whole of human history from hunter-gatherers to global geological force.[10] Both he and the historian Dipesh Chakrabarty wonder who the "we" is, given that humans never experience themselves as a species or as "geological agents." Chakrabarty maintains that a politics of intrahuman justice is still necessary, but a politics adequate to the current crisis must "ground itself in a new philosophical anthropology, that is, a new understanding of the changing place of humans in the web of life and in the connected but different histories of the global and planetary."[11] Thus the multifaceted Anthropocene, in heightening awareness of existential precariousness, has raised many questions, particularly about human orientation on a wildly erratic planet. This article explores two of these questions: Which narratives tend to best reflect realistic assessments of the human condition and what, fundamentally, *is* the human condition? In the Anthropocene Immanuel Kant's unanswered fourth question, "What is the human being?," looms large.

To address such questions, the present article develops an interpretive framework drawn from Blumenberg's theories of myth and metaphor, philosophical anthropology, and philosophy of history.[12] In contrast to the grandiose species-subject *Anthropos*, Blumenberg advances a minimal, deflationary anthropology that begins with the fact that human beings are vulnerable, biologically underdetermined animals whose adaptation over the millennia required becoming second-natured social and cultural beings. Thus the stories humans tell about themselves, and their lifeworldly (*Lebenswelt*) practices and institutions, respond to and compensate for a permanent bioanthropological orientation problem. By underscoring the inherent risk of the "human mode of existence," it is possible to evaluate functionally which stories and capacities

8. See, e.g., Biermann et al., "Down to Earth"; and Lövbrand et al., "Who Speaks for the Future of Earth?"

9. See Moore, *Anthropocene or Capitalocene?*

10. Bonneuil, "Geological Turn," 19.

11. Chakrabarty, "Planet," 13, 30.

12. Nicholls's excellent book *Myth and the Human Sciences*, 24, raises the issue of Blumenberg's contemporary relevance and underscores the inseparability of myth and philosophical anthropology.

have managed that risk. Blumenberg cautions us to "avail ourselves" of the lessons contained in that history (*WM*, 111), lest we succumb to unrealistic fantasies and the excesses of our own instrumental success.

As a species, a rich array of skills supports "resilience"[13] in the face of the "absolutism of reality" (*WM*, 3–4)—a boundary concept representing the loss or threatened loss of control over the conditions of existence. These skills involve distancing ourselves from our impulses through narrativizing, becoming reflexive, empathetic,[14] and cooperative beings. Chakrabarty is correct about needing a new philosophical anthropology. However, this article argues that the Anthropocene is the latest iteration of an old problem: how to cope with the radical asymmetry between human and nonhuman forces or, as Blumenberg would say, the discrepancy between life-time and world-time.[15] Blumenberg's minimal anthropology is a cautionary reminder that even though narratives provide orientation in a confusing world beyond our control, and even though humans are at the center of their stories, they are not the center of the universe, and the predatory instrumental rationality that has brought us to the brink of self-annihilation is not the only skill to cultivate.

Blumenberg argues that the Enlightenment did not banish myth, because the absolutism of reality is never definitively overcome (*WM*, 8). Great myths such as Prometheus, which has been mobilized in the Anthropocene, narrate human struggles with powers that cannot be gainsaid, and their persistence rests on continuing to meaningfully frame the human condition in relation to contemporaneous circumstances—to the extent that the myth is recognized *as* myth. However, historically emergent "absolutisms," such as accelerated change and fears of impending disaster, stimulate desires for new myths, which may not reflect realistic zones of behavior (*WM*, 12). Myths may be no more than mystification, an "absolutism of wishes" (*WM*, 8). Metaphors, such as "God species," "geoagents," and "geological force," become the subjects of narratives, but can a "geoagent" control the Earth system? Specifying the conditions of human existence and drawing on empirically sound lessons contained in our evolutionary history make it possible to evaluate functionally which

13. Blumenberg, *Beschreibung des Menschen*, 591 (hereafter cited as *BDM*).

14. Blumenberg uses the word *consolation* (*Trost*), which clearly presupposes empathy. On this issue, see Pavesich, "Hans Blumenberg: Philosophical Anthropology and the Ethics of Consolation."

15. Blumenberg devotes an entire book to this issue: *Lebenszeit und Weltzeit*. World-time is indifferent to us, which is another way to frame the absolutism of reality concept in *Work on Myth*. Nicholls discusses Blumenberg's analysis in the *Nachlass* writings of Adolf Hitler's attempt to forcibly reduce "world-time back into the dimensions of a life-time," as an "extreme act of violence." Polymyth has been replaced by a dangerous monomyth (*Myth and the Human Sciences*, 238).

accounts of the Anthropocene might preserve a human mode of existence. Reason's function is to "distinguish between wholesome and harmful types of myths [and to resist] the harmful ones,"[16] particularly those that promise a bypass of the absolutism of reality. For example, Paul J. Crutzen and Christian Schwägerl, buying into grandiose versions of the *Anthropos* myth, claim with some hubris that "it's we who decide what nature is and what it will be."[17] Because of the Anthropocene's many uncertainties, it may become extremely difficult to secure what Johan Rockström et al. call a "safe operating space for humanity,"[18] but neither the technocratic, god-species supremacy of the eco-modernists nor a radical nihilism that paralyzes action in the present offers viable ways of coping.

To explore this last claim, the final section of this article draws on Blumenberg's philosophy of history. Chakrabarty has drawn attention to how the unprecedented "rifts" and "ruptures" signaled by the Anthropocene challenge the possibility of historical understanding.[19] However, the Anthropocene can be understood as a "position for consciousness" that responds to what Blumenberg calls "questions" implicit in the expectations and disappointments generated by the previous historical configuration, in this case modernity's dream of self-foundation and progress. Blumenberg views historical change as a process of forming, dismantling, and reconstituting continuities (lifeworlds). Thus the goal of historical understanding is to grasp both continuity (the old) and discontinuity (the new) in terms of how a new historical formation attempts to solve problems raised by its predecessor—as well as the danger posed by mythical "reoccupations" of an earlier position. Blumenberg shifts attention from the specific contents of consciousness to their function in our self-understanding within a historical epoch. For example, the Anthropocene peril is new, but it is continuous in that it represents both the inheritance of unintended consequences and modernity's suppression of the following "questions": the planetary and human time-scale differences effaced by instrumental rationality, our radical dependence on a natural world indifferent to us but in which we are embedded, our failure to adjust liberal individualist politics and economies to limits posed by finite resources, and our lack of specialness in the

16. Marquard, "In Praise of Polytheism," 93. The most dangerous myths, according to Marquard, are those that become "the one true story," for example, "inexorable progress of world history toward freedom" (94).

17. Crutzen and Schwägerl, "Living in the Anthropocene."

18. See Rockström et al., "Planetary Boundaries."

19. For a discussion of this problem, see Chakrabarty, "Climate and Capital"; and Chakrabarty, "Climate of History."

scheme of things. Thus it is mistaken to suppose that a mythical "god species" can continue modernity's utopian dream of mastering nature or to view the Anthropocene as an *entirely* unprecedented rupture with the past. Historical understanding works against myth's seductions: these two extreme options confuse history and myth and are open to critical reflection insofar as they deny the anthropological conditions of existence that will be specified in this article. Thus the interpretive optic derived from Blumenberg's writings accounts for the orienting work that myth accomplishes—as well as its excesses—and demonstrates how the past constrains but does not determine what is still possible. Recognizing reason's limits and the fact that we have a history rather than a mythical repetition of the past are modes of working on myth, modes of orientation and reorientation.

Background: Philosophical Anthropology from Kant and Herder to the Anthropocene

The historical origins of philosophical anthropology are in eighteenth-century disputes between Kant and Johann Gottfried Herder, which also coincided with the emergence of an industrial economy relying on fossil fuels and a growing interest in historical ecology and the human degradation of Earth.[20] Kant worried about the eventual disappearance of the human species—the only one capable of reason—which was an outgrowth of his thinking about species aging generally and of Earth itself.[21] For Kant, all philosophical questions depended on answering the question "What is man?" (Was ist der Mensch?). Kant hoped an answer would emerge from further developments in the natural sciences. The panpsychist Herder, in reaction to Cartesian dualism and Kantian rationalism, favored a holistic conception rooted in nature and biology. Although Herder claimed that human beings were deficient compared with animals, he saw this deficiency as what made reason and self-determination possible. Freedom from instinctually determined behavior meant a gain in freedom and independence from instinct—a free space for reflection.

Kant's unanswered question continues to haunt us, but it was Herder who set the stage conceptually for a reconfigured answer in early twentieth-century

20. Szabo, "Historical Ecology." See also Bonneuil and Fressoz, *Shock of the Anthropocene*, who point out the concern many had during this period. In 1855 Eugene Huzar, a French lawyer, claimed in *The End of the World through Science* that industrialization would lead to climate disasters. See also Fressoz, "Lessons of Disasters." Bonneuil, in "Geological Turn," documents early awareness of environmental degradation and climate change, which, he claims, is ignored by the "standard narrative" promoted by Will Steffen and others.

21. See Clark's discussion of Kant's concerns and Kant's reflection on deep geological time in "Geopolitics and the Disaster of the Anthropocene." Clark adds that Kant's worries never went away and are now back on the table in the Anthropocene.

philosophical anthropology.[22] The question of "man" as a being with no fixed nature preoccupied Max Scheler, Helmuth Plessner, Arnold Gehlen, Paul Alsberg, Erich Rothacker, and others. All rejected the human-nature separation and biological reductionism. Blumenberg works along these lines, highlighting the risks posed by biological underdetermination. Despite their political differences, all agreed that humans had to compensate by becoming cultural and historical beings. Writing about Plessner, the philosopher Fred Dallmayr states their central focus: "Rather than being safely enmeshed in a life cycle or the stimulus-response nexus, man has to 'lead' his life by designing a web of cultural and symbolic meanings—patterns which provide him at best with a fragile habitat."[23] Blumenberg pointedly added that success is not programmed in (*BDM*, 524).

For Blumenberg, the first proposition of a philosophical anthropology must be that "it cannot be taken for granted that man is able to exist."[24] In *Beschreibung des Menschen* he claims that man is the "impossible being" (535, 550). He updates Kant's fourth question as "What made us possible?" He explores answers primarily in *Work on Myth* and in *Beschreibung des Menschen*, offering "an existential description of the human being that science investigates as one particular species of the animal realm." He claimed to exploit "the results of the positive sciences for the elaboration and development of anthropology."[25] Rather than elevate humans, deny their overlap with other species, or propose an essentialism, he appraises the competencies that made them possible. However, the clues for how humans coped with earlier survival challenges are in our evolutionary history. The chemists Will Steffen and Crutzen, who helped popularize the term *Anthropocene*, agree that humans should be placed in a history of life on Earth. However, their "pre-anthropocene" story from hunter-gatherers selectively focuses on the history of energy-mastery efficiency leading up to reliance on fossil fuels, and, as Bonneuil points out, this narrative predetermines humans as naturalized, depoliticized species-subjects.[26] Such stories do not address the full range of human competencies within the deeper history of life. Humans come very late in the history of a planet that was not made for them. A plausible philosophical anthropology must account for survival in a world indifferent and even hostile to humans.

22. Zammito, *Kant, Herder, and the Birth of Anthropology*.

23. Dallmayr, "Return of Philosophical Anthropology," 359.

24. Blumenberg, "Anthropological Approach to the Contemporary Significance of Rhetoric," 118 (hereafter cited as AAR).

25. See Wetz, "Phenomenological Anthropology of Hans Blumenberg."

26. Bonneuil, "Geological Turn," 18–23.

Blumenberg complicates these oversimplified portrayals by understanding humans as an "improbability made flesh"—the ongoing result of adaptations to a wide range of environments, climates, food sources, other people, and so on. No other animal has adapted or tried to adapt to as many variables as humans (*BDM*, 589), and therefore no other animal had to develop so diverse a range of skills to cope with its extreme vulnerability. Adapting to the strange new world heralded by the Anthropocene will push our adaptive capacities to their limits. According to Roy Scranton, it will require new skills, new stories, new ideas, and a new way "of thinking our collective existence . . . a new vision of who 'we' are—a newly philosophical humanism, undergirded by renewed attention to the humanities."[27] Dallmayr, although not discussing the Anthropocene, argues for reviving philosophical anthropology, aiming for a 'subdued, self-critical . . . nonhegemonic view of the 'human,'" supported by the biological and evolutionary sciences.[28] Humanism may be anthropocentric, but it need not be metaphysically grandiose.[29] Blumenberg's anthropology fulfills these requirements.

Myth, Metaphor, and the Absolutism of Reality

Before turning to how the evolutionary and biological sciences support, but do not supplant, the subdued humanism that arguably motivates Blumenberg's entire oeuvre, I turn to the concepts "absolutism of reality" and "lifeworld" drawn from *Work on Myth* in order to frame later sections, particularly how the Anthropocene narratives involve mythical thinking. Additional clarification of Blumenberg's understanding of metaphor's anthropological function follows.

Work on Myth begins with an anthropogenesis, asserting a "sudden lack of adaptation" associated with a change in biotope. Bipedal and no longer able to take refuge in trees, humans became extremely anxious about the "unoccupied horizon of the possibilities of what may come at one," as well as a dire need to "stabilize" the advantage of a widened horizon of (5, 6, 4).[30] This urgent situation (which was not sudden and emerged over millions of years) required cultural adaptations that created "distance" from "the absolutism of reality." To live means to continually move away from this threat, from "what would

---

27. Scranton, *Learning to Die in the Anthropocene*, 19.
28. Dallmayr, "Return of Philosophical Anthropology," 359.
29. Chernilo also argues that we need to consider what is meant by the *Anthropos* in the Anthropocene narrative. If we are capable of "decentering" ourselves, it is possible to appeal to us as moral agents ("Question of the Human," 55).
30. Blumenberg, *Work on Myth* (hereafter cited as *WM*).

make [human life] impossible" (*WM*, 110). The concept of biological insufficiency, emphasized by Gehlen and others and taken up by Blumenberg,[31] has
an important explanatory function. It specifies a limit condition—the *terminus
a quo* of existence. Similar to Kant, the immensity of nature and the awareness
of the insufficiency of our faculties to take in an estimation of this realm force
us to find our own limitations.[32]

Blumenberg's account of philosophical anthropology in *Work on Myth*
contains four elements: the *terminus a quo* (absolutism of reality / creature of
deficiencies), a compensatory lifeworld, self-assertion, and an implicit idea of
humanity as a life between extremes.[33] Because the absolutism of reality marks
the limits of comprehension, it is a boundary concept set in place by our own
biological underdetermination. As such, it becomes the conceptual horizon for
understanding the lifeworld as compensation. Blumenberg summarizes this
initial distancing with the concept "work of myth," the unknowable past's past
(*die Vorvergangenheit*) (3). The work *of* myth—a life-and-death enterprise—
should be distinguished from work *on* myth, or the ongoing historical reception
and reworking of inherited mythical materials.

The lifeworld thus has two meanings: (1) it is a boundary concept, representing an impossible perfect congruence between the creature and its world
(e.g., myths of paradise, immortality, or perfect control of the Earth system),
and (2) it is our familiar world of myths and practices—the "world that serves
life, the hidden, self-givenness in the functional context of self-preservation."[34]
Historical existence occurs between the two limits of no orientation and perfect orientation. Because humans must act to solve the problem of self-
preservation, they must also be "self-assertive."[35] Self-assertion (*Selbstbe-*

31. For example, for Gehlen, it was *Mängelwesen*, or creature of deficiencies; for Plessner, it was
Exentrizität, or eccentricity. According to Blumenberg, the philosophical tradition, particularly Platonism, has obscured this background need for orientation (AAR, 180).

32. Kant, *Critique of Judgment*, §28.

33. Barbara Merker argues that the ideal lifeworld is the primary foundational concept ("Bedürfnis
nach Bedeutsamkeit"). However, because Blumenberg repeatedly refers to the function of myth as a
strategy of distancing *from* what the absolutism of reality represents, this article understands the absolutism of reality as the fundamental limit concept (e.g., *WM*, 4, 16, 19). Blumenberg reasons with other
limit concepts, such as "final myth," and this and the lifeworld refer to the exclusion of the absolutism of
reality. It is therefore a variant of the same idea.

34. Blumenberg, "Life-World and the Concept of Reality," 438.

35. In *The Legitimacy of the Modern Age* Blumenberg thematizes self-assertion as the modern age's
response to deficits in the previous epoch, that is, as a response to theological absolutism and how the
world ceased to have relevance for human orientation. However, *Work on Myth* understands self-
assertion more generally as an anthropological characteristic, given the perennial need to actively
solve orientation problems.

hauptung) resists subsumption by an indifferent reality, whether this is understood as the *terminus a quo* or a historically emergent absolutism, such as being jolted by the "rude shock of the planet's otherness" in the Anthropocene.[36] Furthermore, because self-assertion tends to exceed or fail to acknowledge limits, humans must create balance between the equally impossible extremes of chaos and perfect orientation. Thus Blumenberg's implied concept of human existence is not an essence or a nature (an idea he always resists) but a set of parameters within which human existence becomes possible: a set of self-assertive behaviors, which include symbol and tool use, aimed at self-preservation of a distinctively human life within the limits prescribed by the absolutism of reality and a lifeworld that limits arbitrariness.

For Blumenberg, both myth and metaphor have an anthropological function. Metaphor compensates for the fact that humans have neither definitive knowledge nor existential security. Because humans can only influence a familiar reality, metaphor's function is to create a horizon of meaning. For example, when absolutisms emerge historically, they are experienced as pressing needs to repair a threatened consistency.[37] Metaphors manage chaos by naming the unknown (the threat) and integrating it into a system of the known.[38] For example, to call humans a geological "force" draws on the mechanistic nature presupposed by Newtonian physics, translating force into a human-existential category of power. This translation shifts the problem into human history, incorporating an ethical horizon and time frame absent from geology or physics.[39] Once this shift has occurred, the destabilizations referred to earlier suggest stories (myths) with coping procedures. The mechanism metaphor perpetuates the human-nature dualism and generates futurist fantasies of controlling the Earth system through geoengineering, gene technology, and synthetic biology. Crutzen and Schwägerl write that we are "the masters of planet Earth . . . [through] the immense power of our intellect and our creativity."[40] James Love-

---

36. Chakrabarty claims that the Anthropocene concept is about addressing this shock ("Climate and Capital," 23).

37. Blumenberg, "Prospect for a Theory of Nonconceptuality," 241–42.

38. Blumenberg adopts the term *animal symbolicum* from Ernst Cassirer. However, he takes issue with Cassirer's formalism. Cassirer did not account for the anthropological function of symbolic forms as compensation for biological underdetermination. See AAR, 187. Mythical figures emerge and distance us from a lethal reality. For example, over time pure fear coalesced into the figure Medusa, who now can substitute (be a metaphor) for potentially uncontrolled anxiety. Once named, a story and procedures for dealing with her can be articulated (*WM*, 15), just as the terror of our possible extinction has mobilized stories in the Anthropocene.

39. See Chakrabarty, "Anthropocene Time," 9.

40. Crutzen and Schwägerl, "Living in the Anthropocene."

lock's controversial Gaia metaphor of Earth as a vast self-regulating living system, on the other hand, embeds humans in nature, subject to biological and resource constraints, suggesting that living systems be models for human activities.

Blumenberg understands cultural and historical change generally as structured metaphorically. When significant metaphors emerge, they create the possibility of an ongoing metaphorical substitution of one thing for another. Furthermore, even our constitution is metaphorical. Echoing Kant's assertion of incomplete self-reflexivity, Blumenberg states: "Man comprehends himself only by way of what he is not. . . . It is not only [man's] situation that is potentially metaphorical; his constitution itself already is" (AAR, 207). The *already is* is the dissonance of the deficiency-absolutism of reality heterogeneity that, when stimulated, must be resolved indirectly by drawing on names and meanings from available lifeworldly inventories. Even "action" has a metaphorical structure, because it presupposes mediation of impulse. One action can be substituted for another, such as animal sacrifice for human sacrifice, or symbolic behavior for reactive behavior, or environmental regulations for environmental degradation. "Without this capacity to use substitutes for actions not much would be left of mankind" (AAR, 190). Every account of the human contains a metaphorical surplus that exceeds conceptuality. Whether we are machines, animals, genes, gods, or geological forces depends on the richness or poverty of what is available historically. Each sets the terms of a worldview and expectations motivated by needs emerging from the life world.[41] Blumenberg cautions: we should not try to win every debate with reality (*BDM*, 622).

Thus what characterizes the human animal is not a fixed genetic inheritance or essential nature but insecurity, versatility, flexibility, malleability, and a capacity for initiating action and change—within the range made possible by the accomplishments (a lifeworld) that have been conserved historically over against the absolutism of reality. Whether this highly malleable and creative creature, with its millennia of more or less successful stabilizing adaptations (stories and practices that were not contradicted by reality), can continue to adapt to what scientists refer to as "the Great Acceleration" since the mid-twentieth century is an open question.[42] I return to this problem and to an evaluation of a selection of Anthropocene narratives in the final sections.

---

41. Blumenberg, "Prospect for a Theory of Nonconceptuality," 239–40.
42. See Steffen et al., *Global Change and the Earth System*.

The Biology and Anthropology of Underdetermination and Its Implications: The Need for Distance and Flexible Adaptation

Myth, metaphor, and a lifeworld "distance" humans from threats to their continued existence, but to leave it at that would be to overlook what the biological and paleoanthropological sciences contributed to the renewal of Kant's fourth question. As Nicholls points out, the philosophical anthropologists who influenced Blumenberg had to repose Kant's fourth question in the context of early twentieth-century scientific achievements. Indeed, biological vulnerability and the coping strategies humans developed during their evolutionary history were central to Blumenberg's philosophical anthropology throughout his career and are reflected in his reformulation of Kant's fourth question as "What made us possible?" in *Beschreibung des Menschen*.[43] In addition, a story about anthropogenesis figures prominently in the articulation of his anthropology in *Work on Myth*, which Blumenberg claims is based on all currently accepted paleoanthropological theories. However, philosophical anthropology is not a mere summary of the sciences; early on it aimed to be foundational, drawing on the empirical sciences while lodging a powerful critique of Darwinian selection.[44] Even though philosophical anthropology fell into disfavor during the interwar years for various reasons, such as Gehlen's and Rothacker's ties to National Socialism, disruption caused by the war, and Martin Heidegger's direct attacks on the whole idea of philosophical anthropology, Blumenberg's work testifies to what can be learned from this eclipsed movement. To emphasize our long evolutionary history as integral to philosophical anthropology underscores not only the tremendous achievement that life represents but to set in relief how easily this accomplishment can be destroyed.

The philosopher Kasper Lysemose defends the legitimacy of incorporating paleoanthropology into philosophical anthropology—and by implication other sciences—arguing that even though it remains somewhat speculative, the enterprise is valid for its existential significance. It helps make the phenomenon of human existence appear to us as a form of self-understanding. If we cannot know about ourselves, we require—as Blumenberg would say—a "detour," a hypothesis that gestures toward the phenomenon in question.[45] Blu-

43. For more on philosophical anthropology's debt to the sciences, especially the paleontology and biology of the time, see Nicholls, *Myth and the Human Sciences*, 89–93, 108–16; and Lysemose, "The Being, the Origin, and the Becoming of Man," 118–20, 126, 128.
44. Nicholls, *Myth and the Human Sciences*, 86.
45. Lysemose points out that philosophical anthropology is enjoying a renascence, at least in Europe, and that contemporary philosophical anthropologists engage with paleoanthropology to do even more than discover the origin of humankind: they ask about the origin of the "deficient being"

menberg has special praise for Paul Alsberg's emphasis on paleoanthropology. Alsberg's book *Das Menschheitsrätsel* (*The Riddle of Man*, 1922) was rewritten, updated, and published in 1970 as *In Quest of Man: A Biological Approach to the Problem of Man's Place in Nature*; his paleontological speculations are the backdrop for Blumenberg's anthropogenesis in *Work on Myth*, as well as the further elaboration of his anthropology in *Beschreibung des Menschen*.[46] Alsberg, a critic of Charles Darwin, argues that early humans' increasingly skillful tool use created distance from existential dangers, becoming "the primary mode of adaptation."[47] Tool use freed the body from evolutionary pressures (*Körperausschaltung*), which then led to greater cognitive development and shifted from "the animal to the human principle of evolution."[48] What Blumenberg draws from Alsberg is the emphasis on needing to create "distance" from a lethal reality. Blumenberg adds that using technical means is not a typical solution to the problem of life's self-assertion (*Selbstbehauptung*) on Earth as a way to minimize selection pressures (*BDM*, 585). The upshot was a correlation between increasing biological despecialization and learning to survive in many environments (*BDM*, 589). Neither flight nor fight would solve the problem of being in the savannah visible as prey. However, stereotypic vision and an increased horizon enabled the bipedal species to prevent unwanted occurrences—to shield the "frail body" (*BDM*, 586). Memory and intelligence as forms of action at a distance emerge along with tool use. The ever-increasing development of the capacity to direct attention selectively also prevented the species from being at the mercy of contingencies and overrode reactive behavior, which is a highly adaptive capacity for an unspecialized species.

Blumenberg claimed that his anthropogenesis was speculative, but as Nicholls points out, even though Alsberg got the time scales wrong, he did supply a plausible framework while avoiding biological reductionism.[49] Contemporary research in the biological and other sciences renders Blumenberg's account even more plausible, strengthening the interpretive optic used in this article. For example, the theoretical biologist Mary-Jane Eberhardt, also rejecting the mechanistic assumptions of Darwinism, corroborates the critique that

that becomes humankind, emphasizing "how the species in question *arrived* at this mode of being. . . . How did nature hand man over to man for him to handle?" ("Being, the Origin, and the Becoming of Man," 127, 128, 118, 117).

46. Nicholls, *Myth and the Human Sciences*, 108.
47. Alsberg, *In Quest of Man*, 132.
48. Alsberg, *In Quest of Man*, 136–37.
49. Nicholls, *Myth and the Human Sciences*, 175.

the philosophical anthropologists had lodged against Darwin. She also supports Alsberg's speculative thesis that humans learned to deactivate natural selection by switching over to cultural selection. She places our species in the larger history of planetary life by arguing that distancing is a strategy of life in general. Against the genetic reductionists, she foregrounds epigenesis, claiming that "genes are followers rather than leaders in evolutionary change." As organisms become more complex, they become more "detached" or less integrated into specific environments. Detachment is also the possibility of greater complexity as organisms become more involved in their own niche construction to survive and attain their adult forms. Over vast amounts of time, increasing levels of what Gehlen and other philosophical anthropologists called "world openness," and which we now call "biological plasticity," mandated an adaptive phenotypic response. This led to increased evolutionary novelty, which has a recursive effect such that changes are conserved historically. However, new adaptations—or destabilizations—may emerge quite suddenly, such as the million species at risk, according to a recent UN report, or the accelerating spread of pathogens due to climate instability.[50] Hand in hand with epigenetic models of phenotypic stabilization and inheritance is greater flexibility and degrees of internal freedom plus greater potential for self-generated adaptability in higher-level organisms.[51] However, more complex organisms are also increasingly vulnerable to contingent relationships and perturbations.[52] At the fragile apex is the most detached animal, the human being—the being that Blumenberg stated has no nature but who nonetheless makes itself possible within nature. Detachment is also experienced as anxiety, which motivates storytelling and problem solving but without guarantees that the resulting assessments are accurate. This sensitivity to contingencies reframes what human exceptionalism really means. That is, our species is exceptional partly because of its extreme vulnerability to erratically changing circumstances with a "narrow zone [for] realistic behavior" (*WM*, 12).

50. Burakoff, "One Million Species at Risk of Extinction"; Harvard T. H. Chan School of Public Health, "Coronavirus, Climate Change, and the Environment."

51. See West-Eberhard, *Developmental Plasticity and Evolution*; and West-Eberhard, "Developmental Plasticity and the Origin of Species Differences."

52. See Stock, "Are Humans Still Evolving?," S52. Stock notes that "many animal species are able to accommodate environmental stress simply by changing their behavior in response to environmental conditions, without the need to resort to genetic adaptation" (S52). However, he also draws attention to how "dramatic environmental instability" could be produced by climate change (S54). This may mean that selection pressures, coupled with a failure of the economic and technological means at our disposal, will lead to further biological evolution.

Blumenberg argues that humans became unspecialized in order to develop a maximal ability for adaptation (*BDM*, 548). He identifies four anthropological constants: resilience, the concept, saving time (*Zeitgewinn*), and consolation (*Trost*). Resilience is flexible stability, and each of the other constants support being resilient to environmental and emotional perturbations (*BDM*, 608, 591). This section examines "the concept." The wider horizon associated with the upright posture also meant "the emancipation of the foremost extremities," that is, the hand (*BDM*, 575), which led to toolmaking and expressive gesture. It also led to the capacity to imagine something in its absence and anticipate threats, which is preliminary for the conceptual instrumentality needed for pursuing options and adapting to many environments (*BDM*, 566). As Blumenberg claims in *Work on Myth*, "Reason signifies coming to terms with something—and in the extreme case, with the world" (490). The emergence of the concept refers to "preemption" and foresight fueled by the awareness of scarce life-time (*BDM*, 620).[53]

In *Beschreibung des Menschen*, Blumenberg returns to his claim in the rhetoric essay that humans operate on a "principle of insufficient reason" (AAR, 198). Reason, just like human existence itself, was a contingent adaptation. "Reason may have been the last resort and desperate device of this particular organic system for coming to terms with distressing features . . . that characterize the very conditions of its existence" (*BDM*, 520). Reason is "the sum of all presumptive, anticipatory, and also provisional achievements," a capacity we possess because we have learned to achieve delay and hesitation, not the other way around (*BDM*, 559). Long before it was made into a noble achievement and defining characteristic of the human species, reason was a developmental compensation (*BDM*, 409). This account puts into perspective and deflates the autonomous, self-determining subject that has been at the center of philosophy for centuries; it also casts doubt on the ecomodernist assumption that the problems brought into focus by the Anthropocene can be controlled solely through rational planning.

The cognitive neuroscientist Merlin Donald, whose multifaceted research relies heavily on recent paleoanthropological research—and he corrects the time-scale problem in Alsberg's work—addresses the development of this "generalized cognitive capacity," filling in some gaps in the story so far. He,

---

53. Brad Tabas claims that "prevention" does not capture the nuance of *Prävention*. Blumenberg means something closer to "preemption," which involves planning and "taking measures to avoid an event or encounter" by sorting through various possibilities ("Blumenberg, Politics, Anthropology," 143).

too, asks how plasticity evolved—"presumably to support better learning and memory"—but it would not have had "much adaptive value outside the context of a highly unpredictable cultural world."[54] As the outcome of a long evolutionary process, our cognitive capacities came with the hefty price tag of managing ever more complex and variable circumstances plus our increasingly labile emotions. Successful adaptations, which presuppose the control of emotion through mimesis and public ritual, are conserved phylogenetically and passed on ontogenetically, reflecting a long, slow suite of rehearsing, embodying, and consolidating.

The achievement of this generalized cognitive capacity in the face of extreme vulnerability presupposes the long prehistory condensed in Blumenberg's "work *of* myth," which develops in tandem with the formation of a compensatory lifeworld. The lifeworld is composed of "institutions," which for Blumenberg is an anthropological term,[55] referring to sedimented meanings, habit patterns, languages, and so on that provide both inner and outer stability in the flux of time. He labels them "rhetoric," which refers to all of the above, including myth. The term *rhetoric* draws attention to the insufficiencies of reason, to the reality that not everything can be called into question at once and that definitive knowledge is unavailable. However, rhetoric is a form of rationality, a "rational way of coming to terms with the provisionality of reason" (AAR, 203). "Rhetoric" includes all the "optimized constants" of a lifeworld that have been subjected to cultural evolution. Those that have endured have met certain "burdens of proof," allowing the species to run trial and error experiments behaviorally (*WM*, 163), which is the circumstance of having a history. A being whose main characteristics include a permanent biological insufficiency, great flexibility, and no fixed natural niche faces serious self-preservation problems that go well beyond a need for nutrition. Successful institutions that continue to support self-preservation within the extremes represented by the two boundary concepts mentioned earlier exhibit a "sufficient" rationality. This applies to pedagogical issues as well, such as learning which plants and animals were poisonous, how to control fire and cook food, how to protect against the elements, and so on. But pedagogy was and is possible only when humans have semireliable constants. The downside to our general-purpose cognitive capacity is a tendency to fragment experience and threaten the "optimized" constants we need. Dangerous myths and stories (ideologies,

54. Donald, *A Mind So Rare*, 211. For the time scale issue, see esp. chaps. 5, 7, and 8.
55. Although Blumenberg adopts this term from Gehlen, he rejects what he calls Gehlen's "absolutism of 'institutions'" (AAR, 118).

tribalism) lead humans astray, but stories are both a necessary stage in human cultural development and an ongoing need because the bioanthropological problem is never definitively solved. The burden of proof is always on the new story or practice in relation to what has already stood the test of time. Thus how we frame the crises signified by the term *Anthropocene* matters.

Cognitive complexity also depends critically on having managed—and continuing to manage—the affective challenges that accompany biological vulnerability. Blumenberg claims that metaphor and myth, which are precursors to concepts, pave the way by regulating affect, particularly in times of real or perceived emergencies.[56] At the beginning of *Work on Myth*, Blumenberg states that anxiety had to be resolved into fear, that humans had to learn to resist fight or flight responses, and so on, through the "substitution of the familiar for the unfamiliar . . . of names for the unnamable" (6), which is the anthropological basis for metaphor and then myth. Once there is a name, a story can be told. The Anthropocene narratives reflect this affective dimension—our latest terrors about our possible extinction have coalesced and been given a name.

More can be said about managing affect by turning to Blumenberg's discussion of consolation rituals in *Beschreibung des Menschen*. Blumenberg claims that consolation (*Trost*) played a decisive role in anthropogenesis, because it helped make human contingency bearable (*BDM*, 626). Consolation soothes the anxieties that arise when faced with existential vulnerabilities that cannot be gainsaid. Furthermore, consolation is a "special category" that leads into the complex of "characteristics that philosophical anthropology thematizes" (*BDM*, 623), which means the cultural prostheses that emerged because "man cannot get help in elementary ways" (*BDM*, 626). Furthermore, the capacity for receiving and giving consolation reveals something distinctive about our species (*BDM*, 623).

As an emotionally labile species, humans often need reassurance, especially during breakdowns of relied-on continuities, such as the developmental stages of childhood, natural disasters, illnesses, loss of families and friends, oppressive situations that aggravate a feeling of powerlessness, or the disintegration of any taken-for-granted lifeworld formation. Reassurance makes bearing brushes with the absolutism of reality tolerable. So attention from receptive others can be consoling (*BDM*, 624), and so might myths and stories

---

56. The evolutionary anthropologist Michael Tomasello and Merlin Donald focus, from different perspectives, on the importance of collective rituals and mimesis to help regulate emotion and as precursors to cognitive development—both phylogenetically and ontogenetically. See Tomasello et al., "Understanding and Sharing Intentions," 681; and Donald, *A Mind So Rare*, 263.

that "delegate" our suffering or consolation rituals that diffuse suffering and facilitate emotional processing. For example, funeral and bereavement rituals compensate by showing "respect" and therefore have a "protective function" (*BDM*, 628). Ultimately, consolation derives its significance from the fact that at our limit (*terminus a quo*), there is inconsolability (*Untröstlichkeit*). "Consolation appears when reality cannot be changed" (*BDM*, 624), but there is a moment of "freedom," because there is distance (*BDM*, 631).

Thus consolation presupposes a complex intersubjective and cognitive reflexivity as well as empathetic perspective taking within a community. So the preservation of a human world and even happiness (*BDM*, 646) depend on compensating for the losses referred to above. Both the evolutionary anthropologist Sarah Hrdy and the primatologist Frans de Waal speak directly to the role of emotional orientation in anthropogenesis.[57] According to de Waal, empathy is deeply wired into older parts of the mammalian brain,[58] which means that it, too, preceded the formation of the unspecialized human creature. Like Blumenberg, Hrdy maintains that natural selection does not aim for future payoffs. Rather, adaptations try to solve emergent problems. Hrdy asks why our species, more than any other, engages in elaborate modes of cooperation, despite its often bellicose behavior. "The emotional qualities that distinguish modern humans from other apes, especially mind reading combined with empathy and developing a sense of self, emerged earlier in our evolutionary history than anatomically modern humans did," and emotion sharing had to precede the emergence of language.[59]

Hrdy emphasizes the critical formation of attachment systems both phylogenetically and ontogenetically. It is well documented that human brain development is dependent on attachment systems.[60] Blumenberg phrases it this way: the young need "specific environments" because of the "plastic variability of the capacity of this organic system": the mother-child relationship is a shield against the raw pressures of space-time contingency (*BDM*, 636, 640). Attachment systems are integral to how the species learned to manage fight or flight impulses, develop extensive modes of cooperation and inner stability, and solve

57. Hrdy, *Mothers and Others*.

58. See de Waal, *Age of Empathy*, 11. De Waal argues for "a complete overhaul of assumptions about human nature" and maintains that the maternal bond provides an "evolutionary template for all other attachments" (7, 11).

59. Hrdy, *Mothers and Others*, 137–38.

60. Allan Schore documents an "epigenetic sequence of adaptive issues which must be negotiated by the caregiver-infant dyad to achieve self-regulation" via neurophysiological maturation (*Affect Regulation and the Origins of the Self*, 31–32).

self-preservation issues that not only have not gone away but have taken on new and lethal forms in the Anthropocene. Donald claims that accelerated change has "driven our conscious capacity to the wall."[61] What took millennia to achieve can be quickly undone. As Blumenberg claims in *Beschreibung des Menschen*, the multiplicity of the achievements of humanity can be grasped with a single principle: maintaining sufficient distance from both external and internal threats in order to create an environment in which options can be tested (569). We are arguably, at this point in time, at an inflection point and in uncharted waters due to the speed of change on just about every front, both internally and externally.

Modernity, Acceleration, and Anthropos

Lysemose has drawn attention to the close relation between the rise of philosophical anthropology and modernity. Skepticism about the progress narrative and anxiety about the speed of change, coupled with the loss of traditional answers to the question of what man is, led to "philosophical reflection on the historical experience of the loss of all such theories."[62] What Scheler said in 1928 has been amplified in the Anthropocene: "It can be said that man at no point in history has become so problematic for himself than is presently the case."[63] Lysemose argues that the loss of essence characteristic of modernity "is the acute historical experience at the root of philosophical anthropology."[64] Understanding "how a being without a nature is possible within nature"[65] then becomes a meditation on the conditions of our possibility in the midst of accelerating forces that Blumenberg calls excessive demands on the creature that must distance itself from absolutes, construct "detours," rely on people, institutions, and myths that contain possible points of attachment or recognition, and within that context engage in critical reflection. Modernity made visible the need for a philosophical anthropology that could specify these requirements in the absence of biological, practical, or metaphysical guarantees. Now, the Anthropocene narratives render these issues blindingly clear insofar as they represent the latest confrontation with the absolutism of reality—the intense pressure on all species resulting from our successful colonization of almost every environment on the planet.

---

61. Donald, *A Mind So Rare*, 259.
62. Lysemose, "Self-Preservation of Man," 49.
63. Scheler, *Man's Place in Nature*, 4.
64. Lysemose, "Self-Preservation of Man," 50.
65. Lysemose, "Self-Preservation of Man," 50.

Even though Blumenberg identifies the need to "save time" as an anthropological constant—one that has produced astonishing technical achievements—acceleration now threatens the possibility of a humane world, a world created by establishing distance. Anthropologically, saving time refers to the transformation of the animal who flees into the animal that creates distance (*BDM*, 616). In our evolutionary history, distancing facilitated cognitive mastery and technical learning, but it also takes time to mediate impulses, process emotions, form attachment bonds, and to assimilate and then transmit cultural learning to offspring. This "saves time" because the species does not begin anew with each generation. Saving time at this point in history would mean *retarding* the pace of change in order not to be used up as a species. The finite subject is not the "theoretical subject [of science and technology, which] is only able to strive for indifference because it is not identical with the individual subject and finitude . . . but has an open temporal horizon. 'Significance' is related to finitude" (*WM*, 67, 68). Modernity fused these two subjects, assuming an open temporal horizon, which has led to delusional fantasies of unlimited growth and progress, a dangerous conflation of life-time and world-time.[66]

It is worth asking Donald's question about whether our species' brains can adapt to such rapid change. In addition to accelerating changes in the environment are accelerating selection pressures from within, both emotionally and physiologically. Hrdy claims that the "fastest-evolving genes in the human genome are those associated with the central nervous system."[67] This raises questions about whether our species can preserve the adaptive capacities that depend on attachment styles. As part of the "rhetoric" of accumulated learning, they must be passed on culturally.

Like Blumenberg, Hrdy refuses to view our species as static, and she links certain behaviors with the persistence of species identity. She draws on research by the evolutionary psychologists John Hawks and Henry Harpending, who date acceleration pressures on our species to the last forty thousand years rather than since just the Enlightenment or the Industrial Revolution, when it became more visible—which provides some backstory for the geoscience narrative that begins the Anthropocene with the "Great Acceleration" since 1945. Hawks and Harpending do, however, say that the fairly recent dramatic surge in human population has created an exponential increase for muta-

---

66. In *Lebenszeit und Weltzeit* Blumenberg calls attention to the vast gulf between world time and human time. Institutions help us cope with the fact that something will continue beyond us, but another response is delusion. See Nicholls's discussion of Hitler in *Myth and the Human Sciences*, 237–38.

67. Hrdy, *Mothers and Others*, 292.

tions to act on. There is no reason why "cognitive and behavioral traits would be any less susceptible to ongoing selection." If an agent of selection is removed, the evolutionary consequences can be rapid, which is certainly now true of other species on this planet.[68] So the question is not only how planetary resources can support an enormous population but whether the empathic behavior and curiosity about others that has been shaped by our heritage of communal care will disappear in the face of this latest challenge.

In addition, Donald examines decreased capacities for rote verbal skills, mental arithmetic, and memorization. Digital media provide "instant access to an infinitely expandable collective memory system," which is not tethered to biology. This is not the memory system represented by rhetoric in Blumenberg's sense, which interferes with and retards accelerated change. According to Donald, digital media "has the potential to seriously violate the ancient co-evolutionary pact between brain and culture which has kept the rate of cultural and technological change within tolerable limits."[69] How does one establish "networks of trust" within an environment of anonymity where people are easily manipulated? This is doubly problematic because digital media have now become essential for survival in our world.[70] Furthermore, without trust, effective cooperation is seriously threatened even though the human need for trust continues to be an anthropological requirement.

As Blumenberg reminds us, the species may be overwhelmed by impulses and fail, partly because of how it represents threats to itself (*BDM*, 550). The implied imperative is to be vigilant about what protects and nurtures both the flexible internal and external stabilities that support resilience in the face of the excessive, destructive pace of change to which we subject ourselves, other animals, and the natural world. Thus the Anthropocene is as much about the need for inner resilience as it is about institutions responsive to changes in the natural world. Making intelligent choices about the latter indeed depends on the former.

The Promethean Anthropocene Reoccupies the Progress Narrative

Prometheus, as a figure who defied limits, has been revitalized in the Anthropocene literature. The theft of fire becomes the theft of fossil fuels and techno-

---

68. Hrdy, *Mothers and Others*, 292, 293.

69. Donald, "Digital Era," 68.

70. Chakrabarty references the work of P. K. Haff, who also argues that it would not be possible to sustain billions of people on the planet without "modern forms of energy and communications technology touching all our lives in some significant way." Without the "technosphere," human populations would collapse ("Climate and Capital," 14).

logical prowess, with all their unintended material and psychological consequences. Unsurprisingly, the myth continues to resonate given the new historical realities. Because I claim that Blumenberg's anthropological framework allows us to clarify and gain distance from the crises reflected by the phenomenon of the Anthropocene narratives, an obvious place to turn is the central place occupied by the Prometheus story in *Work on Myth*.[71] Blumenberg traces its reception history from antiquity to Kafka, who seems to bring the myth to an end by merging a weary, bored Prometheus with a rock. Blumenberg's final sentence in *Work on Myth*, following his remarks on Kafka, is "But what if there were still something to say, after all?" (636). Will a technological Hercules emerge to solve the vulnerabilities that Prometheus' theft unleashed? Or will more benign narratives gain a foothold?

The great myths evolve in time by conserving, or "optimizing," a position by adapting to circumstances; a great myth is a revisable rhetorical consensus about how things stand with existence, and in this capacity, myth is a trope for the conditions of cultural survival generally. The limit case is movement away from the *terminus a quo*. All we have is the "slender stock" of what has survived, which is a model for all "rhetoric" that has survived and met a "burden of proof." Blumenberg calls this optimizing process "work *on* myth." Myths' transformations are shaped historically by needs and situations that "test" what can "no longer be dispensed with in a unit myth" (*WM*, 174). The mythical figure and stories it makes possible are like themes and variations in music. History or "time brings things out" in myths (*WM*, 69), in relation to problems posed by the epoch in question, such as those dramatized by the Prometheus-Anthropocene nexus.

From Blumenberg's point of view, we could say that the Promethean Anthropocene stories have led us once again to Kant's unanswered fourth question. They have brought out (figuratively) a set of parameters bracketed by two limits: rock, which suggests surrender, eclipse, or the futility of human agency, on the one hand, and geoengineering mastery, on the other. For example, stratigraphers such as Jan Zalasiewicz write that "to be useful to geologists, the Anthropocene must be thought of not just as history, but as rock, as strata . . . that geologists can map."[72] Analyzing the metaphor, Lauren Rickards writes that stratigraphers position "human bodies in deep time as ultimately geologi-

---

71. For a detailed account of Blumenberg's tracking of the Prometheus story in *Work on Myth*, see Nicholls, *Myth and the Human Sciences*, 153–82. Nicholls claims that Blumenberg's *Nachlass* examines the political dimensions of myth that are implicit in *Work on Myth* but explicit in later writings that he refused to publish while he was alive.

72. Quoted in Rickards, "Metaphor and the Anthropocene," 282.

cal objects," as though the human species has died out. Zalasiewicz's popular writing imagines a posthuman time, as seen in the title of his book *The Earth after Us: What Legacy Will Humans Leave in Rocks?*[73] At the other extreme, ecomodernists imagine humans as geological "forces" who are as, or more, powerful than other forces, such as volcanoes and tectonic plates. Humans compete with and potentially dominate the forces of nature, which naturalizes the Christian model of human domination and extends the progress narrative into a nonhuman open temporal horizon. A further iteration is the planetary steward: technological and scientific prowess enabling us to become a geological force for good, but this too has an open temporal horizon. According to Steffen, Crutzen, and John R. McNeill, humans may even, far into the future, "deflect meteorites and asteroids before they could hit the Earth."[74] Somewhat imperiously, Crutzen and Schwägerl claim that we live in the "Age of Men," and with bioengineering we will decide "what nature is and what it will be."[75] These two extremes, rock and mastery, roughly parallel Blumenberg's *terminus a quo* and a perfect lifeworld, neither one of which adequately describes or supports the human realm that philosophical anthropology has shown our species needs.

However, these two extremes do signify the arena within which human self-assertion must occur, delineating metaphorically the absolutes specific to this historical period from which the species must distance itself. The problem is that "what we need from history [and cannot get] tends toward indicators having the clarity of mythical models, indicators that enable the individual subject, with his finite time, to determine how he can set himself in relationship to the large-scale structures that reach far beyond him." Great myths may be "high karat work[s] of logos" (*WM*, 128), because they tell stories that have not been contradicted by reality, but all kinds of myth suspend the need for explanations and fill empty positions with a high degree of density (*WM*, 128), and the subjective conclusiveness characteristic of myth may encourage submission rather than thinking for oneself. Radical disorientation often leads to mythicizing or remythicizing (*WM*, 29), which may be no more than "an absolutism of wishes" set up against the "abomination." For example, imagining control of the Earth system with human tools and technologies within the time frame of *human* history, believing that climate change or the pandemic is a hoax, or

73. Rickards, "Metaphor and the Anthropocene," 283, 284. See also Zalasiewicz, "Epoch of Humans," 9; and Wallace-Wells, *Uninhabitable Earth*. To examine metaphors is not to say that the epoch in which we live cannot be called the Anthropocene in a scientific sense.

74. Steffen, Crutzen, and McNeill, "Anthropocene," 620.

75. Crutzen and Schwägerl, "Living in the Anthropocene."

that there is no scientific consensus on anthropogenic climate change are all examples of denial, of refusals to take up burdens of proof.[76] Critics on both sides accuse each other of propagating myths, which are seductive in an age without cosmic or any other kind of assurances. The rude shock of the Anthropocene is about realizing that there are planetary histories that have nothing to do with human time or human exceptionalism. We can ask, along with Blumenberg: What would count as a realistic zone of "as if" behavior for running trial and error experiments (*WM*, 12)? What would count as Rockström's "safe operating space for humanity" now that philosophical anthropology has clarified a set of parameters and nonnegotiable limits? Philosophical anthropology is as much a stance from which to interrogate and clarify as it is a theory of human existence.

Blumenberg has established that we do not adapt to reality solely through reason—either as a form of self-foundation or in the form it takes in science. He has also demonstrated that myth and theory have different anthropological functions, as well as pointing out the dangers of confusing the two. For example, when René Descartes insisted on the intuitive certainty of clear and distinct ideas, reason was asked to assume the function of myth. Myth does not try to give rational grounds for anything; it preempts questions rather than answering them (*WM*, 234). Reason's job is to prevent unreason from occupying empty space, to examine myths' self-evidences, to ask which questions have been preempted. For example, to what unstated question(s) are *Anthropos* and the Anthropocene an answer? Clearly, the vastly different time scales of human and planetary history, our radical dependence on the natural world, and our lack of specialness in the broader scheme of things, which were suppressed by the modernist narrative, exert pressures that need to be addressed. This invites consideration of Blumenberg's philosophy of history. Although the Anthropocene seems to be an unprecedented rupture, it is instructive to examine analogues in the past that suggest ways of framing both these pressures and the time-scale dilemmas that Chakrabarty says test the limits of historical understanding. Historical knowledge connects pasts and futures and assumes that there is both continuity and discontinuity to human experience, which has to be grasped within the time frame of *human* history.

76. For a sample of Fox News reporting on climate and the environment, see Lott, "Five Most Over-the-Top Climate Warnings." In addition, the Heritage Foundation, the Cato Institute, the Manhattan Institute, and other conservative US think tanks have become influential in setting US environmental policy by manipulating data to cast doubt on such phenomena as climate change, ice melting, and species extinction.

Blumenberg can speak to Chakrabarty's dilemma given how he addressed similar problems in *The Legitimacy of the Modern Age*. By shifting attention away from the contents of consciousness to their functions, and by distinguishing between myth and history, Blumenberg understands history, like rhetoric and shifts in metaphor, as a series of substitutions. History is a series of questions and answers that transform each other temporally.[77] The answers, which do not always precede the questions, are "positions for consciousness," or consolidated lifeworldly orientations. Answers are identifiable because of their inertia; they endure *long enough* through change such that change can be recognized and evaluated in relation to them. These positions generate "expectations" for the future, which bridge the discontinuities that inevitably emerge.[78]

In times of disorientation, expectations and fears are also a readiness to receive what myth, in all its forms, offers. Disorientation produces a "vacancy" or question. Significant content then preemptively fills the vacancy with meanings that *appear* to assume the same function, that is, continue to answer what is or appears to be the same question. For example, the expectation of progress was generated from scientific advances and therefore independently of a medieval synthesis dependent on salvation as the meaning of history. When the Scholastic version of monotheism broke down under pressure from nominalist critiques, the expectations associated with the salvation story remained. The progress idea in the wings had been sufficiently validated by experiential success that it could "occupy" this emptiness with a density of meaning. The position had become "questionable" because the salvation story as fulfillment in the beyond ceased to address human orientation needs. However, the moderns overextended and overgeneralized the idea of progress as the answer to the implicit "question" about the meaning of history overall. Furthermore, the

---

77. Blumenberg reminds us not to take the metaphor literally: "'Philosophy of history' only thematizes the structure of the process" (AAR, 202). Although he is making an argument about epochs, this model is applicable to the study of historical change generally. His reception and reoccupation theories also reflect his appropriation of Cassirer's framework of formalist substance, function question, and answer. For a discussion of Blumenberg's anthropological reinterpretation of Cassirer's framework, see Pavesich, "Hans Blumenberg's Philosophical Anthropology: After Heidegger and Cassirer."

78. Blumenberg argues that "rhetoric has to do not with facts but with expectations" (AAR, 201), which he associates with the prospect of actively intervening in events. Blumenberg is probably referring to Reinhart Koselleck's anthropological schema in *Future's Past*. Koselleck argues that we have the past through "experience," which he defines as the "present past," and the future anticipated through "expectations": "These two categories are indicative of a general human condition; one could say that they indicate an anthropological condition without which history is neither possible nor conceivable" (270).

Enlightenment saw itself as discontinuous with the past, a completely new self-grounding project that rejected the past, as well ushering in what Carolyn Merchant refers to as the "death of nature."[79] Progress thus "reoccupied" the position. The medievals had no reason to question history's meaning because the salvation story preempted it. Nonetheless, the question was implicit in the idea of salvation in a transcendent realm. The moderns then substituted postponement (with its open temporal horizon) for transcendence. In this sense, Blumenberg claims questions do not always precede their answers; it is possible for "totally heterogeneous contents to take on identical functions in specific positions in the system of man's interpretation of the world and himself."[80] This is not arbitrary because humans necessarily inherit the problems and expectations associated with a previous epoch.

Hindsight allows us to see that the new form of self-assertion did not just occupy the space, which would have been the "anthropological minimum under the conditions of the theological maximum" (*LM*, 196); it reoccupied it mythically. Theological absolutism produced a legitimate orientation problem for humankind, because the loss of cosmic orientation as a result of God's arbitrary absolute power required a countermobilization of forces, a compensatory interest in the human world—just as the waning of the progress narrative has given way to a parallel orientation problem as a result of anxieties about the arbitrariness of the Earth system in the Anthropocene. The moderns overlooked the fact that a less grandiose solution was available, a fallible notion of reason that more adequately reflected human capacities.[81] When the Enlightenment and the philosophy of history tried to answer the medieval question, they masked the anthropological significance of self-assertion, which could have meant renouncing absolutist claims and exercising limited dominion over a natural world in which they were embedded. "The criterion of leaving nothing unsaid [what myth aims to do]" is what qualifies a reoccupation as mythical (*WM*, 176). *R*eoccupations "restore continuity" (*LM*, 463), which they achieve by *appearing* to be repetition. Reoccupation may strive to be mythical repetition (e.g., control of planetary systems that matches modernist

---

79. Merchant, *Death of Nature*.

80. Blumenberg, *Legitimacy of the Modern Age*, 64 (hereafter cited as *LM*).

81. Blumenberg respects science's fallible idea of reason and points out that humans often do not want to pay the price of renouncing definitive answers. He notes that when the ideal of consensus, as "agreement subject to later revocation," was transferred from rhetoric to the scientific "method" of the modern age, "philosophy too was not spared the renunciation on which all rhetoric is based" (AAR, 185). This is connected to an attack on Descartes, whose starting point "forbids itself to have a history" (*LM*, 146).

expectations), but it is precisely not this, which the functional explanation of continuity as the substitution of one "position" for another that distinguishes history from myth reveals. We could say that *knowledge* of reoccupation rather than repetition is a form of work on myth and an exercise of reason. One way to work on myth is to cultivate a sense of history by exploring the questions implied by contemporaneous historical configurations.

In the rhetoric essay, Blumenberg implies that the theory of reoccupation—the question and answer sequence, positions, and so on—is a series of rhetorical transactions and part of a broader anthropological system (AAR, 194). He refers to a neediness of consciousness (*LM*, 9, 64, 89, 131, 469; *WM*, 29) and to "a constant matrix of needs" (*LM*, 463). Thus philosophical anthropology is integral to his historical logic and has nothing to do with human essences or constant meanings. There are elementary self-assertion needs on both sides of the threshold of change. Such needs are "reflected in mythical configurations . . . that keep it in a state of unease and agitation" (*WM*, 273–74).[82] This is its own deficiency and constant need to repair a fragile lifeworld by consolidating "positions for consciousness" or answer positions that resist humankind's demise.

In this context Blumenberg claims both that history makes itself and that we make history. Having a sense of history means knowing what humans do not make in order to have a sense of what they can make. Humans do not make the iconic constants, burdens of proof, or answer positions. However, "we must proceed from the assumption that man makes history—who else shall make it for him? . . . [But] the principle that man makes history certainly does not mean that which is made depends solely on the intentions and the precepts as a result of and according to which it was produced" (*LM*, 477). History is not identical with human intentions, because actions and outcomes cannot be unambiguously coordinated (*LM*, 478). Unintended consequences have their own historical productivity, which, as Chakrabarty claims, means facing up to facts, such as "Soil, fossil fuel, and biodiversity [loss] are not renewable on human time scales"—at least not on a large-enough scale to support several billion human beings. "The narrative of world history has now collided (in our thoughts) with the much longer-term geological history of . . . the Earth system,"[83] and we face the problem of discovering modes of distance from what Blumenberg would call an "absolutism."

82. In this context he is responding to possible objections to his theory of myth, that is, why myths all over the world resemble each other is explained by a constant problem and not by archetypal meanings (*Work on Myth*, 274).

83. Chakrabarty, "Climate and Capital," 22, 23.

Chakrabarty points to "rifts" and "fault lines" "in the landscape of our thought," which correspond to questions inherited from the previous epoch. He articulates a number of these questions: How do we think in terms of probabilities in modern economies while taking into account the "radical uncertainty of the climate"? How are our "necessarily divided lives" related to our "collective life as a species"?[84] How do we supplement our anthropocentric thinking while putting the needs of the planet first? These rifts involve three histories that operate on different time scales and at different speeds,[85] as well as the problems I outlined at the beginning of the article and in the last section. Of a piece with the obvious widespread dislocations associated with globalization, climate change, migration, inequality, resource conflicts, population increase, and now a pandemic is the emotional distress caused by accelerated pressures on our nervous systems, plus the propensity of large numbers of people to believe illusions. The Anthropocene refers to this radical multifaceted destabilization, to the entire cluster of ecological and psychological fault lines that the progress narrative, self-foundation, and separation from nature suppressed and cannot adequately address.

If resistance to absolutisms in the Anthropocene requires a "countermobilization of self-assertion" on behalf of humans as historically situated beings, then there is no built-in necessity that it become a mythical *re*occupation that teleologically preordains either complete collapse or complete mastery. Blumenberg defines *countermobilization* as "an existential program, according to which man posits his existence in a historical situation and indicates to himself how he is going to deal with the reality surrounding him and what use he will make of the possibilities that are open to him" (*LM*, 138). This definition must be read next to the anthropological requirements that leave an increasingly smaller margin for error. Apocalyptic thinking and restorations of paradise, such as floating islands with private armies and exile to new planets, or ecofascism will not ameliorate the suffering of most people and are also pipe dreams. There are no easy answers because of the vast number of unknowns, and as Chakrabarty claims, there is "no silver bullet that solves all the problems at once." Wisely, he asserts that we may diagnose but not be able to solve all these problems.[86] Blumenberg would agree and assess whether the stories create distance, the reflective space necessary for appraising our prospects realistically. In other words, the focus should be on keeping in view, as a constant

84. Chakrabarty, "Climate and Capital," 3.
85. Chakrabarty, "Climate and Capital," 3, 4, 9.
86. Chakrabarty, "Whose Anthropocene? A Response," 107.

reminder, the anthropological minimum that Blumenberg gestured toward in *The Legitimacy of the Modern Age* and more fully articulated in *Work on Myth* and *Beschreibung des Menschen*.

The massive multifaceted literature on the Anthropocene is a beginning insofar as it represents a collective process of labeling, digesting, and debating the fissures that opened in the modernist narrative. With Blumenberg, we can ask which stories are dangerous. Which stories threaten to become monostories? Which stories efface the difference between human time and planetary time, either preordaining outcomes or offering technofixes modeled unreflectively on progress narratives, such as assuming that scientists will find the silver bullet? And what about the white-supremacist ecofascists who desire "lebensraum" and those who prefer antidemocratic means plus a drastic reduction in nonwhite populations?[87] Rather than tell stories that reflect reality, we may try to make reality fit the stories. For example, in his popular book *Homo Deus: A Brief History of Tomorrow*, Yuval Noah Harari describes a trajectory, not unlike that of Crutzen and Schwägerl, which is perfectly continuous with the modernist technological mastery narrative in which artificial intelligence and bioengineered humans and other organisms become the primary reality, and Homo sapiens as we have known it dissolves into a massive data network.[88]

In *Die Vollzähligkeit der Sterne* (*The Completeness of the Stars*), Blumenberg proposes stopping and listening, meditating on the immensity of time and space (innumerable galaxies) and the powerlessness of *Wissen*. The size of the universe is an index of the loss of our significance and the improbability of our form of existence. So it is precisely this meditation that could deflate narcotizing grandiose metanarratives and turn us back onto ourselves and realize that Earth is "the life-worldly ground of our existence."[89] Awareness of the immensity of space and time can also remind us that planetary time is not human time and that life is precious and limited.[90] Although already on this side of the absolutism of reality, we can never reach "the turning point in history at which the relative predominance of reality over . . . consciousness and . . . fate has turned into the predominance of the subject" (*WM*, 9). It is worth asking what it would mean to resist the trajectory Harari sees as a possibility, that is, to turn technical prowess toward actualizing stories that recognize the embeddedness of humans in nature while living in human time and

87. See Wilson, "Eco-fascism Is Undergoing a Revival."
88. Harari, *Homo Deus*, 151.
89. Bajohr, "Anthropocene and Negative Anthropology."
90. See Wetz, "Abscheid ohne Widersehen." Wetz tends to read these passages pessimistically, which is not surprising. Another way to read this is that Blumenberg is soberly confronting us with the challenge we face.

while soberly appraising which anthropogenic disasters can and cannot be influenced to the extent that our limited knowledge allows. It is entirely possible that systems supporting life will become too degraded to support life as we know it, including our own. A big problem is that many do not know *that* they do not know (*BDM*, 478). However, we do know that the Anthropocene is producing and will continue to produce suffering, such as the extinction and displacement of humans and other species because of drought, fire, and flooding, but we do not know the long-term outcome. Perhaps as Scranton has written: we can accept the end of our civilization without despair and work toward a change in collective consciousness. "We need not just biological arks, to carry forward endangered genetic data, but also cultural arks, to carry forward endangered wisdom."[91] This is not unlike Jonathan Lear's analysis in *Radical Hope*. Lear is not writing about the Anthropocene, but he asks what would count as hope in an age characterized by an "uncanny sense of menace and vulnerability" without the concepts with which to think about how to project a meaningful future. To be courageous going forward means accepting this loss in the face of overwhelming forces, not in ignorance of them, and responding to reality rather than to the "wishful omnipotence one often sees in dreams."[92]

There is not space in this article to address the early critics of the progress narrative and mechanism metaphors or attempts to reinvigorate old background metaphors that draw attention to our embeddedness in nature. For example, the influential environmentalist Aldo Leopold cautioned us to "think like a mountain," to take a long, broad view and contemplate the interconnectedness of everything in the natural world. Lovelock's Gaia, Earth as a living system, is perhaps the best known. Freya Mathews and Arne Vetlesen urge revisiting panpsychism.[93] Others examine indigenous peoples' worldviews, and so on, and many of these metaphors and critiques have mobilized new technologies, such as biomimicry.[94] New respect for gardens, green spaces, the healing powers of nature, and transitions to renewable energies all aim to support resilience within the time frame of human history. We do not know how much difference these self-assertive efforts will make in the big picture of things. It is best to keep in mind Chakrabarty's view that the Anthropocene is an informal category capable of bearing multiple stories, as well as Blumenberg's claim that there might still be something to say after all. That "something" is the oppor-

91. Scranton, *Learning to Die in the Anthropocene*, 109.
92. Lear, *Radical Hope*, 7, 41, 44, 132.
93. Vetlesen discusses Mathews, his inspiration for panpsychism, in *Denial of Nature*.
94. See the Biomimicry Institute website at biomimicry.org.

tunity to continue working on myth through the lens of the anthropological minimum, exploring and often implementing strategies embedded in the stories that preserve distance from absolutes.

Vida Pavesich teaches in the philosophy department at the California State University, East Bay.

References

Alsberg, Paul. *In Quest of Man: A Biological Approach to the Problem of Man's Place in Nature*. Oxford: Pergamon, 1970.

Anthropocene Working Group. "Anthropocene GSSP Project." *Newsletter of the Anthropocene Working Group* 10 (2020): 4. quaternary.stratigraphy.org/wp-content/uploads /2021/03/AWG-Newsletter-2020-Vol-10.pdf.

Bajohr, Hannes. "Anthropocene and Negative Anthropology: Return of Man." Institute for Interdisciplinary Research into the Anthropocene, August 11, 2019. iiraorg.com/2019 /08/11/anthropocene-and-negative-anthropology.

Baskin, Jeremy. "The Ideology of the Anthropocene?" MSSI Research Paper No. 3. Melbourne Sustainable Society Institute, University of Melbourne, May 1, 2014. sustainable .unimelb.edu.au/publications/research-papers/the-ideology-of-the-anthropocene.

Bauer, Andrew M., and Erle C. Ellis. "The Anthropocene Divide: Obscuring the Understanding of Social-Environmental Change." *Current Anthropology* 59, no. 2 (2018): 209–27.

Biermann, Frank. *Earth System Governance: World Politics in the Anthropocene*. Cambridge, MA: MIT Press, 2014.

Biermann, Frank, et al. "Down to Earth: Contextualizing the Anthropocene." *Global Environmental Change* 39, no. 2 (2016): 341–50.

Blumenberg, Hans. "An Anthropological Approach to the Contemporary Significance of Rhetoric," translated by Robert M. Wallace. In *History, Metaphors, Fables: A Hans Blumenberg Reader*, edited and translated by Hannes Bajohr, Florian Fuchs, and Joe Paul Kroll, 177–208. Ithaca, NY: Cornell University Press, 2020.

Blumenberg, Hans. *Beschreibung des Menschen*. Frankfurt am Main: Suhrkamp, 2006.

Blumenberg, Hans. *The Legitimacy of the Modern Age*, translated by Robert M. Wallace. Cambridge, MA: MIT Press, 1985.

Blumenberg, Hans. "The Life-World and the Concept of Reality." In *Life-World and Consciousness: Essays for Aron Gurwitsch*, 425–44. Evanston, IL: Northwestern University Press, 1972.

Blumenberg, Hans. "Prospect for a Theory of Nonconceptuality," translated by Hannes Bajohr. In *History, Metaphors, Fables: A Hans Blumenberg Reader*, edited and translated by Hannes Bajohr, Florian Fuchs, and Joe Paul Kroll, 239–59. Ithaca, NY: Cornell University Press, 2020.

Blumenberg, Hans. *Work on Myth*, translated by Robert M. Wallace. Cambridge, MA: MIT Press, 1985.

Bonneuil, Christophe. "The Geological Turn: Narratives of the Anthropocene." In *The Anthropocene and the Global Environmental Crisis: Rethinking Modernity in a New Epoch*, edited by Clive Hamilton, François Gemenne, and Christophe Bonneuil, 15–31. New York: Routledge, 2015.

Bonneuil, Christophe, and Jean-Baptiste Fressoz. *The Shock of the Anthropocene: The Earth, History, and Us*, translated by David Fernbach. London: Verso, 2016. Kindle.

Burakoff, Maddie. "One Million Species at Risk of Extinction, Threatening Human Communities around the World, U.N. Report Warns." *Smithsonian*, May 6, 2019. www .smithsonianmag.com/science-nature/one-million-species-risk-extinction-threatening -human-communities-around-world-un-report-warns-180972114.

Chakrabarty, Dipesh. "Anthropocene Time." *History and Theory* 57, no. 1 (2018): 5–32.

Chakrabarty, Dipesh. "Climate and Capital: On Conjoined Histories." *Critical Inquiry* 41, no. 1 (2014): 1–23.

Chakrabarty, Dipesh. "The Climate of History: Four Theses." *Critical Inquiry* 35, no. 2 (2009): 197–222.

Chakrabarty, Dipesh. "The Future of the Human Sciences in the Age of Humans: A Note." *European Journal of Social Theory* 20, no. 1 (2017): 39–43.

Chakrabarty, Dipesh. "The Planet: An Emergent Humanist Category." *Critical Inquiry* 46, no. 1 (2019): 1–31.

Chakrabarty, Dipesh. "Whose Anthropocene? A Response." In "Whose Anthropocene? A Response to Dipesh Chakrabarty's 'Four Theses,'" edited by Robert Emmett and Thomas Lekan. *Rachel Carson Center Perspectives: Transformations in Environment and Society* 2016, no. 2. www.environmentandsociety.org/perspectives/2016/2/whose -anthropocene-revisiting-dipesh-chakrabartys-four-theses.

Chernilo, Daniel. "The Question of the Human in the Anthropocene Debate." *European Journal of Social Theory* 20, no. 1 (2017): 44–60.

Clark, Nigel. "Geo-politics and the Disaster of the Anthropocene." *Sociological Review* 62, no. S1 (2014): 19–37.

Clark, Nigel, and Yasmin Gunaratnam. "Earthing the Anthropos? From 'Socializing the Anthropocene' to Geologizing the Social." *European Journal of Social Theory* 20, no. 1 (2017): 146–63.

Crutzen, Paul J., and Christian Schwägerl. "Living in the Anthropocene: Toward a New Global Ethos." *Yale Environment 360*, January 24, 2011. e360.yale.edu/features /living_in_the_anthropocene_toward_a_new_global_ethos.

Dallmayr, Fred. "The Return of Philosophical Anthropology." In *Philosophy and Anthropology: Border Crossing and Transformations*, edited by Ananta Kumar Giri and John Clammer, 357–64. London: Anthem, 2013.

Davison, Nicola. "The Anthropocene Epoch: Have We Entered a New Phase of Planetary History?" *Guardian*, May 30, 2019. www.theguardian.com/environment/2019/may /30/anthropocene-epoch-have-we-entered-a-new-phase-of-planetary-history.

de Waal, Frans. *The Age of Empathy: Nature's Lessons for a Kinder Society*. New York: Crown, 2009.

Donald, Merlin. "The Digital Era: Challenges for the Modern Mind." *Cadmus* 2, no. 2 (2014): 68–79.

Donald, Merlin. *A Mind So Rare: The Evolution of Human Consciousness*. New York: Norton, 2004.

Harari, Yuval Noah. *Homo Deus: A Brief History of Tomorrow*. London: Random House, 2015.

Harvard T. H. Chan School of Public Health. "Coronavirus, Climate Change, and the Environment: A Conversation on COVID-19 with Dr. Aaron Bernstein, Director of Harvard Chan C-CHANGE." www.hsph.harvard.edu/c-change/subtopics/coronavirus-and-climate-change (accessed November 1, 2020).

Hrdy, Sarah H. *Mothers and Others: The Evolutionary Origins of Mutual Understanding*. Cambridge, MA: Harvard University Press, 2011.

Kant, Immanuel. *Critique of Judgment*, translated by J. H. Bernard. New York: Prometheus, 2000.

Koselleck, Reinhart. *Future's Past: On the Semantics of Historical Time*, translated by Keith Tribe. Cambridge, MA: MIT Press, 1985.

Lear, Jonathan. *Radical Hope: Ethics in the Face of Cultural Devastation*. Cambridge, MA: Harvard University Press, 2006.

Lott, Maxim. "Five Most Over-the-Top Climate Warnings." *Fox News*, May 28, 2019. www.foxnews.com/science/five-most-over-the-top-climate-warnings.

Lövbrand, E., S. Beck, J. Chilvers, T. Forsyth, and J. Hedrén. "Who Speaks for the Future of Earth? How Critical Social Science Can Extend the Conversation on the Anthropocene." *Global Environmental Change* 32 (2015): 211–18.

Lysemose, Kasper. "The Being, the Origin, and the Becoming of Man: A Presentation of Philosophical Anthropogenealogy and Some Ensuing Methodological Considerations." *Human Studies* 35, no. 1 (2012): 115–30.

Lysemose, Kasper. "The Self-Preservation of Man: Remarks on the Relation between Modernity and Philosophical Anthropology." In *Philosophy and Anthropology: Border Crossing and Transformations*, edited by Ananta Kumar Giri and John Clammer, 39–56. London: Anthem, 2013.

Marquard, Odo. "In Praise of Polytheism (On Monomythical and Polymythical Thinking)." In *Farewell to Matters of Principle: Philosophical Studies*, translated by Robert M. Wallace with the assistance of Susan Bernstein and James I. Porter, 87–110. New York: Oxford University Press, 1989.

Merchant, Carolyn. *The Death of Nature: Women, Ecology, and the Scientific Revolution*. New York: HarperCollins, 1985.

Merker, Barbara. "Bedürfnis nach Bedeutsamkeit: Zwischen Lebenswelt und Absolutismus der Wirklichkeit." In *Die Kunst des Überlebens: Nachdenken über Hans Blumenberg*, edited by Franz Josef Wetz and Hermann Timm, 68–98. Frankfurt am Main: Suhrkamp, 1999.

Moore, Jason W., ed. *Anthropocene or Capitalocene? Nature, History, and the Crisis of Capitalism*. Oakland, CA: PM Press, 2016.

Nicholls, Angus. *Myth and the Human Sciences: Hans Blumenberg's Theory of Myth*. New York: Routledge, 2015.

Pavesich, Vida. "Hans Blumenberg: Philosophical Anthropology and the Ethics of Consolation." In *Naturalism and Philosophical Anthropology: Nature, Life, and the Human between Transcendental and Empirical Perspectives*, edited by Phillip Honenberger, 66–93. London: Palgrave Macmillan, 2015.

Pavesich, Vida. "Hans Blumenberg's Philosophical Anthropology: After Heidegger and Cassirer." *Journal of the History of Philosophy* 46, no. 3 (2008): 421–48.

Rickards, Lauren A. "Metaphor and the Anthropocene: Presenting Humans as a Geological Force." *Geographical Research* 53, no. 3 (2015): 280–87.

Rockström, Johan, et al. "Planetary Boundaries: Exploring the Safe Operating Space for Humanity." *Ecology and Society* 14, no. 2 (2009). www.ecologyandsociety.org/vol14/iss2/art32.

Scheler, Max. *Man's Place in Nature*, translated by Hans Meyerhoff. New York: Noonday, 1961.

Schore, Alan. *Affect Regulation and the Origins of the Self: The Neurobiology of Emotional Development*. Hillsdale, NJ: Erlbaum, 1994.

Scranton, Roy. *Learning to Die in the Anthropocene*. San Francisco: City Lights, 2015.

Steffen, Will, Paul J. Crutzen, and John R. McNeill. "The Anthropocene: Are Humans Now Overwhelming the Great Forces of Nature?" *Ambio* 36, no. 8 (2007): 614–21.

Steffen, Will, et al. *Global Change and the Earth System: A Planet under Pressure*. www.igbp.net/globalchange/greatacceleration.4.1b8ae20512db692f2a680001630.html.

Stock, Jay T. "Are Humans Still Evolving?" *EMBO Reports* 9 (2008): S51–S54.

Szabo, Peter. "Historical Ecology: Past, Present, and Future." *Biological Reviews* 90, no. 4 (2014): 997–1014.

Tabas, Brad. "Blumenberg, Politics, Anthropology." *Telos*, no. 158 (2012): 135–53.

Tomasello, Michael, Malinda Carpenter, Josep Call, Tanya Behne, and Henrike Moll. "Understanding and Sharing Intentions: The Origins of Cultural Cognition." *Behavioral and Brain Sciences* 28, no. 5 (2005): 675–91.

Vetlesen, Arne Johan. *The Denial of Nature: Environmental Philosophy in the Age of Globalization*. New York: Routledge, 2015.

Wallace-Wells, David. *The Uninhabitable Earth: Life after Warming*. New York: Crown, 2019.

West-Eberhard, Mary Jane. *Developmental Plasticity and Evolution*. New York: Oxford University Press, 2003.

West-Eberhard, Mary Jane. "Developmental Plasticity and the Origin of Species Differences." *Proceedings of the National Academy of Sciences* 102, suppl. 1 (2005): 6543–49.

Wetz, Franz Josef. "Abscheid ohne Widersehen: Die Endgültigkeit des Verschwindens." In *Die Kunst des Überlebens: Nachdenken über Hans Blumenberg*, edited by Franz Josef Wetz and Hermann Timm, 42–47. Frankfurt am Main: Suhrkamp, 1999.

Wetz, Franz Josef. "The Phenomenological Anthropology of Hans Blumenberg." *Iris: European Journal of Philosophy and Public Debate* 1, no. 2 (2009): 389–414. www.fupress.net/index.php/iris/article/view/3309/2912.

Wilson, Jason. "Eco-fascism Is Undergoing a Revival in the Fetid Culture of the Extreme Right." *Guardian*, March 19, 2019. www.theguardian.com/world/commentisfree/2019/mar/20/eco-fascism-is-undergoing-a-revival-in-the-fetid-culture-of-the-extreme-right.

Zalasiewicz, Jan. "The Epoch of Humans." *Nature Geoscience*, January 2013, 8–9.

Zammito, John. *Kant, Herder, and the Birth of Anthropology*. Chicago: University of Chicago Press, 2002.

The Vanishing Reality of the State:
On Hans Blumenberg's Political Theory

Hannes Bajohr

Jürgen Habermas's two-volume *This, Too, a History of Philosophy* (2019) offers a grand vista over the history of "post-metaphysical thought." The central distinction between its two main lineages is the weight each accords historical thought: only the intersubjectively focused heirs of Immanuel Kant, not the subject-centered descendants of David Hume, theorize a historically situated reason. Reflecting on one's own historical standpoint while acknowledging that such reflection is itself the result of a historical learning process gives *theories of modernity* a central position.[1] However, most such approaches in the twentieth century reject the modernity they theorize. Habermas names only *one* philosopher who comes close to his own affirmative stance: Hans Blumenberg, with his 1966 *Legitimacy of the Modern Age*.[2] Yet, despite the agreement on the defense of modernity, Habermas dismisses his work: because Blumenberg conceives of modernity as a solution to eternal anthropological problems, he in the end "seeks refuge in a rhetoric of the *Work on Myth*."[3] The reference to Blumenberg's 1979 book implies that what appears as a pro-

I wish to thank Julia Pelta Feldman, Rieke Trimçev, Dorit Krusche, and an anonymous reader for their advice as well as Bettina Blumenberg for the permission to cite unpublished material from the Hans Blumenberg Papers at the German Literary Archive in Marbach.

1. Habermas, *Auch eine Geschichte*, 35–38, 40–74. All translations mine unless otherwise noted.
2. Habermas, *Auch eine Geschichte*, 64; Blumenberg, *Legitimacy*.
3. Habermas, *Auch eine Geschichte*, 65–66, 41.

New German Critique 145, Vol. 49, No. 1, February 2022
DOI 10.1215/0094033X-9439657   © 2022 by New German Critique, Inc.

gressive position in *Legitimacy* later revealed itself to have been conservative all along, dealing with eternal anthropological constants, not with historical change.

Habermas's verdict is symptomatic of a certain puzzlement in the face of Blumenberg's oeuvre that results from the difficulty of placing him politically. When Habermas suggests that historically reflexive theories mostly come in the shape of or at least imply a political theory,[4] it is not immediately clear where Blumenberg would have formulated his. Blumenberg's interpreters are indeed divided about the status of politics in his work: he is either seen simply not to have a political theory,[5] to be only a reactive commentator of the secularization theories he attacks (mostly Karl Löwith's and Carl Schmitt's),[6] or to possess a more substantial, yet hidden, political theory that can be extracted from his theory of myth.[7] In this latter case, the main works to be considered are his 1979 *Work on Myth* (which did not deal with politics) as well as two recent posthumous publications, *Rigorism of Truth* and *Präfiguration* (which did).[8]

In Habermas's estimation, the third position eventually won out against the second, and he is not alone in this view of Blumenberg's political thought. Yet it is incomplete—not only because it is difficult to plausibly relate the Blumenberg of *Legitimacy* to the Blumenberg of *Work on Myth*, and that means to connect his more liberal *theory of history* with his more conservative *philosophical anthropology*, but also because Blumenberg *did* write about political theory, and not in a merely reactive mode, nor only in texts hidden among his papers. In 1968, two years after *Legitimacy* and eleven years before *Work on Myth*, he published the essay "The Concept of Reality and the Theory of the State" in the liberal *Schweizer Monatshefte*—in its May issue, as he later pointed out gleefully.[9] Astonishingly, this long and dense text has virtually been ignored by those in search of Blumenberg's thoughts about political

4. Habermas, *Auch eine Geschichte*, 73.

5. Wetz, *Hans Blumenberg zur Einführung*. This is a recurring stance in the more popular writing on Blumenberg. For instance, Uwe Justus Wenzel calls Blumenberg "nonpolitical" ("Meister des Problemkrimis").

6. Bragagnolo, "Secularization"; Ifergan, "Cutting to the Chase."

7. Nicholls, *Myth and the Human Sciences*; Nicholls, "Hans Blumenberg on Political Myth"; Heidenreich, "Political Aspects"; Kirke, *Hans Blumenberg*.

8. Blumenberg, *Work on Myth*; Blumenberg, *Rigorism of Truth*; Blumenberg, *Präfiguration*.

9. Blumenberg, "Wirklichkeitsbegriff und Staatstheorie"; Blumenberg, "The Concept of Reality and the Theory of the State." The *Neue Zürcher Zeitung* journalist Martin Meyer recounts how he received a copy of this text from Blumenberg in the 1980s, with the date of the issue—May 1968—circled in red ("Der Kandidat," 54).

theory.[10] It draws out the *political* implications of his theory of modernity, and it does so without any hint at anthropology, which for Habermas always risks a conservative proclamation of traits eternal to human nature.[11] Rather, "Theory of the State" builds on a theory of history.

In this article I aim to rectify this oversight by giving "Theory of the State" the attention it has missed. In it, Blumenberg develops a rhetorical approach to politics that is connected to his theory of history, which he called "historical phenomenology."[12] Only later would he articulate this rhetorical theory with reference to his philosophical anthropology, which he called "phenomenological anthropology."[13] In what follows, I contextualize the essay in Blumenberg's oeuvre and show how it propounds an innovative approach to politics as anti- or nonperformative speech acts, analyzes the slow dissolution of the state, and advocates for supranational structures to replace it; in line with his ideas in *Legitimacy*, Blumenberg describes the situation of politics in the technical age. I conclude by addressing the differences between the historical and the anthropological approaches; the turn from the former to the latter marks the main change in Blumenberg's work.

The State and Its Discontents: A Historical Phenomenology of Politics
Blumenberg's biography hardly allowed him to be apolitical. His experience of totalitarianism, his classification as a "Half Jew" by the Nazis, and his internment in a labor camp shortly before the liberation left a lasting mark on his life and shaped his political outlook.[14] He became a strong skeptic of state power, and even if he accepted that the new Germany had a stable parliamentary democracy, the distanced stance toward the country that had once declared him an enemy remained remarkably consistent throughout his life: in 1948 he wrote to a friend that "in my most formative years, they tried to drill into me the idea that by nature I could not be a German—and lo and behold: today, now that I am allowed to be a German, I indeed cannot be one."[15] Four months before his death in 1996, in a letter to a former student, Blumenberg still rejected

---

10. Felix Heidenreich and Angus Nicholls mention the text only as a corollary to Blumenberg's anthropology ("Nachwort der Herausgeber"), as does Oliver Müller ("Beyond the Political"); only Jean-Claude Monod has given it some attention in its own right and as a part of a historical phenomenology rather than a phenomenological anthropology ("Préface").

11. For a similar point, see Gordon, "Secularization," 164.

12. Blumenberg et al., "Diskussion," 226.

13. Blumenberg, *Beschreibung des Menschen*, 167.

14. See Zill, *Der absolute Leser*, 37–134.

15. Blumenberg to Eric Orton, December 20, 1948, DLA Marbach.

the idea that Germany was a *Heimat* to him: "This country has remained uncanny to me, although I have left it only rarely. . . . What had made Hitler possible in this country has not melted into thin air."[16]

Such skepticism of the state as a locus of political identity finds its counterpoint in what one could call Blumenberg's political anti-absolutism. It comes to the fore most succinctly in his confrontation with Schmitt in *Legitimacy*. The story of this intellectual standoff has been told many times, and here I give only a brief recapitulation.[17] Schmitt's notion that "all significant concepts of the modern theory of the state are secularized theological concepts"—part of his "sociology of concepts" that assumes an isomorphism of a time's "metaphysical image" and its political terminology[18]—led him to suggest that sovereignty and the state of exception defining it correspond to the ideas of divine omnipotence and the miracle. Since "the rationalism of the Enlightenment rejected the exception in every form,"[19] the modern age no longer has an adequate conception of politics understood as sovereignty-as-decision. Implied herein is the need for a political theology that would replace any political theory.

Both the interpretation and the demand are objectionable to Blumenberg: rather than adopt theological concepts by turning them into political ones, the modern age commences as an epoch of "human self-assertion" against a theology of an all-powerful nominalist God and brings forth the rationality of "self-preservation" embodied in scientific and technological progress. It was precisely the unbearable omnipotence of the "decisionist" God against which modernity was founded and which disqualified this structure as a model for politics. No substantial but a "linguistic secularization" had taken place, which had transferred the divine attributes to the state retrospectively and with legitimizing intent—a tactic Blumenberg also suspected with Schmitt. "Political theology" is for Blumenberg a matter of metaphorics in its justificatory function.[20]

To Blumenberg, Schmitt imputed illegitimacy to liberal modernity and advertised what was unacceptable in a less-concealed rhetorical form: absolutist political structures. Indeed, for Schmitt to posit that "the political is the total"[21] means to advocate for a total state, a state whose self-organization as

16. Blumenberg, "'Und das ist mir von der Liebe zur Kirche geblieben,'" 178–79.

17. Schmitz, "Legitimacy of the Modern Age?"; Bragagnolo, "Secularization"; Hammill, "Blumenberg and Schmitt"; Ifergan, "Cutting to the Chase."

18. Schmitt, *Political Theology*, 36, 45–46.

19. Schmitt, *Political Theology*, 37.

20. Blumenberg, *Die Legitimität der Neuzeit*, 58. I quote the German first edition here, since the English translation is based on the substantially revised second edition.

21. Schmitt, *Political Theology*, 51.

well as its ability to mobilize are not dependent on any other ground than sovereignty-as-decision. In broader terms, Schmitt's political vision is aimed against what he sees as an "age of neutralizations,"[22] in which the state had been undermined by liberalism's worship of trade, technology, and parliamentarianism. Schmitt deems deficient the pure self-authorization of modernity through the scientific curiosity that Blumenberg praised: "This seems to be simply grounded in a justification issuing from the novelty."[23] A world of pure scientific immanence, a constant "process-progress," is for Schmitt a horrifying vision.[24]

Blumenberg, however, has a much more positive view of scientific progress and the notion of an autonomous self-authorization of modernity. Against Schmitt's absolutism of the total state and his anti-Enlightenment stance, Blumenberg suggests that the real task is "to destroy [*destruieren*] the absolute qualification of political situations as anachronisms."[25] In this "radicalization of Enlightenment,"[26] as Robert Wallace has called it, Blumenberg declares the "'worldliness' of the modern age" not only a positive achievement but also an achievement that must be shielded against absolutist theoreticians of retheologization—it is "not a secure historical characteristic, but its continuing critical *officium* [duty]."[27] Modernity, in other words, must be defended, without recourse to theological references, but solely from the norm of human self-assertion.

In formulating his objections against Schmitt, Blumenberg revealed little of his own, positive political theory. And although he defended his notion of a legitimacy that is independent of continued historical substances, he did not present alternatives to Schmitt's other basic categories such as the political, sovereignty, neutralization, or decisionism. In the 1968 essay "The Concept of Reality and the Theory of the State," however, Blumenberg went on to offer counterpositions on all these points. Defending a version of liberalism that places Blumenberg within a "constellation de pensée post-souverainiste,"[28] he embraces the very neutralization Schmitt abhors. Three basic theses stand out: politics in the strong sense is losing its status of master *episteme* in the present; it takes on a rhetorical function that performs by *not* performing anything; and

22. Schmitt, *Political Theology*, 80.
23. Schmitt, *Political Theology II*, 118.
24. Schmitt, *Political Theology II*, 120.
25. Blumenberg, *Die Legitimität der Neuzeit*, 61.
26. Wallace, "Translator's Introduction," xxv.
27. Blumenberg, *Die Legitimität der Neuzeit*, 61.
28. Monod, "Préface," 32.

the state is dying off, to be replaced by supranational structures. Despite its hermeneutical difficulties, this fascinating text is the most detailed exposition of Blumenberg's thoughts on the historicity of the state, the conditions of its demise, and the role of rhetoric as a technique of politics.[29]

Already in the title, Blumenberg draws attention to *reality* as a criterion of politics. Schmitt is frequently called a "political realist," and more than the split between politics and morality that comes with this appellation, Schmitt's realism relies on the normative force of reality itself: the decisive reality is what is produced by the decision over the state of exception. Blumenberg challenges the historical stability of this reality: "If the assessment of realities is one of the elementary preconditions of political action, then the *concept of reality* that such assessment *implies* matters, especially if it should not be the trivial *constant* as which it might appear at first glance—if, in other words, the concept of reality itself possesses a historical dimension."[30]

The "concept of reality" is the operative term in what Blumenberg came to call "historical phenomenology." He first introduced the concept of reality in the early 1960s as a historicized version of Edmund Husserl's notion of the "life-world."[31] For transcendental phenomenology, the life-world is the correlate to the "natural attitude," the horizon-like, pretheoretical understanding of reality that forms the unexamined background of all reflection.[32] Historical phenomenology is the study of *historical* life-worlds; the concept of reality is what structures the understanding of reality in a given epoch. Introducing both in "The Concept of Reality and the Possibility of the Novel" (1964), he distinguishes four concepts of reality. In antiquity it is "reality as instantaneous evidence," in which what is real is immediately felt and is in no further need of proof, as with the sun of the good and true in Plato's cave allegory. In the Middle Ages reality is conceived of as "guaranteed reality," in which God becomes

29. Blumenberg prepared three versions of this essay: a first draft; a job talk for a professorship in social and political philosophy he gave in November 1967 at the University of Zurich; and a final version that appeared in the May 1968 issue of *Schweizer Monatshefte* (Blumenberg, "The Concept of Reality and the Theory of the State"). For the first and second drafts, see "WST" and "WST II," folder "Wirklichkeitsbegriff und Staatstheorie," DLA Marbach. As Blumenberg's biographer, Rüdiger Zill, relates, the essay was an outlier. When in 1967 Blumenberg was invited to give the job talk in Zurich, he suggested three topics, of which the theory of the state was his least favorite. Yet it was chosen, and with much misgiving he wrote the talk he had not yet prepared (Zill, *Der absolute Leser*, chap. 2). It appears to have been deemed too complicated by the audience. See Meyer, "Der Kanditat," 54.

30. Blumenberg, "WST II," 1.

31. Blumenberg, "The Concept of Reality and the Possibility of the Novel." See also Blumenberg, *Realität und Realismus.*

32. Husserl, *Crisis of European Sciences*, §51.

the final ground for everything that is. Modernity has two concepts of reality that are dialectally related: the first has a structure of "the actualization of a context in itself," a consistency realized over time—in the absence of immediate self-evidence or a transcendent guarantor, reality is real until disproved. This structure brings forth the final concept of reality, reality as the "experience of resistance." Here it is the rupture of this context that appears to be the actual mark of the real.[33] Concepts of reality, while never directly stated, implicitly structure what in a given epoch is conceived of as real, and come to the fore in vastly different areas, such as art and literature, technology, science,[34] and, indeed, in politics. Therefore any conception of the state, too, is bound to the epoch's reigning concept of reality: "For the construction of the state there is no model that would be equally binding and self-evident in every phase of the historical process. . . . It is not a static, but a dynamic reality."[35]

For this reason, any call to "realism" must be suspect, as "every realism can itself be instrumentalized. The label 'reality,' attached to what is to be designated as authoritative, authenticates the positive proposition as that which is meant to be thought of as possible."[36] Blumenberg, the metaphorologist, had already charged Schmitt with dissimulation, passing off theology as politics. Blumenberg, the historical phenomenologist, enacts a similar critique of ideology by questioning the political realist's concept of reality. For before one can "realistically" decide on the state of exception, one has already decided on what should count as reality.[37] Thus Blumenberg begins "Theory of the State" with the observation that the state always stands in "reference to reality in a twofold sense: first, to that reality the state claims for itself and manifests in political actions, and second, to that reality it grants to *that* which it itself is *not*."[38]

By dissecting the contingency of the state and its underlying rationality, Blumenberg counteracts Schmitt's claim that the state is a supratemporal entity, a natural form, or an eternal necessity. His rebuke of the state, then, is a most direct rebuke of Schmitt's doctrine of political sovereignty. Yet even beyond

33. Blumenberg, "The Concept of Reality and the Possibility of the Novel," 501–6. See also Blumenberg, "Preliminary Remarks." Emphasis deleted.

34. Blumenberg, "'Imitation of Nature'"; Blumenberg, "Phenomenological Aspects"; Blumenberg, *Legitimacy*, pt. 3.

35. Blumenberg, "WST," 19–20.

36. Blumenberg, "Preliminary Remarks," 118.

37. As Blumenberg puts it in an unpublished manuscript: "The decisive question is who decides what is realism and who may call himself a realist. (Analogous to Carl Schmitt: Sovereign is he who decides the state of exception)" ("Aufzeichnungen und Notizen zum Wiener Kreis und zum Realismus," DLA Marbach).

38. Blumenberg, "The Concept of Reality and the Theory of the State," 83.

Schmitt, Blumenberg also attacks an entire tradition of German political theory. Against this ahistorical notion, Blumenberg begins his text by juxtaposing the notion of the state in the ancient and the modern concepts of reality. In the ancient model—in which reality is understood as nature, identical with a cosmos whose truth is "instantaneously evident" and to which no alternative exists—the state is a direct part of nature. This is why Plato can argue for an isomorphism between the polis and the soul (in the *Republic*), and between the polis and the cosmos (in the *Timaeus*). In political Platonism, truth, morality, and politics form a unit, and so the state, too, is sanctioned as both true and good insofar as it is "founded on the self-evidence of [its] relation to reality."[39] This notion of political Platonism—as well as its resultant rejection of pluralism—remains influential for much of Western history, Blumenberg holds.

In the Middle Ages, the naturalness of the state is refashioned into a natural law that is ultimately sustained by God, as in the political thought of Thomas Aquinas. While reality now relies on a transcendent guarantor, little changes in the quasi-natural, divinely legitimized status of the state. Only the modern concept of reality that appears in the Renaissance ruptures this notion. No longer describing a well-ordered, necessary cosmos, it is determined by radical contingency. It requires human self-preservation, not as an anthropological achievement, but as the constant "realization of a context," which Blumenberg defends as a notion of nonteleological progress as continuation from the given. This epochal threshold was the focus of *Legitimacy*, where the response to theological absolutism had been human self-assertion. Something similar, Blumenberg argues, happens in political philosophy with the almost simultaneous writing of Niccolò Machiavelli's *Prince* (1513, published 1532) and Thomas More's *Utopia* (1516). In both texts, the state is no longer natural or divinely sanctioned but appears as an artificial construction that needs to be actively sustained. Both authors express a reality that, rather than the phenomenal reflection of an ideal noumenal order, has merely become "a hyletic stock that must be arranged by humans for humans."[40] Machiavelli and More are the first political instances of this new concept of reality.[41]

For Blumenberg, More's *Utopia* is the origin of the revolutionary strand of modern political theory. Instead of offering a Platonic ideal state based on true knowledge, *Utopia* is first and foremost "aimed critically against the fac-

39. Blumenberg, "The Concept of Reality and the Theory of the State," 89.
40. Blumenberg, "WST," 6.
41. Blumenberg, "The Concept of Reality and the Theory of the State," 93–94.

ticity of what is."[42] If nothing new could come into the world before, because the world was complete, now the new is a distinct possibility, and can be made by humans.[43] "If the alternative to the self-evidence of the cosmos is chaos, the alternative to contingency is the possibility of the other, and that also means, of revolution."[44] With this affirmation of human freedom, however, epistemic skepticism enters the political realm. While "the ideal Politeia is a norm spelled out," utopia states only what could, not what must, be.[45] And where More attacks the naturalness of politics by highlighting contingency, Machiavelli does so by turning politics into a techne: questions of legitimacy remain as left-over elements of the old system but are now open to being manipulated; the art of politics furnishes "the appearance of unbroken continuity and unquestioned naturalness" after the fact.[46] This in turn results in a new concept of power as something human in origin, no longer entwined with the Platonic triad of nature, truth, and morality as reflections of the ordered cosmos. Both More and Machiavelli therefore rehabilitate the phenomenal against the noumenal in modernity's world of contingency.

The strange duality of the modern concept of reality also plays a role in politics. The work of sustaining a context must break down at some point, and this experience of resistance can itself become a sign of reality. "Reality is not what looks like nature" but must constantly be made; at the same time, it is also "what cuts deeper into life than anything ever could that seems natural to it."[47] This reality puts the state, too, into a new situation. It can no longer claim an inherent legitimacy because it mirrors the order of the cosmos, but must per-petually legitimize itself. And it has to "cut deeper into life" just to be felt as real and to prove its necessity. Both qualities follow from what Blumenberg calls the rationality of the modern concept of reality: self-preservation. "Con-sistency, immanent harmony with itself [*immanente Einstimmigkeit*], is the mark of the modern concept of reality. Self-preservation (instead of a transcen-dent *conservatio*) is the principle of this consistency and thus the principle of the idea of the state that corresponds to it."[48]

Self-preservation is, one can argue, the structural equivalent to the "self-assertion" *Legitimacy* had seen in the struggle against the nominalist god.[49] If

42. Blumenberg, "The Concept of Reality and the Theory of the State," 90.

43. Blumenberg discusses the possibility of the new in the modern concept of reality in "The Con-cept of Reality and the Possibility of the Novel," as well as in "'Imitation of Nature.'"

44. Blumenberg, "WST," 16.

45. Blumenberg, "WST II," 5.

46. Blumenberg, "The Concept of Reality and the Theory of the State," 93.

47. Blumenberg, "WST II," 4.

48. Blumenberg, "WST," 16.

49. See Matysik, "Hans Blumenberg's Multiple Modernities."

self-assertion is an "existential program" in the face of a loss of meaning,[50] then self-preservation is its underlying rationality, the modern (nonaffective, ateleological) constant realization of a context, which is translated into the "rational norm of a process."[51] This is, Blumenberg stresses, not a question of anthropology but only addresses the "logical self-preservation" of the pure continuation of the structure of consistency itself.[52] One of this rationality's expressions is the dynamic of an immanent progress in science and technology: no final truth is to be had, only an incremental progress to be made. This rationality also plays out in the theory of the state, and for Blumenberg, it is best exemplified in Thomas Hobbes: the state of nature must be left behind not because of its being "solitary, poor, brutish, nasty, and short"—that is, not because it is *affectively* disagreeable—but because it makes future actions *logically* impossible. After all, it is the mere affective drive that creates the state of nature, in which everyone has a right to everything, for it fosters the brutishness of everyone claiming their right. The rational self-preservation, on the other hand, abstracts from affect and makes everyone relinquish their natural rights in order to create a new system that will reinstate positive rights within a state.[53]

In Hobbes, Blumenberg thus sees the rationality of self-preservation transferred onto the state. Since it cannot claim naturalness any longer, it must constantly make the case for its own necessity. And because reality is a "contrastive concept," this justification will have to perpetually point out what the rationality of self-preservation is meant to thwart—this is the reality of "*that which it itself is not*" mentioned above.[54] And it is here that Schmitt's total state enters again:

> By way of comparative and *competing presence* it can be understood what it means to say the state claims reality and grants it to that which exists "beside, above, and beyond the state, and often enough even against it." . . . It is in war that the state sees an upswing of its own reality as the most extreme and exclusive bindingness, of the self-evidence of its necessity and its right, which tends toward absolutism; this occurs not only in war but also on the brink of war, also in the simulation that anticipates war as a "cold" one. *Only the crisis essentializes the state's existence*; the state of emergency [*Notstand*] is the textbook case of its vindication.[55]

50. Blumenberg, *Legitimacy*, 138.
51. Blumenberg, "Self-Preservation and Inertia," 219.
52. Blumenberg, "WST 17."
53. Blumenberg, "Self-Preservation and Inertia," 217–19.
54. Blumenberg, "The Concept of Reality and the Theory of the State," 83.
55. Blumenberg, "The Concept of Reality and the Theory of the State," 84. Emphasis mine. Blumenberg quotes Thomas Mann's *Reflections of an Unpolitical Man*.

Thus, just as Hobbes's absolutist state receives its legitimacy—and thus its reality—from the promise to end the unsustainable state of nature, the modern state must continuously point to the state of emergency. The state of emergency is therefore indeed the locus of power and legitimacy for the state, but not in the sense of Schmitt's decisive sovereignty. The result is that Blumenberg presents not a strong but an utterly *weak* state: the modern state is always on the brink of losing its reality and must try to assert it by constantly keeping in consciousness that *against* which it exists—crises, states of emergency, war. Because of this, the state "tends towards absolutism," and this tendency can falsely appear as a sign of strength. Schmitt certainly argues in this sense when he formulates his vision of political theology. Yet in fact, Blumenberg shows, this strength is a sign of dependency and would be a mark of power only under a concept of reality that holds the state to be naturally given or divinely guaranteed. Yet in modernity, human self-assertion has discarded these possibilities. It is for this reason that Schmitt's historical method is flawed: the "sociology of concepts" and its epoch-defining "metaphysical image" claim historicity but are still based on an idea of reality as providing eternal norms or legitimacies.[56] Schmitt tries to transfer assumptions from the past into a fundamentally different present for which they no longer hold. The "sociology of concepts" is anachronistic, wishful thinking. Thus it is not *mastery* of the state of emergency that legitimizes sovereignty—rather, sovereignty *depends* on a perpetual state of emergency for its very survival.

The Immanent Neutralization of the State: Technology and Technization

The paradox of strength necessitated by weakness—a direct consequence of the modern concept of reality as resistance—is in line with *Legitimacy*'s view of the turn from transcendence to immanence in modernity. To be sure, Blumenberg does not formulate a law of history. Rather, he thinks through the consequences of an observation: "My concern is with an analysis of tendencies."[57] One such tendency is the decline of the strong state. In industrialized societies, Blumenberg sees politics—the formerly dominant discourse of their organization—in the process of being either relativized or replaced by some other system. Here Blumenberg is in agreement with other thinkers of functionally differentiated modern societies in the tradition of Max Weber, such as Niklas Luhmann or, indeed, Habermas. As a result of modernity's inherent rationality and its functional complexity, Blumenberg affirms what Schmitt

56. Schmitt, *Political Theology*, 46.
57. Blumenberg, "The Concept of Reality and the Theory of the State," 104.

had seen as the great evil of the state's liberal "neutralization," that is, the role played by the economic sphere, the parliamentary system, and technology in limiting the state.[58] In this respect, Schmitt and Blumenberg agree on facts but not on their evaluation: Blumenberg welcomes neutralization as an immanent development of the modern state. Speculatively following this logic to its end, Blumenberg argues that the current age could petrify the state to the point of its obsolescence. He demonstrates this thought by example of the two things Schmitt abhors, economy and discourse; both, for Blumenberg, are instances of "technization."

It is helpful to remember the political circumstances of 1967, when Blumenberg wrote "Theory of the State," internationally and domestically. After the shock of the Cuban missile crisis in 1962, which pushed the world to the brink of nuclear conflict, the Cold War had entered a phase of détente, with power balanced between the two great blocs and their nuclear arsenals. In Germany the governing grand coalition of Social Democrats and Christian Democrats, formed in 1966, discussed the *Notstandsgesetze*, aimed at changing the constitution to extend the state's emergency powers; a year later the emergency laws would play a decisive role in the student protests. In a rare nod to current events, Blumenberg notes that the plans for the *Notstandsgesetze* only seem to confirm that "the state of emergency [*Notstand*] is the textbook case" of political normalcy in which the "manipulated crisis [is] a tool for [the] inner stabilization" of power.[59] The nuclear threat is another example of the state as a "subject of crises," which retains its reality only if it remains the visible answer to this threat. However, for Blumenberg, this rationality has changed in the present. The idea of *Notstandsgesetze* as well as the grand coalition itself only play the role of a "pragmatic myth" meant to suggest political decisiveness and agency,[60] both of which are no longer given in actuality. Likewise, the fact of mutually assured destruction makes war unthinkable. Both developments signal that politics is losing its status as master episteme. If, in the transition to modernity, nature had been replaced by politics as the reality that "cuts deeper into life,"[61] now "politics in turn seems liable to be surpassed by the relevance of other structures."[62]

One difficulty of "Theory of the State" is that Blumenberg never quite spells out what exactly these other structures are. At first glance, he seems to

58. Schmitt, *Concept of the Political*, 28.

59. Blumenberg, "The Concept of Reality and the Theory of the State," 84.

60. Blumenberg, "The Concept of Reality and the Theory of the State," 96. See also Nicholls, "Hans Blumenberg on Political Myth."

61. Blumenberg, "WST II," 4.

62. Blumenberg, "The Concept of Reality and the Theory of the State," 100.

suggest that it is the dynamics of a globally integrated economy. Not only do "elections, crises, formations of governments increasingly occur under the influence of economic factors and situations," but the "interests of economic existence" serve as criteria for almost all political demands. Economic policy "has increasingly become the substance of politics, or, what is essentially the same, the desubstantialization of its historically sanctioned form."[63] The only function of domestic politics, then, is the control of economic growth, so that neither the *Notstand* nor a grand coalition can restitute actual power to the state. Indeed, the term *politics* itself may simply be a leftover element, one that, reoccupation-like, now refers to economic regulation.[64]

For the anti-absolutist Blumenberg, it is a blessing that there is "almost nothing left of the absolutism of the reality of the state."[65] Yet it is not altogether certain whether it is really economics as such that supplants politics, as Schmitt had feared. In affirming that the state has been reduced only to sustaining the bare necessities of a hegemonic economy, Blumenberg appears to approach Robert Nozick's idea of the night-watchman state; in seeing the economy as truly self-regulatory, he exhibits an affinity to the spontaneous order of free-market theorists like Friedrich von Hayek. In this reading, Blumenberg would be a radical economic libertarian, yet one for whom there is little possibility for political agency. Not committing to any interpretation of Blumenberg's economic persuasion, Angus Nicholls thus interprets him as a proponent of "a disillusioned and melancholy politics."[66] And while Jean-Claude Monod notes that "the whole question of the political capacity of populaces in times of the rule of economies and markets has reached a degree that Blumenberg's text foresaw,"[67] Monod chides him for an all-too-fatalistic approval of this fact. Indeed, one must ask whether Blumenberg reserves any systematic room for agency or political freedom at all—if his plea for postsovereignty is accompanied by an acceptance of postpolitics.

But the role of the economy and the space of freedom are more complicated in this text. Against interpretations that see Blumenberg as a libertarian, I would argue that he privileges not a self-regulating economy but self-regulation as an expression of modern rationality as such. That he does not favor a libertarian economics becomes clear when he writes that Walter Eucken's ordoliberal model of deregulation—partly responsible for the Ger-

63. Blumenberg, "The Concept of Reality and the Theory of the State," 102.
64. Blumenberg, "The Concept of Reality and the Theory of the State," 103–4.
65. Blumenberg, "WST II," 14.
66. Nicholls, "'How to Do Nothing with Words,'" 74.
67. Monod, "Préface," 33.

man *Wirtschaftswunder* of the 1950s—has failed, now that "the automatism of self-controlling systems has evinced alarming fluctuations."[68] In a draft of "Theory of the State," he even praises Karl Schiller, the new social democratic minister of economic affairs, who countered the previous chancellor Ludwig Erhard's ordoliberalism with a Keynesian approach that included increased regulation.[69] In his assessment, Blumenberg has the dialogue and accord between state and economic players in mind, Schiller's "concerted activity" (*konzertierte Aktion*).[70] Rather than any actual control of politics over the economy, Blumenberg highlights the *rhetorical* nature of such politics. It is his main example of the thesis that "to a high degree, economic politics is the politics of words."[71] In fact, all that is left of the old economic politics is the power of rhetoric; "its instrument is essentially the word in public discourse: the trustworthy piece of information, the call to nonintervention by others, guiding principles, planning projections, and encouragements to consume."[72]

Here we approach the center of the essay—the connection between rhetoric and technology, understood as not just technical objects but the core of modern consciousness. Rhetoric, for Blumenberg, is closely related to the notion of technology. To understand this, it is important to keep in mind that for him, two connected but distinct phenomena become increasingly decisive in modernity: the "principle of technicity," on the one hand, and the concept of "technization," on the other.[73] The first simply designates the logic of technological progress, which follows the concept of reality as a purely immanent, ateleological continuity—what Schmitt had derisively called the "process-progress"—instead of operating according to any transcendent criterion or telos.[74] Blumenberg argued at different times that the unfolding of this immanent principle of technicity overcomes the problems that technology itself had created, instead of "dogmatically" rejecting technology altogether.[75] By this he means the notion that the current problems of technology are to be solved not by future technological progress but by stepping out of the continuum of history—by a reversal into the past, or a parallel, that is, utopian, present. He

---

68. Blumenberg, "The Concept of Reality and the Theory of the State," 102.

69. "Rhetoric does not need to take on the naïveté of 'soul massages'; rather, it can be implemented as a more subliminally than morally suggestive jargon of musical metaphorics, such as the current economy minister of the Federal Republic commands so masterfully" (Blumenberg, "WST," 10).

70. See Hochstätter, *Karl Schiller*, chap. 3.

71. "Blumenberg, "WST," 10.

72. Blumenberg, "The Concept of Reality and the Theory of the State," 103.

73. Blumenberg, "Phenomenological Aspects," 362, 359.

74. Schmitt, *Political Theory II*, 120.

75. Blumenberg, "Dogmatische und rationale Analyse," 259.

cites Walter Benjamin, for whom "the realization of the idea of technology is a betrayal of utopia,"[76] precisely because a utopian history must break with the continuity of technological progress. Instead, Blumenberg speculates on the consequences of the principle of technicity on the existence of the state to determine whether "what was supposed to be realized as *human* endeavor would come as *technological* consequence."[77]

If the "principle of technicity" plays out in the realm of technical progress, the second concept, "technization," explains how modern consciousness responds to this progress. Blumenberg borrows the term from Edmund Husserl, just as he had already appropriated the life-world.[78] Like Blumenberg and Weber, Husserl understood modernity as a process of increasing rationalization. Yet where the Marxist critique that took up Weber's analysis saw a problem in the "iron cage" of rationality on the level of social relations,[79] Husserl was more concerned with the rift between scientific and everyday modes of knowledge. This rift was responsible for, as the title of his book has it, *The Crisis of the European Sciences*.[80] The scientific method replaced eidetic knowledge with "'symbolic' concepts,"[81] so that not every step of, for instance, a mathematical operation had constantly to be present to consciousness. And just as Blumenberg welcomes the rationalization of the principle of technicity, so does he embrace technization as the separation of knowing-how from knowing-that. Politics, Blumenberg argues, inevitably morphs into a techne. Against the old Platonism, in which truth was the precondition for action, Blumenberg offers a rejuvenated Sophism that deals with such techniques. And the most politically eminent form of technization for Blumenberg is rhetoric.

Both the principle of technicity and rhetorical technization explain the demise of the state and the rise of a new type of politics. In describing the political consequences that grow out of the principle of technicity, Blumenberg returns to the state as a "subject of crises." Just as Hobbes's absolutist state had not quelled all conflict but projected it "onto the relationship between the

76. Blumenberg, "WST," 13. See also Blumenberg, "The Concept of Reality and the Theory of the State," 109n32. That Blumenberg refers to Benjamin should not be taken to indicate that he knew Benjamin's writings well. This thought—taken from the last segment of *One Way Street*—Blumenberg found in a book by Peter Szondi, as the manuscript shows.

77. Blumenberg, "WST II," 17–18.

78. See Mende, "Histories of Technicization."

79. Weber, *Protestant Ethic*, 123.

80. Husserl, *Crisis of European Sciences*. Often the term *Technisierung* is translated as "technicization." I follow the translation in *Crisis of European Sciences*, which gives "technization."

81. Husserl, *Crisis of European Sciences*, 48. For a metaphorological investigation of technization, see also Blumenberg, *Paradigms*, 75.

now-forming nation states,"[82] it was not only the specter of a *Notstand* but also the external threat of war that rendered the state "evident." This balance of internal and external threat that still dominated Hobbes's era is now exacerbated in the new world order of the Cold War, with its dual centers of power and unprecedented technologies of destruction. If Hiroshima had shown the extent of nuclear devastation, the Cuban missile crisis vividly demonstrated the urgent danger of self-annihilation: "Given, however, a technological state in which real wars endanger the state itself and as such, and in which they can destroy its identity even as a subject of crises, the hypothetical war—the 'phantom war'—becomes a medium that promises to push states to crystalline solidity."[83]

The state's looming "crystalline solidity" approached by the principle of technicity is, however, not the total state of Schmitt: the self-preservation of the individual in the state is acceptable in this situation only as long as the state offers more protection than harm. Once the progress of arms technologies endangers its own existence, this logic collapses. The result is the *impossibility* of a total state, as the solidity of the state cancels out the very quality that defines it, the ability to decide. Under the doctrine of mutually assured destruction, the political loses its meaning, since any decision could trigger a complete annihilation of both parties. This is why, for Blumenberg, "the all-encompassing antithesis of the East/West dualism has only been a short-lived interlude," since it may be "that the experiment of absolute authorities has been *played through to its conclusion.*"[84] The fading away of "the political" (in Schmitt's sense) as the main category of actual politics thus applies not only to domestic politics emaciated by economics but also to international politics. Blumenberg sees Schmittian agonism and decisionism replaced with an "immanent regulation" as the rationality of the technical age.[85] The result might not be an eternal, but at least a "cold" peace. "It does not mean that war as means can no longer be thought, but that this thought can no longer be thought to the end."[86] The sta-

82. Blumenberg, *Die Legitimität der Neuzeit*, 59.
83. Blumenberg, "The Concept of Reality and the Theory of the State," 84.
84. Blumenberg, *Legitimacy*, 91. Emphasis mine.
85. Blumenberg, "The Concept of Reality and the Theory of the State," 95.
86. Blumenberg, "The Concept of Reality and the Theory of the State," 84, 96. In his analysis of the "cold" peace, Blumenberg picks up on a newspaper article by the physicist and "peace researcher" Carl Friedrich von Weizsäcker, who had argued that the arms race required a new morality, for "the technical world does not stabilize itself. Its stabilization is a political task" ("Friede und Wahrheit"). This is exactly what Blumenberg questions. On the international stage, the nuclear deterrence policy seems to him, despite its horrendous risk, to constitute a certain stabilization, which may create "a bad peace but not the worst" ("The Concept of Reality and the Theory of the State," 96). The best peace, Weizsäcker's

bilization of the cold peace through the principle of technicity leads Blumenberg to welcome *rhetorical* technization.

> Let us suppose we were able to approximate this threshold value of immanent regulation, in which case the axiom would gain validity whereby political action best fulfills its purpose by only *simulating* the classical quality of "decisiveness" [*Entscheidungsfreudigkeit*]. . . . This is an irritatingly exaggerated formulation, but it seems useful to me as an antidote against overestimating the traditional scope of political "reality."[87]

Here Blumenberg fully embraces Husserl's notion of technization as the use of "'symbolic' concepts": "The decisions that have become possible today no human can make anymore. This justifies their replacement by symbolic quodlibeta. At least as a model it is thinkable that the state will one day be nothing more than the institutionalized, rule-bound exchange of words and information, of hypotheses about action that never will be necessary."[88] The state, here, is no longer based on true insight, as it was in the Platonic model. It only requires the simulation of decisions, since the decision as the central category of the political can no longer "match our political experience" in a world of mutually assured destruction,[89] and in a world dominated by economics. Examples of that are Karl Schiller's "musical metaphorics" as well as the ways in which the two world powers rhetorically preempt the strikes they cannot execute if they want to survive.[90] One does better to accept "how preferable, particularly with regard to global structures, is the substitution of words for facts and actions, proclamations for decisions."[91]

---

peace born of moral insight, appears not only less likely to him but dangerous. It reintroduces the Platonic dependence of politics on morality and truth. Moreover, this speculative new morality relinquishes what can be anticipated from the logic of modern rationality. Weizsäcker assumes that current problems of technology can be solved only by stepping out of the continuum of history—by a reversal into the past or a leap into a parallel, that is, utopian, present. Blumenberg's criticism is partly a question of theory design: modern rationality can at least be anticipated in its outcome, "played through," while stepping out of its course jeopardizes what is already achieved. The point of "The Concept of Reality and the Theory of the State" is that politics becomes a technique like any other, and morality must be separated from it. What is significant about Blumenberg's rejection of morality in politics is that while Schmitt saw the opponent in the political debate as a moral category (*Political Theology*, 28), Blumenberg wants to develop it from the inherent logic of modernity.

87. Blumenberg, "The Concept of Reality and the Theory of the State," 95.
88. Blumenberg, "WST II," 17.
89. Blumenberg, "WST," 7.
90. Blumenberg, "WST," 10.
91. Blumenberg, "The Concept of Reality and the Theory of the State," 94.

A Politics for the Technical Age: Nonperformative Rhetoric, the Public Sphere, and Postsovereignty

Speech instead of deeds: this is a reversal of the old political "realism" that argued that actions spoke louder than "mere words." For Blumenberg, such realism is a residue of an antirhetorical Platonism that exists even in the otherwise purely modern Machiavelli. "Platonism is a philosophy against the rule of the word, the postulate of visual perception against listening, of self-evidence against persuasion, of *res* [things] against *verba* [words]."[92] It was against the Sophists that Plato pitted the politeia, which was meant once and for all to put an end to politics as a matter of debate and make it into a matter of truth. Yet under the exigencies of the technical world, Blumenberg argues, "the *res-verba* antithesis would have become the *verba pro rebus* thesis—and this in turn would be something like the return of Sophism from its Platonic exile."[93] Instead of a politics based on Platonic evidence in all its varieties—"insight and conviction, fidelity and steadfastness"—politics should be understood as a series of capacities, "as a technique [*Technik*] just like any other technique" that requires only knowing-how, not any deeper knowing-that.[94] Against politics as decision, he offers politics as rhetoric.

I see a strong and a weak interpretation of Blumenberg's theory of political rhetoric. I will start with the strong interpretation. It conceives of rhetoric as the complete *suspension* of decisions, and it must count as one of the most fundamental counterpositions to Schmitt's political theory imaginable. It argues that politics in modernity is defined by a replacement of action through words without ever completely crossing this boundary. As such, it is ultimately untenable as a political theory but heuristically useful in its exaggeration. On the basis of this exaggeration—an "analysis of tendencies"—Blumenberg isolates a concept of the *public* as the locus of politics.

In the strong interpretation of the techne of rhetoric, it has a strange performative structure that undercuts the usual theories of political speech. It does not only contradict the Schmittian decisionism that rejects speech as apolitical, or a Marxist view, which lessens its importance compared with class dynamics, but also goes against the reverse tradition that understands speech itself to be the supreme political action. In the twentieth century, Hannah Arendt most fervently argued that speech is action (and a host of theorists have followed her, not least Habermas).[95] What connects Schmitt and Arendt, and separates them

---

92. Blumenberg, "The Concept of Reality and the Theory of the State," 94.
93. Blumenberg, "The Concept of Reality and the Theory of the State," 100.
94. Blumenberg, "WST," 12.
95. Arendt, *Human Condition*.

from Blumenberg, is that they both see action at the core of the political—be it the discursive speech or the decision (which in most cases is also a speech act). Yet in a strong interpretation of Blumenberg, words are not actions at all: Blumenberg's political thought would be based on a theory of language that is performative by *not* being performative. In a central passage of "Theory of the State," Blumenberg notes: "*How to Do Things with Words* is the title of an important book by J. L. Austin—maybe another one still needs to be written: *How to Do Nothing with Words*."[96]

Blumenberg refers to Austin's theory of speech acts, which looked not only at the semantic dimension of propositions but also at their pragmatic impact—at the effects utterances have in the world once they are uttered. Austin differentiated three elements of speech acts: the locutionary act is the propositional content of a sentence, its meaning; the illocutionary act deals with the "force of the utterance," the communicative significance within a natural language; and the perlocutionary act is the resulting consequences in the world.[97] Political speech also consists in performative acts; their illocutionary force may be that of a declaration or an order, and their perlocutionary effect a change in political reality. What Blumenberg seems to have in mind when he alludes to Austin, however, is radically different. He inserts a hiatus into the structure of the speech act itself, so that it becomes a performative utterance whose illocutionary force is not simply a passive or negative perlocution—as in Austin's example of the utterance "You can't do that!"[98]—but the indefinite delay of any perlocution *at all*. Put differently, in a strong interpretation of Blumenberg, *the perlocution of a political speech act is its own suspension.*

Parallel to Austin's performative, Werner Hamacher has coined the concept of the "afformative." At least in some regards, it seems to come close to what Blumenberg has in mind. According to Hamacher, afformatives "are not a subcategory of performatives." They do not posit but "depose."[99] Hamacher develops his idea following Benjamin's "Critique of Violence." The Benjaminian difference between lawmaking and law-preserving violence is transposed

96. Blumenberg, "The Concept of Reality and the Theory of the State," 106.
97. Austin, *How to Do Things with Words*, 22.
98. Austin uses the example to explain his distinctions: If person A says to person B, "You can't do that!," the locution is the semantic meaning that B is unable to perform a certain action C (Austin suggests that this can be reformulated as "he said that . . ."); the illocution is the act of protesting against C ("he argued that . . ."), and the perlocution may be to stop B from doing C ("he convinced me that . . .") (*How to Do Things with Words*, 102). In this case, the performative utterance indeed may stop an action, but it is still an action itself. This is not the case in Blumenberg's strong conception of rhetoric.
99. Hamacher, "Afformative, Strike," 1139.

onto speech act theory: just as every act that upholds the law has in it the potential to overthrow the law, Hamacher believes that every performative is, at its basis, affirmative, able to turn against its perlocutionary power. His proximity to Benjamin—and Benjamin's to Schmitt—would sit uneasily with Blumenberg, and I do not want to suggest a direct theoretical lineage or a shared political project here; after all, Benjamin's "religious decisionism"[100] and his antiparliamentarianism are exactly the type of positions Blumenberg wants to "depose" in his use of the rhetorical afformative. On the contrary, his hope is exactly that for which Schmitt—and Benjamin—had scolded "the bourgeoisie as a 'discussing class,'" namely, "to evade the decision. A class that shifts all political activity onto the plane of conversation in the press and in parliament is no match for social conflict."[101] Taking the afformative merely as an apt descriptor of Blumenberg's ideal of political speech, one may say that for him, parliamentary democracy can be considered the perpetual deferral of the decision that could potentially be the end of the world. It thus would be, ironically, something like Schmitt's *katechon*, the "restrainer" of the Antichrist, and Nicholls indeed sees the goal of this politics in nothing less than "saving the world."[102] In this strong interpretation of rhetoric, afformative speech acts are the most rational implementation of the imperative of self-preservation in the atomic age.[103]

Of course, if this were to describe the *whole* of political rhetoric, it would be the end not only of decisionism but also of any kind, even nonabsolutist, political activity. It would, indeed, be a formulation of Arnold Gehlen's "posthistoire," which Nicholls assumes that Blumenberg reproduces.[104] In such a world, political speech would only have the effect of preventing irrational agents from disturbing a self-regulating technical equilibrium; it would be a postpolitics. This strong position is a willful exaggeration in line with Blumenberg's methodical approach of an "analysis of tendencies," and while it offers valuable insights, as a political theory it must remain utterly unconvincing. Political decisions are not only made on the level of nuclear war avoidance, and politics as a matter of public debate, negotiation, and deliberation is not even touched on in this model.

100. Honneth, *Pathologies of Reason*, 90.

101. Schmitt, *Political Theology*, 59.

102. Schmitt, *"Nomos" of the Earth*, 59; Nicholls, "'How to Do Nothing with Words,'" 74.

103. *Speech acts* need not be taken to mean singular, identifiable propositions here. With Jean-François Lyotard, one could also say that a specific "phrase regimen" or the "linking together" of different such regimens can have an afformative effect (*Differend*, xii). I thank Rieke Trimçev for suggesting this to me.

104. Nicholls, "'How to Do Nothing with Words,'" 66.

However, Blumenberg's thought also offers a weaker, and more convincing, model of rhetorical technization, and one that includes democratic deliberation and a productive role of the public sphere. It reduces the afformative element to only one in the political process. Rhetoric, here, may delay action or diffuse its effects to gain time for further deliberation, which yields performative results. Such rhetoric retrieves its performativity in the hiatus of the afformative. It provides "a solid technique of at least placing speeches ahead of actions, and information ahead of intervention."[105] Whoever speaks, one could say, does not fight. Thus "the often vilified 'endless discussion' can very well replace and transpose the momentary discharge of a conflict."[106] If the stronger notion of rhetoric is due to the logic of rhetorical technization, the weaker notion is the result of its interaction with the principle of technicity. Together, they allow a reformulation of the notion of political activity that follows a more dialogical model. It relies on the "secure conditions under which pluralistic and non-violent communication can take place,"[107] as Nicholls writes. This kind of political rhetoric is compatible with parliamentary democracy, not only as *katechon* against the potentially annihilating decision but as a safe system for effective deliberation. Here also lies Blumenberg's notion of political freedom within limits: rhetoric acts less as a replacement for action than its regulation through a specific type of public *consensus*—but one quite different from Habermas's understanding of the concept.

Blumenberg describes the full interaction between the principle of technicity as immanent regulation and the afformative tendencies of rhetorical technization in what he calls the "paradox of the powerless power." If technological progress creates a stability between powers internationally, it has domestic effects as well. Any state is now "confronted with the complexity of the problems of a world that is only possible by virtue of technology." This engenders "being forcibly turned toward rationality."[108] In the technical age, power is no longer the exertion of mere physical force by way of sovereign decisions. Rather, the functioning of the technology that undergirds power largely depends on the cooperation of a highly specialized and functionally differentiated society; indeed, it makes sense to include these interrelations between complex social systems under the heading of "technology." "Whatever one may wish to call the powers and qualities that might at this moment

105. Blumenberg, "The Concept of Reality and the Theory of the State," 106.
106. Blumenberg, "The Concept of Reality and the Theory of the State," 104.
107. Nicholls, "'How to Do Nothing with Words,'" 74.
108. Blumenberg, "The Concept of Reality and the Theory of the State," 98.

be the objective of an expansive political will to subdue, they can no longer be separated from the free consent to this will." The fragility of this machinery is the "humane surprise" that hastens the end of Schmittian sovereignty. The "substance of what can be neither won nor ruled by power"—the consent of a public closely integrated into the technical world—"has become crucial, in modern reality, to the continued existence of that very reality."[109] Most surprisingly, it is the creation of political reality itself, once at the hand of the state creating perpetuating crises, that is now a function of this public. In his essay on the novel, Blumenberg thus had written, "Reality as a self-constituting context is a boundary concept of the ideal totality of all selves—it is a confirmative value for the experience and interpretation of the world that take place in intersubjectivity."[110]

Blumenberg repeats this point expressly in a posthumous publication, stating "that the modern concept of reality cannot be interpreted correctly without reference to an interpretive community [*Verständigungsgemeinschaft*] of subjects."[111] This amounts to the notion of the public both as the *regulator* of the political will and the *perpetuator* of political reality—reminiscent of Kant's "transcendental principle of publicity,"[112] according to which only those political decisions are permissible that require public consent—and that its role is most developed in a state so technologically advanced that it is nearly impossible to act against it. Both its functions render "any notion of violence, even of the most conventional kind, risky in the extreme."[113] Instead, they require slow and deliberative processes. In this, Blumenberg comes close to Arendt's notion of the public as a guarantor of reality,[114] or Habermas's discourse theory of politics. However, in Blumenberg, consensus is not the result of a discussion under the assumption of an ideal speech situation. Rather, the consensus marks the *beginning* of any deliberation as a result of the immanent regulation of the technical world—it is the consent *to* deliberate rather than the consent *by* deliberation. Instead of being situated within dialogue, technical rationality makes dialogue possible in the first place by ruling out any alternative to it.

"Theory of the State" is very much in line with Blumenberg's thinking since *Legitimacy*. He sees as the result of modern rationality's immanent

109. Blumenberg, "The Concept of Reality and the Theory of the State," 99.
110. Blumenberg, "The Concept of Reality and the Possibility of the Novel," 504. Emphasis deleted.
111. Blumenberg, *Realität und Realismus*, 29.
112. Kant, "Toward Perpetual Peace," 104–9.
113. Blumenberg, "The Concept of Reality and the Theory of the State," 96.
114. See Bajohr, *Dimensionen der Öffentlichkeit*, chap. 3.

dynamic an eventual increase in individual freedom and a decrease in volatility. Although his model can at times look almost cybernetic in its reliance on self-regulation, Blumenberg is far from suggesting a postpolitical or posthistorical future. Instead, he tries to reformulate the situation of politics in the technical age. This means both the rejection of Platonism as a still-subcutaneously virulent concept of reality and the recognition of the conditions under which political action is possible in industrialized and technicized societies. The reintroduction of premodern notions of reality, as in Schmitt, are deemed dangerous because they risk exploding a trajectory that promises at least some stability and predictability. Likewise, Blumenberg rejects utopian notions of history because they sidestep the rationality of self-preservation.[115] Utopia, as already in More, highlights the contingency of reality, and for Blumenberg this is useful only in its critical function.[116] But modernity must constantly reshape contingency into consistency, and one way of doing this is, as Machiavelli had found out, through the use of political language. Rhetoric may not only replace or suspend action; it is also the most fundamental way of world making in the absence of the norms of nature. No utopia, Blumenberg argues, can provide guidance toward such consistency because it assumes a radical discontinuity in history.[117]

Here, then, lies the task of politics for Blumenberg: to rationally deliberate within the limits of what is implied in the modern concept of reality. For despite all his talk of "immanent regulation," Blumenberg does not suggest any historical determinism. The "immanent regulation" is the consistency of the modern concept of reality projected into the future, and marks the logic one *should* follow—or at least not act against—not a prediction of events to come. Blumenberg is well aware that a relapse into past concepts of reality is always possible, and that, in the long run, ruptures are bound to occur in history, because the integrity of such immanent logic is always at risk of being punctured. This is why his attack on Schmitt on the basis of the latter's false historical epistemology—his "sociology of concepts"—is so significant: it fulfills the "continuing critical *officium*" of modernity.[118] It must indeed be continued, constantly made, since the modern notion of progress is neither teleological nor automatic. It is the logic of a process that can only be differentially detected, by comparing past and present states, but without any final goal.[119]

---

115. Blumenberg, "Dogmatische und rationale Analyse," 272–73.
116. Blumenberg, "The Concept of Reality and the Theory of the State," 110.
117. Blumenberg, "The Concept of Reality and the Theory of the State," 110–11.
118. Blumenberg, *Die Legitimität der Neuzeit*, 61.
119. Blumenberg, "Dogmatische und rationale Analyse," 261–64.

This is why Blumenberg was more of a liberal in the mold of Max Weber, as Charles Turner has suggested, and not simply a Whig historian, as Richard Rorty believed, for whom progress is a given.[120]

Instead of stepping outside the dynamic of modernity, Blumenberg argues, a politics cognizant of this dynamic should follow the immanent logic of the technical world. While one can see Luhmannian undertones in this, another way to look at it would be to call Blumenberg, in a strange way, something of an accelerationist.[121] His suggestion is that technization as well as the principle of technicity accelerate the reduction of state sovereignty to such a degree that at some point a supranational system guided by international law will result. To be clear, Blumenberg remains vague on this notion. He neither refers to any contemporary theorist of postnational politics, be it Alexandre Kojève, whose Schmittian roots and Hegelian outlook he would have found suspicious, or Ernst Jünger and his idea of the *Weltstaat*, whose biologistic undertones he would have abhorred.[122] Characteristically, Blumenberg sidesteps the debates of his time. Instead, he retraces a thought by the French eighteenth-century political theorist (and inventor of the word *ideology*) Antoine Destutt de Tracy, who had suggested that after Hobbes the state of nature between individuals had only been transposed onto the situation between states. "What the states lacked to reach a condition of a 'society which is organized and perfected,'" Blumenberg summarizes Destutt de Tracy, "was the founding of a common court of law and a superordinate coercive power." This thought, however, only becomes convincing once the "threat to everyone by everyone" that Hobbes had assumed for the relationships between individuals also goes for the relationship between states. And this, of course, describes the political situation after the atom bomb.[123]

In 1967, the year of Blumenberg's first draft of the essay, the Brussels Treaty went into effect, consolidating the development of the European Union as a supranational organization. We do not know how Blumenberg thought about it, but it is not unlikely that he deemed it agreeable. Such a supranational entity shows, quite in line with Blumenberg's thinking, "that sovereignty and

120. Turner, "Liberalism"; Rorty, "Against Belatedness."

121. Williams and Srnicek, "#ACCELERATE MANIFESTO for an Accelerationist Politics." Williams and Srnicek define *accelerationism* as the notion of speeding up and exacerbating productive relations within capitalism; they see it as an alternative to the messianic utopianism that puts such a premium on temporal rupture.

122. Kletzer, "Alexandre Kojève's Hegelianism"; Jünger, *Der Weltstaat*. On Blumenberg's political distance to Jünger, see Blumenberg, "Ernst Jünger—ein Fazit."

123. Blumenberg, "The Concept of Reality and the Theory of the State," 113.

sovereign states . . . have been but the passing phenomena of a few centuries, that their passing is by no means regrettable, and that current developments in Europe exhibit the possibility of going beyond all that,"[124] as Neil MacCormick put it. Postsovereignty is the logical result of modern rationality: of self-preservation and the immanent principle of technicity, on the one hand, and of publicness and intersubjectivity, on the other. And postsovereignty is achieved through language in the form of political rhetoric: "The iteration of the state contract through the state contract among states appears in this instance not as an externally introduced utopia, but as the internal consequence of a reality that has been established not only with the contractual act, but with language as the first instrument of social reciprocity."[125]

Conclusion: From History to Anthropology

Blumenberg has since been proved right on some of these points, such as the strengthening of supranational bonds both in international relations and in institutions like the European Union (despite its recent setbacks), and wrong on others, like the self-healing properties of technological progress. Although Blumenberg does not mistake "immanent regulation" for teleology, he puts much faith in the willingness of political agents to act according to the inherent rationality of modernity. The challenges of slowing, if not reversing, climate change—a direct product of technical progress—demonstrate that the reasonable is not necessarily the politically feasible.[126] What is more, the fundamental, and essentially game-theoretical, assumption of his argument—the stability of nuclear deterrence—is anything but certain in a multipolar world. Nuclear deterrence today is not a "foolproof and reliable global security mechanism," if it ever was one; it may eliminate nuclear war, but not the "limited war," itself the product of new technologies, that often proliferates into endless ones.[127]

What is more, while Blumenberg briefly touches on the demagogical potential of rhetoric,[128] his trust in the self-regulating power of a public discourse limited by the necessities of the technical world is unsuited for the present. In the end, he presupposes a base consensus too easily, so that his desire to put Schmittian decision at a distance requires him to subscribe to what Judith

124. MacCormick, "Beyond the Sovereign State," 1.

125. Blumenberg, "WST," 19.

126. For the argument that Blumenberg can nevertheless be brought to bear on the topic of the Anthropocene, see Vida Pavesich's contribution to this special issue.

127. Brown and Arnold, "Quirks of Nuclear Deterrence," 293, 298.

128. Blumenberg, "The Concept of Reality and the Theory of the State," 106.

Shklar has called the "ideology of agreement," which underestimates the challenges of reaching consent in a pluralistic society.[129] In this, his distrust of state power and his private fear of a political climate that "made Hitler possible" were not matched by his theoretical writings, even though his hope for postsovereignty was a strong endorsement of postnationalism.

In the end, "Theory of the State" offers insightful notes toward a political theory of rhetoric without spelling out such a theory once and for all. While this may be consistent with the analysis that politics is losing its central status in contemporary modernity, the plausibility of this very analysis is questionable. However, keeping in mind Blumenberg's method of following tendencies rather than merely describing actualities, it is possible to read "Theory of the State" less as a farewell to politics than as a study of the structural transformation of *modes* of the political. It sketches the move away from Schmittian power politics to a more rhetorical and rhetorically mediated politics. This concentration on modes rather than substances, nevertheless, is in line with a liberal outlook more interested in safeguarding political structures and processes than in dictating positive concepts acting as criteria for the contents of these structures. In this, Blumenberg was closer to skeptical liberals like Shklar and Rorty than to the engaged republicanism of Arendt.

In a curious way, Blumenberg's work runs parallel to the Left's post-1968 melancholia, as his optimism about the rationality of immanent regulation and the power of language, which he formulated in "Theory of the State" (1968), was soon succeeded by a more pessimistic view, exemplified in the 1971 text "Anthropological Approach to the Contemporary Significance of Rhetoric." The reasons for this shift are still debated, but Blumenberg's biographer Rüdiger Zill points out that the student unrest of 1968—and especially the change in student-teacher relations that Blumenberg came to feel in the 1970s—shook him deeply.[130] While the Left never played a role in his thinking before, he was increasingly hostile to anything that showed signs of a Marxist zeitgeist. This included the theory of history, which was now unmistakably a domain of the Frankfurt School. Odo Marquard has suggested that the philosophy of history and anthropology are mutually exclusive alternatives,[131] and there are good reasons to believe that Blumenberg's turn toward anthropology was led by this view.

The anthropological dimension constitutes a genuinely new development in Blumenberg's work. "Anthropological Approach" at first glance appears as

129. Shklar, *Legalism*, 88–110.
130. Zill, *Der absolute Leser*, 302–3.
131. Marquard, *Schwierigkeiten*.

a mere complement to "Theory of the State," adopting its praise of rhetoric as a replacement of action. But the basic assumptions have shifted from a historical onto an anthropological fundament.[132] If the earlier text had focused on the rationality that rests within the historical concepts of reality, to which rhetoric is only the proper *response*, in "Anthropological Approach," rhetoric—an "anthropological 'radical'"[133]—*becomes* a new rationality. Blumenberg sees the situation of human beings as characterized by both a "lack of self-evidence" and the "compulsion to act."[134] Human beings are always under pressure to respond to the situation they find themselves in but are never in possession of enough information to know whether their actions are adequate. Rhetoric here becomes a type of technization that deals with the possibly permanent state of incomplete rationality and thus "a form of rationality itself—a rational way of coming to terms with the provisionality of reason."[135] It is obvious that this expands the concept of rhetoric far beyond its applicability as a political notion. Instead, Blumenberg argues for rhetoric as a genuinely *human* type of rationality. It still may be afformative, replacing *res* with *verba*, but its necessity is now not merely a matter of historically changeable concepts of reality. Rather, it is deeply situated in the human condition, the dearth of human life-time.[136]

Blumenberg's anthropological turn raises the concerns that Habermas, in *This, Too, a History of Philosophy*, hints at. The historicity of Blumenberg's notes toward a political theory, which builds on a historically situated reason, now seems to stand in conflict with the lasting features of the human condition. By only focusing on the later, anthropological Blumenberg, however, Habermas ignores his earlier positions. As this interpretation of "Theory of the State" has shown, Blumenberg's historical phenomenology provides a rich and insightful take on political theory—even if it does not quite become one itself—especially in developing a powerful, *non*anthropological notion of rhetoric. The alternative to a limited view of his thought is to periodize and to pluralize him.[137] There is more than one Blumenberg at work, and the liberal Blumenberg of *Legitimacy* and "Theory of the State" can still be an ally to Habermas's theory of modernity without involving the anthropology of the

132. For a detailed analysis of this shift, see Bajohr, "Shifting Grounds"; and Bajohr, "Gebrochene Kontinuität."

133. Blumenberg, "Anthropological Approach," 187.

134. Blumenberg, "Anthropological Approach," 191, 186.

135. Blumenberg, "Anthropological Approach," 203.

136. Blumenberg expands on this idea in *Lebenszeit und Weltzeit*.

137. I make the case for such an approach in Bajohr, "Shifting Grounds."

more conservative later Blumenberg. After all, both Habermas and Blumenberg are connected in a defense of modernity that was so rare among philosophers of the twentieth century; while diverging on many points, they are united in their "critical *officium*."

Hannes Bajohr is a postdoctoral researcher in the Department of Arts, Media, Philosophy at the University of Basel.

References

Arendt, Hannah. *The Human Condition*. Chicago: University of Chicago Press, 1998.

Austin, J. L. *How to Do Things with Words*. Oxford: Oxford University Press, 1962.

Bajohr, Hannes. *Dimensionen der Öffentlichkeit: Politik und Erkenntnis bei Hannah Arendt*. Berlin: Lukas, 2011.

Bajohr, Hannes. "Gebrochene Kontinuität: Neues über Hans Blumenbergs Werk." *Merkur*, no. 860 (2021): 71–81.

Bajohr, Hannes. "Shifting Grounds: Hans Blumenberg's Immanent and Transcendent Modes of Thought." In *Describing Cultural Achievements: Hans Blumenberg's Literary Strategies*, edited by Ulrich Breuer and Timothy Attanucci, 35–56. Heidelberg: Winter, 2021.

Blumenberg, Hans. "An Anthropological Approach to the Contemporary Significance of Rhetoric." In *History, Metaphors, Fables: A Hans Blumenberg Reader*, edited by Hannes Bajohr, Florian Fuchs, and Joe Paul Kroll, 177–209. Ithaca, NY: Cornell University Press, 2020.

Blumenberg, Hans. *Beschreibung des Menschen*, edited by Manfred Sommer. Frankfurt am Main: Suhrkamp, 2006.

Blumenberg, Hans. "The Concept of Reality and the Possibility of the Novel." In *History, Metaphors, Fables: A Hans Blumenberg Reader*, edited by Hannes Bajohr, Florian Fuchs, and Joe Paul Kroll, 499–524. Ithaca, NY: Cornell University Press, 2020.

Blumenberg, Hans. "The Concept of Reality and the Theory of the State." In *History, Metaphors, Fables: A Hans Blumenberg Reader*, edited by Hannes Bajohr, Florian Fuchs, and Joe Paul Kroll, 83–116. Ithaca, NY: Cornell University Press, 2020.

Blumenberg, Hans. *Die Legitimität der Neuzeit*. Frankfurt am Main: Suhrkamp, 1966.

Blumenberg, Hans. "Dogmatische und rationale Analyse von Motivationen des technischen Fortschritts." In *Schriften zur Technik*, edited by Alexander Schmitz and Bernd Stiegler, 258–76. Berlin: Suhrkamp, 2015.

Blumenberg, Hans. "Ernst Jünger—ein Fazit." In *Der Mann von Mond: Über Ernst Jünger*, edited by Marcel Lepper and Alexander Schmitz, 24–27. Frankfurt am Main: Suhrkamp, 2007.

Blumenberg, Hans. "'Imitation of Nature': Toward a Prehistory of the Idea of the Creative Being." In *History, Metaphors, Fables: A Hans Blumenberg Reader*, edited by Hannes

Bajohr, Florian Fuchs, and Joe Paul Kroll, 316–57. Ithaca, NY: Cornell University Press, 2020.

Blumenberg, Hans. *Lebenszeit und Weltzeit*. Frankfurt am Main: Suhrkamp, 1986.

Blumenberg, Hans. *The Legitimacy of the Modern Age*, translated by Robert M. Wallace. Cambridge, MA: MIT Press, 1983.

Blumenberg, Hans. *Paradigms for a Metaphorology*, translated by Robert Savage. Ithaca, NY: Cornell University Press, 2010.

Blumenberg, Hans. "Phenomenological Aspects on Life-World and Technization." In *History, Metaphors, Fables: A Hans Blumenberg Reader*, edited by Hannes Bajohr, Florian Fuchs, and Joe Paul Kroll, 358–99. Ithaca, NY: Cornell University Press, 2020.

Blumenberg, Hans. *Präfiguration: Arbeit am politischen Mythos*, edited by Felix Heidenreich and Angus Nicholls. Berlin: Suhrkamp, 2014.

Blumenberg, Hans. "Preliminary Remarks on the Concept of Reality." In *History, Metaphors, Fables: A Hans Blumenberg Reader*, edited by Hannes Bajohr, Florian Fuchs, and Joe Paul Kroll, 117–26. Ithaca, NY: Cornell University Press, 2020.

Blumenberg, Hans. *Realität und Realismus*, edited by Nicola Zambon. Berlin: Suhrkamp, 2020.

Blumenberg, Hans. *Rigorism of Truth: "Moses the Egyptian" and Other Writings on Freud and Arendt*, translated by Joe Paul Kroll. Ithaca, NY: Cornell University Press, 2018.

Blumenberg, Hans. "Self-Preservation and Inertia: On the Constitution of Modern Rationality." In vol. 3 of *Contemporary German Philosophy*, edited by Darrell E. Christensen, Manfred Riedel, Robert Spaemann, Reiner Wiehl, and Wolfgang Wieland, 209–56. University Park: Pennsylvania State University Press, 1983.

Blumenberg, Hans. "'Und das ist mir von der Liebe zur Kirche geblieben': Hans Blumenbergs letzter Brief." *Communio* 43, no. 3 (2014): 173–81.

Blumenberg, Hans. "Wirklichkeitsbegriff und Staatstheorie." *Schweizer Monatshefte* 48, no. 2 (1968–69): 121–46.

Blumenberg, Hans. *Work on Myth*, translated by Robert M. Wallace. Cambridge, MA: MIT Press, 1985.

Blumenberg, Hans, Herbert Dieckmann, Günter Gawlick, Dieter Henrich, Max Imdahl, Wolfgang Iser, Hans Robert Jauss, Clemens Heselhaus, Wolfgang Preisendanz, and Jurij Striedter. "Diskussion: Wirklichkeitsbegriff und Möglichkeit des Romans." In *Nachahmung und Illusion: Kolloquium Giessen, Juni 1963; Vorlagen und Verhandlungen*, edited by Hans Robert Jauss, 219–27. Munich: Eidos, 1964.

Bragagnolo, Celina María. "Secularization, History, and Political Theology: The Hans Blumenberg and Carl Schmitt Debate." *Journal of the Philosophy of History* 5, no. 1 (2011): 84–104.

Brown, Andrew, and Lorna Arnold. "The Quirks of Nuclear Deterrence." *International Relations* 24, no. 3 (2010): 293–312.

Gordon, Peter E. "Secularization, Genealogy, and the Legitimacy of the Modern Age: Remarks on the Löwith-Blumenberg Debate." *Journal of the History of Ideas* 80, no. 1 (2019): 147–70.

Habermas, Jürgen. *Auch eine Geschichte der Philosophie*. Vol. 1. Berlin: Suhrkamp, 2019.

Hamacher, Werner. "Afformative, Strike." *Cardozo Law Review* 13, no. 4 (1991): 1133–57.

Hammill, Graham. "Blumenberg and Schmitt on the Rhetoric of Political Theology." In *Political Theology and Early Modernity*, edited by Graham Hammill and Julia Reinhard Lupton, 84–101. Chicago: University of Chicago Press, 2012.

Heidenreich, Felix. "Political Aspects in Hans Blumenberg's Philosophy." *Aurora*, no. 41 (2015): 521–37.

Heidenreich, Felix, and Angus Nicholls. "Nachwort der Herausgeber." In *Präfiguration: Arbeit am politischen Mythos*, edited by Felix Heidenreich and Angus Nicholls, 83–146. Berlin: Suhrkamp, 2014.

Hochstätter, Matthias. *Karl Schiller: Eine wirtschaftspolitische Biografie*. Saarbrücken: Müller, 2008.

Honneth, Axel. *Pathologies of Reason: On the Legacy of Critical Theory*. New York: Columbia University Press, 2009.

Husserl, Edmund. *The Crisis of European Sciences and Transcendental Phenomenology: An Introduction to Phenomenological Philosophy*, translated by David Carr. Evanston, IL: Northwestern University Press, 1970.

Ifergan, Pini. "Cutting to the Chase: Carl Schmitt and Hans Blumenberg on Political Theology and Secularization." *New German Critique*, no. 111 (2010): 149–71.

Jünger, Ernst. *Der Weltstaat*. Stuttgart: Klett, 1960.

Kant, Immanuel. "Toward Perpetual Peace: A Philosophical Sketch." In *Toward Perpetual Peace and Other Writings on Politics, Peace, and History*, edited by Pauline Kleingeld, 67–109. New Haven, CT: Yale University Press, 2006.

Kirke, Xander. *Hans Blumenberg: Myth and Significance in Modern Politics*. Cham: Springer, 2019.

Kletzer, Christoph. "Alexandre Kojève's Hegelianism and the Formation of Europe." *Cambridge Yearbook of European Legal Studies* 8 (2006): 133–51.

Lyotard, Jean-François. *The Differend: Phrases in Dispute*, translated by Georges Van Den Abbeele. Manchester: Manchester University Press, 1988.

MacCormick, Neil. "Beyond the Sovereign State." *Modern Law Review* 56, no. 1 (1993): 1–18.

Marquard, Odo. *Schwierigkeiten mit der Geschichtsphilosophie*. Frankfurt am Main: Suhrkamp, 1973.

Matysik, Tracie. "Hans Blumenberg's Multiple Modernities: A Spinozist Supplement to Legitimacy of the Modern Age." *Germanic Review* 90, no. 1 (2015): 21–41.

Mende, Dirk. "Histories of Technicization: On the Relation of Conceptual History and Metaphorology in Hans Blumenberg." *Telos*, no. 158 (2012): 59–79.

Meyer, Martin. "Der Kandidat." *Schweizer Monat* 100, no. 2 (2021): 53–54.

Monod, Jean-Claude. "Préface." In *Le concept de réalité*, by Hans Blumenberg, 7–33. Paris: Seuil, 2012.

Müller, Oliver. "Beyond the Political: Hans Blumenberg's Criticism of Carl Schmitt." In *Man and His Enemies: Essays on Carl Schmitt*, edited by Svetozar Minkov and Piotr Nowak, 238–53. Białystok: University of Białystok Press, 2008.

Nicholls, Angus. "Hans Blumenberg on Political Myth." *Iyyun* 65, no. 1 (2016): 3–33.

Nicholls, Angus. "'How to Do Nothing with Words': Hans Blumenberg's Reception of Plato's 'Protagoras.'" In *Prometheus gibt nicht auf: Antike Welt und modernes Leben in Hans Blumenbergs Philosophie*, edited by Melanie Möller, 61–75. Paderborn: Fink, 2015.

Nicholls, Angus. *Myth and the Human Sciences: Hans Blumenberg's Theory of Myth*. New York: Routledge, 2015.

Rorty, Richard. "Against Belatedness." *London Review of Books*, June 16, 1983, 3–5.

Schmitt, Carl. *The Concept of the Political*, translated by George Schwab. Enl. ed. Chicago: University of Chicago Press, 2007.

Schmitt, Carl. *The "Nomos" of the Earth in the International Law of the "Jus Publicum Europaeum."* New York: Telos, 2006.

Schmitt, Carl. *Political Theology: Four Chapters on the Concept of Sovereignty*. Cambridge, MA: MIT Press, 1985.

Schmitt, Carl. *Political Theology II: The Myth of the Closure of Any Political Theology*, translated by Michael Hoelzl and Graham Ward. Cambridge: Polity, 2008.

Schmitz, Alexander. "Legitimacy of the Modern Age? Hans Blumenberg and Carl Schmitt." In *The Oxford Handbook of Carl Schmitt*, edited by Jens Meierhenrich and Oliver Simons, 705–30. Oxford: Oxford University Press, 2017.

Shklar, Judith N. *Legalism: Law, Morals, and Political Trials*. Cambridge, MA: Harvard University Press, 1986.

Turner, Charles. "Liberalism and the Limits of Science: Weber and Blumenberg." *History of the Human Sciences* 6, no. 4 (1993): 57–79.

Wallace, Robert M. "Translator's Introduction." In *The Legitimacy of the Modern Age*, by Hans Blumenberg, xi–xxxi. Cambridge, MA: MIT Press, 1983.

Weber, Max. *The Protestant Ethic and the Spirit of Capitalism*, edited by Richard Swedberg. New York: Norton, 2009.

Weizsäcker, Carl Friedrich von. "Friede und Wahrheit." *Die Zeit*, June 30, 1967.

Wenzel, Uwe Justus. "Meister des Problemkrimis: Der große Philosoph Hans Blumenberg wird gerade neu entdeckt." *Die Zeit*, July 9, 2020.

Wetz, Franz Josef. *Hans Blumenberg zur Einführung*. Hamburg: Junius, 2004.

Williams, Alex, and Nick Srnicek. "#ACCELERATE MANIFESTO for an Accelerationist Politics." *Critical Legal Thinking*, May 14, 2013. criticallegalthinking.com/2013/05/14/accelerate-manifesto-for-an-accelerationist-politics.

Zill, Rüdiger. *Der absolute Leser: Hans Blumenberg; Eine intellektuelle Biografie*. Berlin: Suhrkamp, 2020.

Decoding Aesop:
Blumenberg's Fabulistic Turn

Florian Fuchs

Hans Blumenberg never shied away from controversies and quibbles with members of the academic community, but he rarely aimed such critique, whether collegial or hostile, at more than one individual. This makes it a unique occurrence when, in the 1974 essay "The Protophilosopher's Plummet," he launched an attack on the academic field of philosophy that spared none of his colleagues and turned out to be symptomatic for a deeper shift in his work that surfaced during the 1980s. This shift culminated in one of his last books from 1987, *The Laughter of the Thracian Woman*, ending a phase in which Blumenberg argued emphatically against academic philosophy and proposed a mode of thinking based on the reading of fables. This fabulistic turn amounts to a corpus of texts, many of them short and essayistic, that proposes a storytelling practice for philosophy, mostly by demonstrating in medias res how such a practice would newly ground thought in lived reality. Like the concept of metaphor, whose definitory elasticity Blumenberg had exceeded for his metaphorology phase around 1960, he considered fables a type of story not limited to the Aesopic canon. Blumenberg's fabulistic turn centers on an archaeology of the Aesopic fable as a lost medium of an original philosophy. Read as a constella-

An earlier version of this article was presented at the conference "Hans Blumenberg: Neue Zugänge zum Werk" at the ZfL Berlin in October 2019. I am grateful to the conference participants for their helpful comments, in particular to Melanie Möller. In addition, I would like to thank an anonymous reviewer for energizing remarks and questions.

New German Critique 145, Vol. 49, No. 1, February 2022
DOI 10.1215/0094033X-9439671   © 2022 by New German Critique, Inc.

tion, these texts written roughly between 1980 and 1990 seek to discover such fabulistic remnants as surviving beneath the universal stories of the lifeworld, that is, embedded in the anecdotes, letters, and diaries of the everyday.

Fables beneath Anecdotes

The first marker of Blumenberg's attack against academic philosophy is often attributed to his 1979 *Shipwreck with Spectator* and the book's organizing image. The scene of an observer who contemplates in purported safety and certainty the shipwreck of others demonstrated for Blumenberg the contingencies of any possibility for thought. While this "metaphor for existence" exhibits the limits of philosophy from the outside,[1] it is not the most noteworthy scene of contemplation that Blumenberg dissects during the 1970s. His criticism of a university philosophy increasingly removed from thinking about the world, contemplating instead only its own purely academic problems, goes back to his training and research in the Husserlian tradition, which pressed for a fresh grounding of philosophical problems in lived reality, specifically opposing learned schools and their jargons. While already his first short article "The Linguistic Reality of Philosophy" (1947) demands, in explicit recourse to Edmund Husserl's manifesto "Philosophy as Rigorous Science," a critique of philosophy's metalanguage that his "metaphorology" project would take on during the late 1950s, such a purely linguistic critique is no longer Blumenberg's goal in the 1970s.

In the precursor to his fable studies, written in 1974 for the seventh colloquium of the prominent interdisciplinary research group Poetik und Hermeneutik, Blumenberg offered his first systematic treatment of a fable. The text "The Protophilosopher's Plummet: On the Comedy of Pure Theory, with Recourse to a Reception History of the Thales Anecdote" is dedicated to an Aesopic fable that early on was turned into an anecdote. Blumenberg traces its reception through the history of philosophy, from Aesop up to Martin Heidegger, to show how each reception also brought about a slight variation to the story's plot. In each retelling, different particularities of the fable were accentuated, suppressing some of its aspects by overlaying them with new ones, effectively altering the story's stock and appearance over time. Blumenberg calls this phenomenon "reoccupation" (*Umbesetzung*),[2] which, in a surprising adaptation, extends the use of this term, which he had introduced in 1962 for the false smoothing of ruptures in the lineage of an idea, to the narratological

---

1. Blumenberg, *Shipwreck with Spectator.*
2. Blumenberg, "Der Sturz des Protophilosophen," 28.

reoccupation occurring during the retelling of a story.[3] This misuse of his own former central concept is a simple yet crucial indication for the beginning fabulistic turn in his thought. It foreshadows that successions of stories, not of ideas, concepts, or metaphors, will become Blumenberg's focus, shifting the scene of his work from the diachronicity of notions to the synchronicity of philosophizing by storytelling.

In terms of the reception of the Aesopic story, the strongest result of these *reoccupations* is that one of its earliest variations caused a permanent change of the story's genre from fable to anecdote. Consequentially, Blumenberg begins his article by retelling the story in the oldest version drawn from the Aesopic corpus of fables. Consistent with their genre, no names are assigned to the protagonists in this original version: while looking at the stars, an astronomer falls into a well, causing a passerby to ask how he can possibly deal with the matter of the stars above if he cannot even properly deal with the matter of the earth below.[4] For this universal and timeless story, whose close relation to life gives it the function of a parable, being linked to a specific historical individual is a radical transformation that results in something closer to a case story. This shape-shifting happens in Plato's *Theaetetus*, where it is Socrates who tells the Aesopic fable with a completely new historical identifier. It was Thales of Miletus, he claims, who is the fallen philosopher in the fable. The outcome of this genre metamorphosis is that from that point on the story is called "Thales anecdote." As Blumenberg already outlines in his 1974 essay, the historic scene with Socrates as the agent of this metamorphosis is crucial. Blumenberg deduces from it one of the most pervasive defects of philosophy, which he will later call Socrates's "betrayal" of Aesop: the overlooked opposition between anecdote and fable, on which he subsequently based his program of a critique of academic philosophy.

Before Blumenberg turns to the deeper metaphilosophical meaning of the fable, he reiterates the particular conditions of this reception and why it entered into the history of philosophy. Whether true or not, Socrates's revelation of the name of the plummeted contemplator of the heavens not only caused further "reoccupations" but also made them possible in the first place. Through this act of naming, Blumenberg explains, Socrates, on the one hand, acknowledged that philosophy originated from an earlier phase where thinking was

3. Remarkably, Blumenberg published another somewhat anti-academic and partly overlooked essay in the same year, 1974, "On a Lineage of the Idea of Progress," in which he opposes philosophy with astronomy and argues that the latter might be favorable for understanding the concept of progress. On this essay, see Adelson, *Cosmic Miniatures and the Future Sense*, 208–10.

4. Blumenberg, "Der Sturz des Protophilosophen," 17.

significantly linked to the act of telling a certain kind of story that, unlike other genres such as anecdote or gloss, had neither author nor specific protagonists; these stories that we still call "fables" would later form the so-called Aesopic corpus. On the other hand, and more important, Socrates actively brings philosophy's storytelling phase to an end by introducing names of philosophers into the history of philosophy. In Socrates's act Blumenberg recognizes a de facto declaration that all nameless and nongenealogical retelling of philosophical stories shall be discontinued in favor of accumulating the opinions and deeds of individual philosophers. This clarifies the opposition between fable and anecdote. Rather than thinking again and again through anonymous stories drawn from life, philosophy is held to increasingly refine its knowledge by recourse to the thoughts of recognized philosophers, whose teachings first circulate in anecdotes and related genres naming authors and protagonists.

In the 1974 colloquium on "the comical," the subdued critique of institutional philosophy included in this thesis created a controversy, likely in Blumenberg's interest. A tone of agonal amusement can be sensed in his defenses against Karlheinz Stierle, Manfred Fuhrmann, and Harald Weinrich, which are transcribed in the appendix to the conference volume. As if their polemics verified his hypothesis about the unwillingness of philosophy to think through stories and then laugh about its own pitfalls, Blumenberg takes recourse to the earlier colloquium in the 1987 book version on the Thales complex, *The Laughter of the Thracian Woman: A Protohistory of Theory*. The colloquium turned out to be Blumenberg's last with the Poetik und Hermeneutik group, which makes it less surprising that he incorporates the stubborn seriousness of Weinrich and the others into the subsequent book as just another instance where reception of an anecdote prevented the contemplation of the thoughts it contains.[5] Coming from the leading figures of West German postwar humanities and philosophy, the nonunderstanding of the anecdote's underlying fable had fallen all too perfectly in line with Blumenberg's fundamental critique of philosophy's reliance on pure theory. In the aftermath of the 1974 colloquium, Blumenberg seems to almost have been astounded at how his provocation had revealed more problems about academic philosophy than expected. The favoring of anecdotes over fables became a key to the situation of the humanities of his day. In the years after he left Poetik und Hermeneutik, Blumenberg returned once more to Socrates's transmutation of fable into anecdote, this time, however, to clarify programmatically on which side he is.

5. Blumenberg, *Laughter of the Thracian Woman*, 130–32.

Fables, not anecdotes, will increasingly become Blumenberg's model for philosophy. This required laying out how fables could again become philosophy, since it was not enough to merely point to the decline of philosophical storytelling before it was excluded from the academies by Socrates. Academic philosophers indebted to names and their genealogies, Blumenberg explains in the 1987 book, can observe life only in the theoretical distance dissociated from the world and the thinker's position in it. They will not burst into laughter about their own obliviousness, but only about that of others, who were so lost in thought to fall to the ground while thinking about the world. That the meaning of the Thales anecdote, that is, its fabulistic content, could pass unseen for his colleagues is interpreted by Blumenberg as the need for a new kind of philosophy. "The interdisciplinary reception of the reception [of the Thales anecdote]," he writes in the book's last sentence, "supports the diagnosis that the end of philosophy is announced just as it sees its own task in the treatment of its beginning."[6] This outlook indicates the dialectic of two-step lessons demanded by fables. Like the contemplator in the fable, philosophers should lose themselves in thought to leave the reality of the common people and then rise into heavenly transcendence. But they must not forget the second part of the dialectic, namely, to let themselves be returned to the thicket of things once reality strikes and welcome the humor of sober bystanders. The laughter of these common folk is representative not only of this thicket of things but also of the unrealistic steps philosophy takes, which cause the subsequent stumbling back into reality. Both are included in the bystander's laughter: the amplified call of reality and the signal to interrupt philosophical transcendence. Both calls imply that philosophy must accept its own worldliness, which is fundamentally different from the setting of philosophical articles and colloquiums. Blumenberg also points to what is not included in the dialectic of the fable, namely, a third-degree observer, which hence must be excluded from philosophy. In the fable, there is no place for the interdisciplinary humanities. These disciplines conceive of philosophy not as the practice of finding relevant questions through autonomous thinking; instead, they consider themselves a closed scene of observing other observers. Instead of thinking about life and the world always anew, a humanities built exclusively along lines of reception, whether it did so explicitly or not, can always only revisit prior thoughts and discern them only from a distance of theory and irony.

This act of distancing that philosophy as an observational "pure theory" performs is somewhat reminiscent of Blumenberg's parallel definition of myth

6. Blumenberg, *Laughter of the Thracian Woman*, 132.

as a cultural formation for distancing absolute entities in his 1979 *Work on Myth*. While he never relates myth and fable at length, one passage in *Work on Myth* speculates that the Aesopic story might historically have served as a correction to the distancing effects of myth, particularly when it came to rendering human behavior. While the anthropomorphization of gods in myth had occupied the figure of the human for storytelling, the fable achieved its reversal, Blumenberg argues, namely, using the humanization of animals to render humans for what they are and accentuate their "typicalness." In consequence, "the fable, though related to the residues of the mythical transformation of monsters into animals and men, would at the same time be opposed, as a type [*der Gegentypus*], to the all too easily accomplished poetic humanization of the gods in the epics."[7] Whereas myth's narratives are rarely aimed at human anthropology as such and instead regulate the horizons humans are behaving toward, a fable-type story centers on how human behavior repeats itself irrespective of any modulations of absolute entities or horizons. In light of this *Gegentypus* or "antitype" function of the fable, Blumenberg's critique of philosophy might very well be aligned with his critique of myth when it comes to the fable, as the fable's selective stories potentially perforate the grand narratives of both.

Blumenberg's interest in the fable, however, does not end with such basic calls for philosophy to leave its second- or third-degree observer positions to return to the actual metaphysical questions. Blumenberg's "metaphorology" project of the 1960s had proposed that philosophy must begin by understanding its own medium, which he identified to be that of imaginative language and, more specifically, of metaphor. While the project for a "metaphorology" never went far beyond the exemplary analysis of his 1960 *Paradigms for a Metaphorology*, Blumenberg's interest in fables marks a significant return to his earlier attempts to reground philosophy by observing the reliance of thought on language. What is different in regard to metaphorology, however, is that Blumenberg no longer plans or expects the inception of a theoretically defined academic subfield for the history of concepts (*Begriffsgeschichte*). On the contrary, the stories told from the lifeworld are based on the contingencies of life and thus necessarily forgo systematization; Blumenberg envisions no "fabulology" that would inherit his projected "metaphorology."[8] It has been noted that

7. Blumenberg, *Work on Myth*, 132.
8. As is well known, Blumenberg never developed a strict metaphorology further than the initial 1960 *Paradigms*. But unlike his later work on fables, which centers on the *activity* of telling fables, the proposal for a metaphorology implies a final project that would demand an at least somewhat organized *systematization* of metaphors and their reception. This is also hinted at when Blumenberg calls his work in *Paradigms* part of a "typology." See Blumenberg, *Paradigms*, 62–63, 78, 99, 115.

Hans-Georg Gadamer's 1958 rebuttal and Joachim Ritter's categorical 1971 refusal of metaphorology seem to have deeply disappointed Blumenberg, whose project had aimed to initiate a widely practiced critique of philosophical language that should arrive also inside academe.[9] The same aspiration is tangible in the fable project, despite its fundamental critique of existing systematizations. But unlike metaphors or anecdotes, whose study necessarily has to take their respective reception histories into account, philosophizing with fables and fable-type stories ultimately requires no context besides what is always already present in the lifeworld. Instead of theoretically opposing pure theory, Blumenberg projects a mode of thought that is structurally incongruent with the accepted tools and methods of academe. What could be called the strategy of Blumenberg's fable project is to reject academe's alleged expertise about the human in favor of the fables' know-how about life.

Aesop's Secret

The alternative philosophical practice resulting from this attack on academic philosophy is documented by the corpus of fable-related texts Blumenberg published in newspapers and journals throughout the 1980s. After a first phase of writing philosophical and literary essays during the 1950s, the fable texts initiate Blumenberg's second phase of writing for the feuilleton and are announced by the programmatic 1980 essay "Pensiveness," which he published in the *Neue Zürcher Zeitung*. Written after the 1974 essay and before the 1987 book, these texts often combine readings of fables with theoretical remarks about the philosophical and epistemological status of fables.[10]

In one 1985 *Neue Zürcher Zeitung* piece called "Unknown Aesopica: From Newly Found Fables," Blumenberg proposes an even more radical correction to the Thales complex than he would later include in the book. In line with reading the fables against the grain of Western philosophy, he argues that the fable's primary function is the bystander's call to the philosopher for his "return to realism."[11] This human utterance acquires heightened importance

9. Blumenberg, "Thesen zu einer Metaphorologie," "Diskussion zum Vortrag Blumenberg"; Ritter, "Vorwort"; Haverkamp, "Scandal of Metaphorology."

10. Compared to the erudition presented in his books, this other format of publication should perhaps be seen as the format he favored over the book for putting forth new philosophical paradigms. While his late books are themselves mostly compilations of shorter texts on one problem or anecdote, the particular selection of texts makes these books read like treatises. With regard to his idea of metaphorology, one could say that those books appear as the rather solidified surface of his philosophy, whereas the liquid substratum of his antidefinitional thought and style is much more palpable in the over one hundred short pieces on anecdotes and fables he published after 1980.

11. Blumenberg, "Unknown Aesopica," 567.

for the fable genre, Blumenberg explains, because the appearance of human protagonists in the Aesopic canon is rare to begin with. Also, Socrates realized the exception of this configuration, Blumenberg alleges, when he practically destroyed the functionality of the fable with his interpretation. Socrates's coup was to have recognized that the fable about the fallen philosopher contained what Blumenberg calls "the secret of Aesop": "The forefather of all philosophy was also that of all fables."[12] This is the message encoded in the story, and the epistemological status of this very fable, the Thales anecdote, is therefore that of a hyperfable, which provides the argument to understand the quality of knowledge contained in all other fables of Aesop. This realization causes Blumenberg to spell out in more detail his critique of the common practice of philosophical reception. The origin of philosophy, he argues, is at the same time the origin of the Aesopic tale, and vice versa. Socrates understood this secret and sought to eradicate it by suppressing it with another tradition. To prevent exactly this from happening, pre-Socratic fabulistic philosophy had maintained the form of a storytelling folk tradition. Blumenberg hence calls Socrates's and especially Plato's trick the "betraying of the secret of Aesop," since it allowed Plato to insert his teacher and himself into a powerful position in this new order of philosophical lineages: Thales, Socrates, Plato, Diogenes Laertius, and so forth. Against his own interest, Thales was placed as the first named philosopher that replaced the mythical folklore storyteller Aesop. In the interest of founding a genealogy of thinkers since Socrates, Plato deemed Aesop unworthy of initiating such a lineage, as he was not a historically reliable fact and his storytelling unsuited to heralding the dialogical Socratic method and its subsequent generations of schools.

With this fundamental claim, Blumenberg seems to advise his own late modernity to reconnect with the nameless pre-Socratic and non-Socratic fabulistic philosophy that the genealogical dictum had left dormant. Already Immanuel Kant, but also Husserl, had raised doubts about the reliability of the original philosopher Thales. While Kant is not sure "whether he was called *Thales* or had some other name," it is clear for him that the first a priori concepts in mathematics were based on "the happy inspiration of a single man."[13] Husserl, however, solves the paradox of the apparent historicity of the ideal objects of geometry by refusing to ever think again of "such a supposed Thales."[14] Instead, he ascribes a "historical a priori" to ideal objects in the

---

12. Blumenberg, "Unknown Aesopica," 567.
13. Kant, *Critique of Pure Reason*, 107–8.
14. Husserl, "Origin of Geometry," 372.

mind, like those of geometry, which thus always already imply historical tradition once they have been produced in experience. Like Blumenberg's antigenealogical fable project, Husserl eliminates the Kantian necessity of a first Thales-type philosopher whose thoughts would have entered into reception. But unlike Blumenberg, he is still bound to presuming such historicity for philosophy's ideal notions. Blumenberg, however, intends to do away with lineages altogether and has a rather anarchic answer when he proposes storytelling to be the true perennial medium of philosophy. Interestingly, Blumenberg's critique of the origin of Thales corresponds well with Jacques Derrida's 1962 interpretation of Husserl's "Origin of Geometry," which deconstructs the historical a priori as always already requiring the intersubjectivity of a living present and, for that matter, of language for its ideal objects to disappear and reappear throughout history.[15] While Blumenberg does not explicitly connect his critique of the Thales anecdote with Husserl's elimination of Thales, he is structurally reinforcing Husserl's critique of the forgotten origins of ideas in the European sciences and academies. As a result, Blumenberg's revelation of "the secret of Aesop" gestures toward a reversal of Socrates's and Plato's institutionalizing act, namely, Blumenberg demands to eliminate the historical person and their names from the sphere of philosophy altogether. The universal nameless story known as the "fable," not the particular indexical anecdote, conjures up the realism that philosophy persistently needed and needs.[16]

Blumenberg's diachronic study of the Thales anecdote in his 1987 book therefore aims to display the primacy of the fable content, even when it is only the anecdote that seems to be retold. The underlying thesis is that the Aesopic fable has an irreducible presence, which is exhibited in each point of the anecdote's reception. A persistence of a fabulistic philosophy becomes therefore tangible, despite the omnipresent institutionalization of philosophical reception. Whereas the 1974 article was interested in the multifold ways the same anecdote could be retold and underlined its flexibility, the 1987 book is interested in the persistence of the anecdote's recurring stock, as this has a certain congruence with the fable. What is worse is that each person who retold and reinterpreted the story was effectively misled and deluded by Plato's method of naming. It caused them to believe implicitly that their own reception of the Thales anecdote would also add their name into the history of philosophy,

---

15. Derrida, *Edmund Husserl's Origin of Geometry.*
16. Unfortunately, the significance of the difference between fable and anecdote for Blumenberg has so far received scant notice. A few observations are contained in Fleming, "On the Edge of Noncontingency"; and Zill, "Anekdote."

when all they should have been doing was contemplate a fable, that is, to have stayed within philosophy's original medium. The specificity of the fable-turned-anecdote is hence one of a double deception. It not only deceives its receiver of the true origin of philosophy but also prevents the fable from ever taking up again its foundational role for philosophy. Blumenberg's radical recasting of philosophy is deduced from this reconstruction of its misplaced origin in fables. Speaking about a philosophical anecdote or focusing on the moral sentence attached to a fable have been two techniques that erected academic philosophy, but effectively kept any thinker away from wrapping herself in thought, that is, in what a fable would have to say.

Fabulistic Philosophy

Blumenberg's view of this historical originality of the fable is underlaid with more methodological groundwork in "Das Lebensweltmißverständnis" ("The Lifeworld Misunderstanding"), a longer essay from 1986. In it Blumenberg engages with the idea of the lifeworld, Husserl's concept of an imperceptible yet omnipresent background of metaphysical assumption in relation to which all human thought, belief, and culture always already occur. As nothing in the lifeworld can be known directly, Husserl hoped to regain fundamental philosophical questions by finding them via reductions of ideas only implicitly present in the lifeworld. Blumenberg varies this heuristic constraint by suggesting that the lifeworld's lack of expressivity and predication does not preclude it from possessing a form of language. Fable-type stories are expressions of the lifeworld, and, given the decoded beginning of philosophy in Aesop, his claim could be extended to suggest that fables are preliminary forms not only of philosophical anecdotes but also of logical conclusions, moral maxims, even of universals, and perhaps paradigmatic of any form of philosophy.[17] Consequentially, this text, also written during the conception of the 1987 book, contains the most concise programmatic layout of Blumenberg's "fabulistic philosophy," proceeding step by step from pre-Socratic Aesop to Cartesian modernity:

> [The lifeworld] has its stories that might institute pensiveness, but they make thinking as a conditional relationship between question and answer obsolete. To draw a "moral" from a story and attach it to a fable is to us perhaps the sole remaining trace of the transgression of a particular condition [*Überschreitung*

---

17. While Blumenberg did not argue for a "fabulistic world philosophy," he had still criticized Husserl for focusing only on the European traditions. At the same time, folklore studies and non-Western philosophical genealogies, for example, Confucianism, show a much stronger awareness that their beginnings lay in a kind of fabulistic philosophy.

eines Zustandes], namely, when it was obvious [*von selbst zu verstehen*] what was meant by a story. That is why long ago we began to be amused by the inadequacy of inherited moral conclusions and the rich meaning of ancient fables these morals seem to be attached to, like helpless annotations. At some point, transportable sentences were needed that made the story seem superfluous, and then questions to these sentences were needed, to which they could have been given as answers. This procedure might have been shorter and helped save time, since stories always have a degree of circuitousness. But no one could know that the short circuit between question and answer triggered a new and more vast circuitousness, namely, to put all given answers to the same question in competition, to play them off against each other in order to get closer to the distant goal of the exclusiveness of one single valid answer.[18]

At the end of this essay on the lifeworld, Blumenberg presents a morphology of Western philosophy in nuce, which he frames as a history of the decline of philosophizing in fables. He begins with the pre-Socratic, Aesopic fable and ends with the counterpoint of a failed "short circuit" relationship between question and answer that Descartes demanded. This genealogy of philosophy ends with a state in which every response to a question must exist independently of time or place and leaves the philosopher diametrically opposed to the storyteller's here and now. In this hunt for perfect definitions that is reminiscent of a central argument in the introduction to *Paradigms for a Metaphorology*,[19] the philosophical fables have become unreadable and can cause nothing else but laughter: "That is why long ago we began to be amused by the inadequacy of inherited moral conclusions and the rich meaning of ancient fables." Instead of seeking freestanding, straightforward answers, Blumenberg argues that the multitude of questions and answers potentially contained in a fable should be detected and formulated, even if they are self-contradictory.

Blumenberg's idea of a philosophy radiating from fable-type stories is thus a proposition to return to a speculative storytelling practice, which can elicit questions from the realism of any life situation, whether this situation is a historical or the ongoing everyday. As a consequence, his books *Care Crosses the River, The Laughter of the Thracian Woman*, the posthumous

18. Blumenberg, "Das Lebensweltmißverständnis," 67–68 (my translation).

19. Compare the similarity to Blumenberg's depiction of the Cartesian ideal in the *Metaphorology*, which again shows how the "fabulistic philosophy" picks up the central concerns of the earlier project: "In its terminal state, philosophical language would be purely and strictly 'conceptual': everything can be defined, therefore everything must be defined; there is no longer anything logically 'provisional,' just as there is no longer any morale provisoire. From this vantage point, all forms and elements of figurative speech, in the broadest sense of the term, prove to have been makeshifts destined to be superseded by logic" (*Paradigms*, 1–2).

Lions, and arguably *Cave Exits* could be called fable books, because they are exercises for this fabulistic reduction of philosophy. Each is a training ground to study how perennial fables must be discovered beneath the historical anecdotes told of individuals and their deeds. In each subchapter, Blumenberg excavates how the nameless and thus antigenealogical fable behind the respective anecdote has been obscured. As a result, every anecdote, every story told by a philosopher has an unknown sibling, a forgotten predecessor: a nameless story that, however, could never have been transported by citing names and people and therefore did not survive. The return to telling such unknown stories would require suppressing a reception based on authors and citations, but hence would radically require each storyteller to think through such a story before it can be retold, rethought, and thus transmitted to others as a vessel of enacted philosophy.

Sticking to this project and steering clear of established philosophical terminology, Blumenberg proposes "nonunderstanding" (*Unverstand*) and "pensiveness" (*Nachdenklichkeit*) as the two notions that describe the fable's phenomenality in the mind. Both account for the decisive effect that the condition of thinking through fables produces. On the one hand, "nonunderstanding" works as the opposite to "obviousness" (*Selbstverständlichkeit*), the Husserlian term of the pregiven, always already perception of the lifeworld. "Pensiveness," on the other hand, is an idle condition consisting of passive and active knowing, where thinking does occur with interruption, but never on methodical paths. Yet "pensiveness" does not denote the activity of "thinking about something" but describes a mood of an insistent, not-yet-resolvable contemplation that yearns for answers, as implied in the German *Nachdenklichkeit*, which literally means "to retrace something in thought." With both word choices, Blumenberg emphasizes that the mode of thinking he tries to define occurs in the actual lived situation in which one is faced with a fable. In the Socratic tradition of the philosophy of names, this fabulistic situation would have been transmitted by the bystander who retold an anecdote about the historical persons involved. Yet in what Blumenberg outlines, a fabulistic situation must be told as a first-degree story in discussion or in writing. This emergence of thought out of quotidian experiences and stories recalls the embodied efficacy of Archaic Greek prose narratives that has been often associated with the term *ainos*, meaning "word" but also "advice."[20] Blumenberg does not

20. Adrados, "Terminology of the Ancient Fable." See also Scheuer, "Ainos." On the general debate about the genre of the Aesopic fable and its location in the Archaic Greek lifeworld, see Kurke, *Aesopic Conversations.*

seem to rely much on research on fables, but the *ainos* concept provides significant support for his project because it was used for the Aesopic fables before Aristotle's *Rhetoric* changed the Greek term to be *logos*, all but burying the Aesopic tradition on the conceptual level.[21] To write the reception of a fable is therefore, to put it pointedly, to write the history of a particular pensive mood about a particular human incident or situation as storytellers across time have recorded it.

In his "Pensiveness" essay that most succinctly laid out his fabulistic turn in 1980, Blumenberg closely develops a theory or, rather, tells a story about how fables emerge as semantic agents in the world. The here and now of a fable situation is a middle ground that lies within the edges of the lifeworld but outside the edges of self-evident life, as only on this unstable ground is insight given into both. The anecdotes and fables Blumenberg investigates therefore cause narrative frictions within the self-evidence of the lifeworld, as they point to unexpressed contingencies and thus cause *nonunderstanding* and especially *pensiveness* for their readers.[22] Blumenberg outlines these two important poles that mark the emergence of pensive philosophy:

> Humanists and philologists have always been struck by the inadequate or non-existent proportion between these maxims and the stories to which they are assigned. If one has surrendered to the pensiveness that the story induces, then its "moral," the result that is supposedly to be derived from it, is often not only sobering, but dismaying and annoying in its nonunderstanding [*Unverstand*]. Although almost none of the teachings can be declared completely wrong, they are in themselves somewhat peculiar and inexplicably inappropriate.[23]

Here nonunderstanding is the refusal or inability to give oneself over to the fable's pensiveness; "pensiveness is . . . exhibited in the incongruity between the fable and its moral."[24] But at the same time, nonunderstanding is also the reason for turning back to the original fable itself, posing questions to the nonunderstanding left by former commentators.

Among Blumenberg's various shorter pieces about fables is also an article called "Of Nonunderstanding: Glosses on Three Fables," which presents

---

21. Aristotle's *Rhetoric* does not use *ainos* but already uses *logos* as the term for Aesopic stories when he writes, "λόγοι, οἷον οἱ Αἰσώπειοι καὶ Λιβυκοί" (logoi, hoion hoi Aisōpeioi kai Libykoi; fables [*logoi*], such as those of Aesop and the Libyan). Aristotle, *Art of Rhetoric*, 272–73.

22. See Fleming, "On the Edge of Non-contingency."

23. Blumenberg, "Pensiveness," 528.

24. Blumenberg, "Pensiveness," 529.

three brief essays about three fables that are merely concerned with the possible nonunderstanding that their factual (or imagined) commentators have had.[25] Nonunderstanding thus negatively denotes the space between a fable and its possible answers, an incomprehension the fable opens between life and lifeworld that pensiveness can positively occupy. "One of the descriptions of pensiveness," explains Blumenberg, "is that whatever comes to mind is allowed to pass through one's head. Pensiveness is an experience of freedom, especially the freedom of digression." Deeply opposed to this fabulistic pensiveness is systematic thought, unless it invalidates existing answers and leads to perplexity and helplessness. Reminding thought of its need for pensiveness is the only function of ordering your mind, "leading thought back to its origin and base in pensiveness."[26] To illustrate pensiveness, Blumenberg can thus only once more turn to a concrete example, the Aesopic fable *The Old Man and Death* that also includes a human protagonist: "An old man who had travelled a long way with a bundle of sticks found himself so weary that he cast it down and called for Death. Death came straightway at his call and asked him what he wanted. The old man answered, 'Help in loading my burden on my back again.'"[27] This fable represents for Blumenberg "the smallest possible story" (die kleinstmögliche Geschichte), the minimum of a narrative prose form that still causes a maximum of disturbance against the lifeworld. That fables can interrupt and disturb is a programmatic definition, and Blumenberg subsequently develops the term (*Störung*) at length in his writings on the lifeworld, including in the following brief passage that illustrates the phenomenological significance of pensiveness: "Disturbance of the conduct of life remains the incentive for philosophy. If one wants to understand philosophy's emergence from the lifeworld, one has to behold the kind of thinking that occurs in the lifeworld. For example, that which we call the arising of pensiveness."[28] The more compact the fable, the more disturbance and the more pensiveness it can create. Precisely here Blumenberg's text points us to the fable's ability to radiate pensiveness that can in no way be described, summarized, or separated from the act of telling. In this moment, the fable appears as an agent, carrying out something that could be called an act of prose. In this activity, a speaker or listener is addressed by opening up existing questions about the burden of life and the burden of death. The fable can create a high tension toward its possible con-

25. Blumenberg, "Of Nonunderstanding."
26. Blumenberg, "Pensiveness," 527.
27. Blumenberg, "Pensiveness," 528.
28. Blumenberg, "Theorie der Lebenswelt," 61 (my translation).

texts and environments, allowing the listener to associate it with any personal experience currently present in their lifeworld. "We think about where we stand because we were disturbed in not thinking about it" is Blumenberg's minimal description of this emergence of pensiveness out of nonunderstanding.[29]

Blumenberg Rescues Aesop

Finally, Blumenberg's consequence for this alternative philosophy is to write his own variations of fables. His aforementioned newspaper piece "Unknown Aesopica: From Newly Found Fables" contains three short para-fables written in dialogue, in which three animals complain to Aesop about the way his fables misrepresented them. Taking the position of a fictive editor,[30] Blumenberg remains at a distance from the brief tales, which he undoubtedly wrote himself, and thus follows the separation of fables and their author that he had demanded from a "fabulistic philosophy." The mythical Aesop himself appears in these pieces, and Blumenberg therefore gives them an unstable genre definition, calling them "intermediate forms between animal fable and anecdote."[31] They are the perfect fusion of the two genres at stake in Blumenberg's proposal for a fabulistic philosophy, rendering them unfit for any direct reception. Rather, they conjure up the everyday potential for fabulistic philosophy by their location in the ephemeral medium of the newspaper and demand what could be called indirect reception. Both their narrative and medial form add to pensiveness, telling us that we are in a singular fleeting contact with the "inventor" of the fable, performing as it were the origin of philosophy out of the lifeworld of the reader.[32] Additionally, each of the three *complaints* is a self-reflection, allowing the fables to investigate the rise of pensiveness by causing pensiveness about the way fables are written.

The third para-fable, "The Fox's Complaint," is different because the plaintiff uses his wit to speak so thoroughly that his arguments reach beyond

29. Blumenberg, "Pensiveness," 530.

30. The "Postscript" reads: "The Frankfurt publisher to whom I offered these unknown Aesopica declined on the grounds that Aesop was not a German classic" (Blumenberg, "Unknown Aesopica," 570).

31. Blumenberg, "Unknown Aesopica," 567.

32. Almost as a side project to the fable studies, Blumenberg in the late 1980s had begun a series of short newspaper pieces for the *Frankfurter Allgemeine Zeitung*, each of which tried to turn a common concept of daily life such as "emancipation" or "health" into a fabulistic tale about the instability of everyday speech. Like the fable project, these miniatures criticized academic philosophy already with their title "Concepts in Stories" ("Begriffe in Geschichten"), which mocked the philosophical subdiscipline of the history of concepts (*Begriffsgeschichte*) that had rejected Blumenberg's metaphorology in the 1960s. These pieces were posthumously republished in Blumenberg, *Begriffe in Geschichten*.

the limits of the fable, revealing most strikingly—and with a similar interest as the fable of the fallen philosopher—how fables work:

> The Fox, too, complained to Aesop. He made him look ridiculous with all the cleverness he imputed to him. "I am not smarter," the Fox said, "than I need to be in order to survive."
>
> "In return you are preventing others from surviving," Aesop pointed out to him. "Think about the chickens you are stealing."
>
> "They have their own art of survival," the Fox protested. "They have invented the easiest procedure to reproduce—they pursue it while seated."
>
> Aesop did not want to let the Fox get away with that. "You are confusing two things there. The chickens that you feed on can no longer make their kind by sitting. But you live on each time, and even better, meal by meal."
>
> The Fox did not relent. "But for my devouring chickens, the world would be full of chickens, as easy as it is for them to become many."
>
> Aesop took the objection in good grace. "That wouldn't be bad. Then even we slaves would have our daily egg and our chicken on Sundays."
>
> "But," the Fox triumphed, "you could no longer invent fables, because the interpreters and exegetes think they have recognized that your little stories are cryptic outcries of a slave's misery."
>
> From Aesop's own hand we find the addition: Here Aesop was silent. He never told of just how clever he really had to find the Fox to be.[33]

Aesop's own fable creation amuses him so much that he falls silent or, better yet, falls into a pensiveness, less about his own fable than about his own life before the background of his lifeworld. On the formal level of genre, this para-fable actively undoes the two levels of anecdote and fable by collapsing the name-based history of philosophy into ephemerality. On the diegetic level, it provides us with the scene of a double effect. The storyteller is struck by the way his fable points him to the condition of his own storytelling, as we are struck by the fact that this story points us toward how a philosophy of story-telling should and could be developed. We are left with a pensiveness about metapensiveness, that is, with a reduction of presumed anecdotal knowledge to the mere fabulistic disturbance.

As the self-reflexivity of this example underlines, Blumenberg limited publishing such applications of his "fabulistic philosophy" to cases that stand in for their own theory and do not require any second-degree theory. His

33. Blumenberg, "Unknown Aesopica," 569–70. This excerpt is reproduced with permission from Suhrkamp Verlag as well as from Cornell University Press, where this English translation appeared first.

"Unknown Aesopica," or "Pseudo Aesopica," as they are called in his papers at Marbach, are not simply additions to the Aesopic corpus but specifically variations of the original fable turned Thales anecdote. Like the fable about the plummeted contemplator, Blumenberg's three fables of complaint are stories about a fallen philosopher, yet they stay within the Aesopic canon by creating an internal dialogue between Aesop and his animals. Their humor intends to cause exactly the kind of laughter that overcame the bystander in the fable, interrupting the theory caused by a fable. By using the characters from the fable universe as interlocutors, Blumenberg demonstrates how a cascade of fables could be told that continue theoretical thought, and hence a first- or second-degree observation of the world and of life, but that fall in no danger of spinning into third-degree observation in which the reality of the world is no longer accessible. Such newspaper pieces are test runs for a nonacademic philosophy based on storytelling and self-observation.

Together with the underlying fable theory, these three fables appear to be more directly aligned with Blumenberg's own intentions for a philosophical program than his texts on anecdotes. Focusing on his anecdotes, Paul Fleming has argued that for Blumenberg the Thales anecdote points to the margin of lifeworld because "the anecdote of Thales and the Thracian woman concerns not the lifeworld in isolation but the *tension* between lifeworld and theory, between the (non-contingent) 'motivating support' of all theory and the necessary contingency of thought."[34] According to this definition, anecdotes are markers of this metaphysical tension throughout history. Their historical particularity allows research into specific situations of the lifeworld. But as Fleming also remarks, only the anecdote's named characters have ensured its traceability throughout history. As Blumenberg exhibits in *The Laughter of the Thracian Woman*, however, this practice is by definition limited to historical work. In light of the ahistorical and proactive fable project, the various corpora of anecdote studies Blumenberg produced therefore have to be understood as preparatory explorations of the persistence of fable stock. Beneath each of his readings of specific anecdotal situations, there is a fable that all anecdote appearances have in common. Such reappearing fable stocks are, for example, the theorist's fall, the contemplation of the skies, the philosopher's quotidian temptations, or the faith of the natural scientist. Many, if not all, of Blumenberg's historical archaeologies of everyday situations, whether these can be already called "anecdotes" or not, are interested in extracting such implicit statements about the margins of the lifeworld, that is, about the tensions of theory and real-

---

34. Fleming, "On the Edge of Non-contingency," 30.

ity, and must effectively be understood as archaeological expeditions aiming to unearth prototypical fable-type situations. With Aesop defunct for millennia, storytellers could tell new fables only in disguise of anecdote lineages. The fact that *The Laughter of the Thracian Woman* reads like "paradigms to an anecdotology," as Fleming characterized it, that is, as a preparation for his many other texts on anecdotes, must be thus countered with the question of whether Blumenberg was not ultimately interested in overcoming anecdotes. His archaeologies of anecdotal parables from the lifeworld are, rather, excavations of the fables always already active as the blueprint of anecdotes.

A final clarification about the relation between anecdote and fable can be drawn by comparing Blumenberg's 1980s work with his historical readings of metaphors. In the metaphorology, the ultimate goal was not limited to writing more and ever more metaphorologies of new metaphors, but the project's systematic critique was aimed at enhancing the academic philosophical practice of concepts with a sensibility for philosophy's own language. Already in his 1947 essay "The Linguistic Reality of Philosophy" as well as in his 1950 habilitation, Blumenberg pressed philosophers to make use of the full poetic range of language when theorizing, demanding that the "plasticity"[35] of words be taken into account before they congeal into technical terminologies. "Doing metaphorology" is hence not the ultimate goal of metaphorology but only the method to prepare another philosophy that can consciously behave with and make use of its metaphoricity. In the same vein, an "anecdotology" or "fabulology" is not Blumenberg's ultimate goal, but his theory of fables is only the preparation to regain another mode of philosophical storytelling by making use of the specific language of the lifeworld.

In terms of quantity, of course, Blumenberg's three para-fables and their accompanying essays are seemingly no match for his extensive corpus of anecdote studies on Goethe, Theodor Fontane, Friedrich Hebbel, Ludwig Wittgenstein, Thomas Mann, Heidegger, Ernst Jünger, and others, which amount to a few hundred different readings in freestanding texts and within larger works. Despite what some of the posthumous editions of these anecdotes suggest, such as the books on Goethe, Fontane, or Jünger, Blumenberg did not write anecdotes with the individuals in mind who experienced them. It was less an alleged intellectual brilliance than their writerly output that caused these individuals' everyday actions and utterances to become recorded in anecdotes by themselves and by others. For Blumenberg, these anecdotes are interesting not as insightful biographical episodes of their subjects or collections of bon mots

35. Blumenberg, *Die ontologische Distanz*, 10c (my translation).

but as archives of fable-type stories. They were recorded as stories because they had incited disturbance between a particularly well-documented reality of an intellectual and this individual's latent lifeworld. Given Blumenberg's fabulistic program, his anecdote corpus must, rather, be understood to be organized by the recurrences of specific fable stock, such as the editors of the two posthumous volumes *The Completeness of the Stars* or *Lions* have realized.[36] What underlies this programmatic attempt to shift the mode of philosophy is that Blumenberg aimed to take philosophers to a specific pensive form of thought, one that is "leading thought back to its origin and base in pensiveness, the terrain from which it took leave, but to which it must also always return."[37] As Philipp Stoellger has explained, this means that for Blumenberg thought in its origin is related to pensiveness, and so "Blumenberg's pensiveness about 'pensiveness' intends to regain this relation [of thought]."[38] In the "Pensiveness" essay, Blumenberg merely provides once more the program for this thought and takes his readers through one Aesopic fable to perform exemplarily what this shift from theory to diegetic storytelling would look like. In the later *Neue Zürcher Zeitung* fables, however, he is no longer demonstrating but takes the first steps toward this new philosophy of fables, leading the way to an anti-academic, antireceptionist philosophy that would be based solely on storytelling and pensive thought.

Like many proposed radical philosophical turns, Blumenberg's preparation of a "fabulistic philosophy" never reached the length of a book, despite the existence of a thin folder in his estate at the German Literary Archive in Marbach titled "Fables without Animals" ("Fabeln ohne Tiere"). One possible reason may be the impossibility of a systematic fabulology; fabulistic philosophy is always already at work. To follow his own premise that fable philosophers must be unnamable would also have meant that Blumenberg had to have published all such fables and possible meta-fables under a pseudonym, as he did for the three fables in the *Neue Zürcher Zeitung*. Rather than looking for reasons why there is no fable book by Blumenberg, it seems more consequential to declare his anecdote studies as the convolutes from which a fable book could be compiled or, rather, in which it still lies dormant. With the rule of anonymity in mind, we can understand those anecdote studies as camouflages of "fabulistic philosophies" that need not declare whether they have an author. Masked by a reader of anecdotes who calls himself "Hans Blumenberg," an unknown,

36. Blumenberg, *Die Vollzähligkeit der Sterne*; Blumenberg, *Lions*.
37. Blumenberg, "Pensiveness."
38. Stoellger, *Metapher und Lebenswelt*, 333 (my translation).

unnamed thinker of the fabulistic a priori of anecdotes can be observed underneath these convolutes. By following this alleged "Hans Blumenberg," the reader of these presumed anecdotologies is thrown into a pensiveness about revealing further "unknown Aesopica" at the substratum of the history of philosophy.

Florian Fuchs is a postdoctoral researcher in German and comparative literature.

References

Adelson, Leslie. *Cosmic Miniatures and the Future Sense*. Berlin: de Gruyter, 2018.

Adrados, Francisco Rodríguez. "Terminology of the Ancient Fable." In *History of the Graeco-Latin Fable*, 3–47. Leiden: Brill, 1999.

Aristotle. *The Art of Rhetoric*, translated by J. H. Freese. New York: Putnam's Sons, 1926.

Blumenberg, Hans. *Begriffe in Geschichten*. Frankfurt am Main: Suhrkamp, 1998.

Blumenberg, Hans. "Das Lebensweltmißverständnis." In *Lebenszeit und Weltzeit*, 7–68. Frankfurt am Main: Suhrkamp, 1986.

Blumenberg, Hans. "Der Sturz des Protophilosophen: Zur Komik der reinen Theorie— anhand einer Rezeptionsgeschichte der Thales-Anekdote." In *Das Komische*, edited by Wolfgang Preisendanz and Rainer Warning, 11–64. Munich: Fink, 1976.

Blumenberg, Hans. "Die ontologische Distanz: Eine Untersuchung über die Krisis der Phänomenologie Husserls." Habilitationsschrift, University of Kiel, 1950.

Blumenberg, Hans. *Die Vollzähligkeit der Sterne*. Frankfurt am Main: Suhrkamp, 1997.

Blumenberg, Hans. *The Laughter of the Thracian Woman: A Protohistory of Theory*, translated by Spencer Hawkins. New York: Bloomsbury, 2015.

Blumenberg, Hans. *Lions*, translated by Kári Driscoll. London: Seagull, 2018.

Blumenberg, Hans. "Of Nonunderstanding: Glosses on Three Fables," translated by Florian Fuchs. In *History, Metaphors, Fables: A Hans Blumenberg Reader*, edited by Hannes Bajohr, Florian Fuchs, and Joe Paul Kroll, 562–65. Ithaca, NY: Cornell University Press, 2020.

Blumenberg, Hans. "On a Lineage of the Idea of Progress." *Social Research* 41, no. 1 (1974): 5–27.

Blumenberg, Hans. *Paradigms for a Metaphorology*, translated by Robert Savage. Ithaca, NY: Cornell University Press, 2010.

Blumenberg, Hans. "Pensiveness," translated by David Adams. In *History, Metaphors, Fables: A Hans Blumenberg Reader*, edited by Hannes Bajohr, Florian Fuchs, and Joe Paul Kroll, 525–30. Ithaca, NY: Cornell University Press 2020.

Blumenberg, Hans. *Shipwreck with Spectator: Paradigm of a Metaphor for Existence*, translated by Steven Rendall. Cambridge, MA: MIT Press, 1997.

Blumenberg, Hans. "Theorie der Lebenswelt." In *Theorie der Lebenswelt*, by Hans Blumenberg, edited by Manfred Sommer, 7–108. Berlin: Suhrkamp, 2010.

Blumenberg, Hans. "Thesen zu einer Metaphorologie" and "Diskussion zum Vortrag Blumenberg." In "Begriffsgeschichte Institutionell: Die Senatskommission für Begriffsgeschichte der DFG (1956–1966)," edited by Margarita Kranz. *Archiv für Begriffsgeschichte* 54 (2011): 186–89, 189–93.

Blumenberg, Hans. "Unknown Aesopica: From Newly Found Fables," translated by Florian Fuchs. In *History, Metaphors, Fables: A Hans Blumenberg Reader*, edited by Hannes Bajohr, Florian Fuchs, and Joe Paul Kroll, 566–70. Ithaca, NY: Cornell University Press, 2020.

Blumenberg, Hans. *Work on Myth*, translated by Robert M. Wallace. Cambridge, MA: MIT Press, 1985.

Derrida, Jacques. *Edmund Husserl's Origin of Geometry: An Introduction*, translated by John P. Leavey Jr. Lincoln: University of Nebraska Press, 1989.

Fleming, Paul. "On the Edge of Non-contingency." *Telos*, no. 158 (2012): 21–35.

Haverkamp, Anselm. "The Scandal of Metaphorology." *Telos*, no. 158 (2012): 37–58.

Husserl, Edmund. "The Origin of Geometry." In *The Crisis of European Sciences and Transcendental Phenomenology*, 353–78. Evanston, IL: Northwestern University Press, 1970.

Kant, Immanuel. *Critique of Pure Reason*, translated by Paul Guyer and Allen W. Wood. Cambridge: Cambridge University Press, 1998.

Kurke, Leslie. *Aesopic Conversations: Popular Tradition, Cultural Dialogue, and the Invention of Greek Prose*. Princeton, NJ: Princeton University Press, 2011.

Ritter, Joachim. "Vorwort." In vol. 1 of *Historisches Wörterbuch der Philosophie*, vii–ix. Darmstadt: Wissenschaftliche Buchgesellschaft, 1971.

Scheuer, Hans Jürgen. "Ainos." In vol. 1 of *Historisches Wörterbuch der Rhetorik*, 295–98. Basel: Francke, 1992.

Stoellger, Philipp. *Metapher und Lebenswelt: Hans Blumenbergs Metaphorologie als Lebenswelthermeneutik und ihr religionsphänomenologischer Horizont*. Tübingen: Siebeck, 2000.

Zill, Rüdiger. "Anekdote." In *Blumenberg lesen: Ein Glossar*, edited by Robert Buch and Daniel Weidner, 26–42. Berlin: Suhrkamp, 2014.

No More Than Seeing:
Hans Blumenberg's Poetics of Spectatorship

Daniela K. Helbig

Only one university visitor had made it all the way out to his writing "den" in Altenberge near Münster, and duly paid the price by passing away a week later—or so Hans Blumenberg informed Hans Robert Jauss, who had been his fellow founding member of the working group Poetics and Hermeneutics (P&H) many years earlier. Jauss would have to take a taxi both ways, since Blumenberg had given up driving. But should Jauss still fail to be deterred from attempting to visit him, Blumenberg will expect him for afternoon coffee the following Monday, even though this will require Blumenberg to set an alarm, something he had "never done since becoming an emeritus; after all, I sleep during the day and mess about typing at night."[1] Blumenberg was an ostentatious recluse, as his letter to Jauss illustrates. He kept a determined distance from academic as much as social engagements—yet, as Julia Amslinger has pointed out, the "Blumenberg myth" of the secular eremite is the product of careful self-stylization.[2] The public image of the recluse has its theoretical counterpart in the figure of the spectator, practicing the "art of keeping out":

I thank Hannes Bajohr, Isabel Gabel, Lily Huang, and the anonymous reviewers for excellent editorial suggestions.

1. Blumenberg to Jauss, May 11, 1987, quoted in Amslinger, *Eine neue Form von Akademie*, 45. All translations are mine unless otherwise noted.

2. Amslinger, *Eine neue Form von Akademie*, 45–46.

New German Critique 145, Vol. 49, No. 1, February 2022
DOI 10.1215/0094033X-9439685   © 2022 by New German Critique, Inc.

one of Blumenberg's lifelong themes.[3] From his cosmological to his anthropological writings, Blumenberg discusses the implications of the distanced, spectatorial position as "one of philosophy's leading tasks," as Melanie Möller puts it.[4] In contrast to the marketable appeal of Blumenberg's image of the recluse, his philosophical spectatorship has not been without criticism, raising the question whether his retreat to an observer position indicates that Blumenberg deemed himself above the need for dialogue or critique.[5]

In what follows, my focus is on Blumenberg's construal of his spectatorial role as an attempt to navigate the challenges he faced, and the strategies he embraced in finding his institutional and intellectual voice in postwar German academe. While Blumenberg refused to practice philosophy as political engagement, his early work with P&H was an attempt at finding ways to do philosophy after 1945, as Anselm Haverkamp has argued.[6] In tracing Blumenberg's figure of the spectator back to his early years with P&H from 1963 on, I seek to follow—indirectly rather than by chronologically reconstructing the development of Blumenberg's thought—the fate of his ambitious attempt to establish a "new practice of scholarship in the postwar wake of an entirely corrupted academic generation."[7] Above all, it is the legacy of Blumenberg's discussion of what is "real"—in his pragmatic sense of effective, *wirksam*—that remains discernible in his spectatorship, on display in his later writings from the margins of academic philosophy. Blumenberg's very own "practice of theory" in the opening volume of P&H not only introduces this concept of reality that proved formative for much of his later work but, in the form of a "bi-level text" containing extensive footnotes, also sets that conceptual move against the group's shared discourse and against "layers of sedimented knowledge"—both to be articulated as the conditions for his own text's actuality, a performance of theory as a "self-thematizing, dialogical procedure."[8]

To the extent that P&H's collective practices were directed "against the authoritarian quality of . . . academic discourses,"[9] Blumenberg had abandoned his hopes for their sustainability alongside his expectations for their intellectual merits by 1976, when he left the group for good, having already

3. The phrase is Blumenberg's. See also Meyer, "Hans Blumenberg, oder: Die Kunst, sich heraus-zuhalten," discussing Blumenberg's withdrawal from the public.

4. Möller, "Zuschauer," 379.

5. Möller, "Zuschauer," 394.

6. Haverkamp, "Nothing Fails Like Success"; see also Haverkamp, "Das Skandalon," 187–88.

7. Haverkamp, "Nothing Fails Like Success," 1224.

8. Haverkamp, "Nothing Fails Like Success," 1222, 1230–32.

9. Haverkamp, "Nothing Fails Like Success," 1227.

withdrawn from its editorial circle in 1967. He had equally abandoned his commitment to philosophy's pedagogical mission. Still insisting in 1961 that "education [*Bildung*] is essentially non-seducibility," by the 1980s he ironicizes any attempt to "align oneself with the Enlightenment's rearguard."[10] His characterizations of philosophy later in his life are notoriously low-key. "Philosophy is the purest expression of one of those disciplines that, even on the pretext of higher and highest aspirations, eventually 'only' serve the goal of increasing and sharpening attentiveness."[11] In another variation on phenomenology's theme, Blumenberg's philosophizing is aimed at "seeing more, no more than seeing."[12] But this social and theoretical retreat to a spectatorial position does not mark the abandonment of Blumenberg's early attempt at probing the possibility of renewing philosophical practice in postwar Germany. The figure of the *theoros*, the spectator, absorbs the ambition of bringing textual actuality into view. If no longer in the social reorganization of the practice of theory, Blumenberg's spectatorship still places hope in the text as the site of always historically conditioned actuality.

Writing therefore turns out to be at the core of Blumenberg's spectatorship. I take as my point of departure the material processes of text production, a very literal sense of poiesis. P&H's collectivization of its writing and publication processes became a reason for Blumenberg's growing discontent with and eventual departure from the group. In the demonstrative solitude of his private writing den, he relied on an elaborate and idiosyncratic set of text production processes (that have since intrigued numerous commentators).[13] Tongue in cheek but not insincerely, Blumenberg's reflections on these processes portray them as the practical equivalent of his theoretical insistence on the historicized preconditions for text making in terms of poetics. At the same time, they are a playful yet important part of his demarcation against another keen theoretician of writing processes: Martin Heidegger, who embodies Blumenberg's figure of the politically and intellectually compromised thinker like no other of his contemporaries.[14] In parallel to his conceptual work on poetics, in particular the concept of reality as an alternative to Heidegger's notion of

---

10. Blumenberg quoted in Müller, *Sorge um die Vernunft*, 334; Blumenberg, *Die Verführbarkeit*, 138 (hereafter cited as *V*).

11. Blumenberg, *Zu den Sachen und zurück*, 190.

12. Blumenberg, *Zu den Sachen und zurück*, 350.

13. See, e.g., Bülow and Krusche, "Nachrichten"; Krauthausen, "Hans Blumenbergs präparierter Valéry"; Voller, "Die Erfindung"; and Helbig, "Life without Toothache."

14. For a recent, brief overview of Blumenberg's lifelong confrontation with Heidegger, see Müller, "Martin Heideggers Verführbarkeit."

Being, Blumenberg's historicization of material text production is a sarcastic take on Heidegger's stylization of the pen, or more literally the quill (*Feder*), as an essential marker of thinking. In pointed contrast, Blumenberg's historical rather than authorial poetics emphasizes the historicized constraints on the spectator who writes.

Blumenberg's insistence on the historicization of the conceptual as well as material prerequisites for text production stems from his early work with P&H, and I turn next to the importance of the pragmatic aspect of his concept of reality for the notion of the spectator. This aspect allows Blumenberg to distinguish his notion of spectatorship, developed from his 1979 *Shipwreck with Spectator*, from Edmund Husserl's phenomenological removal of the spectator from the world-being-watched. While Blumenberg's spectator maintains a distance from the "lifeworld"—that complex concept he inherited from Husserl— he nevertheless remains engaged in that world to some degree. Charged with the task of rendering the elusive "real" sayable, the spectator must deal with rich, messy, historicized detail. Quite practically, Blumenberg's spectator reads and writes to combine the privilege of a distanced position with the world saturation Blumenberg demands of a realistic philosophy; in turn, Blumenberg's spectatorial writing performs the act of bringing into view the "real" via engagement with facticity.

On the other hand, Blumenberg's figure of the spectator is clearly demarcated from understandings of philosophy *as* action, such as that announced publicly in Heidegger's 1933 rectoral address at the University of Freiburg.[15] In his *Genesis of the Copernican World*, Blumenberg chose a loaded term to problematize the "confusion between theory and practice": the "theoretician as perpetrator." As he sums it up, the confusion is a result of the misguided hope that "theory, if indeed it cannot be practical, might at least be an assurance of the possible effects of thought on action."[16] Blumenberg does not deem Heidegger's endorsement of the thinker as perpetrator worthy of explicit critique. But in his numerous short texts on Heidegger, and on the legacy of National Socialism for German philosophy more broadly, he denounces Heidegger's

15. Heidegger's reconfiguration of the relation between theory and practice "in such a way that philosophy is essential action [*wesentliches Handeln*] with the aim of enabling human action as it is required by the historical situation" has been the crucial element in the attempt to reconstruct not just his choice to take political action in 1933 but also the relation between his thinking and his politics beyond the *Rektorat* (Heinz, "Politisierung der Philosophie," 270). On Heidegger's postwar performance of this boundary elision, see Love and Meng, "Political Myths of Martin Heidegger"; and Helbig, "Denktagebücher?"

16. Blumenberg, *Genesis*, 289.

esoteric language as a pose that caricatures the effects of thought on action. As this essay's concluding section shows, this sharp critique delineates Blumenberg's spectatorial task of seeing text as effective—*wirksam* in the poetic sense of reflecting and generating new realities—from Heidegger's fateful caricature of thought as action. In his analysis of philosophical language, Blumenberg makes the most immediately political case for the lasting "necessity of the spectator."[17]

Handiwork? Heidegger's and Blumenberg's Solitary Writing

Blumenberg's retreat to the "den" that was his office near Münster, where he held a professorial appointment from 1970, was also a return to writing as a determinedly solitary act, as opposed to P&H's collective approach to text production. This approach was ambitious in its expectation of all group members to contribute the bulk of their individual work to the joint effort. Long colloquia required participants' attendance at all sessions for the discussion of precirculated texts. P&H's output, the famed *Sammelbände*, were the results of "endless conversations" stretching from colloquia into extensive exchanges of drafts and redrafts, relying on the equipment and staff of "professorial writing offices"—filing systems, typewriters, secretaries.[18] Individual contributions to the *Sammelbände* were complemented by a record of discussion contributions. As Amslinger has shown in her exemplary study of P&H, Blumenberg's aversion to the group's rigid organizational practices—which he placed explicitly in the context of National Socialist forms of labor organization—and the effective disappearance of individual authors' distinct voices in the group's collective publications were important factors in his decision to leave.[19]

At the center of the elaborate text production system that made possible Blumenberg's return to writing alone was his *Zettelkasten*, the slip-card box of roughly thirty thousand entries that he had kept since being expelled from university as a "half-Jew" under the National Socialist Nuremberg laws in 1941. Blumenberg had encountered the slip-card system as a logistical tool during his wartime labor for the respirator manufacturer Dräger, and subsequently adapted it to his own purposes by combining it with another piece of twentieth-century office equipment: a dictation machine.[20] The reluctant writer Blumen-

---

17. Blumenberg, *Ein mögliches Selbstverständnis*, 107 (hereafter cited as *MS*).

18. Amslinger, *Eine neue Form von Akademie*, 153; the chapter's title is "Dauergespräch."

19. Amslinger, *Eine neue Form von Akademie*, 43, 156, 218. On the theoretical controversies preceding Blumenberg's departure, see Müller, "Subtile Stiche."

20. Amslinger, *Eine neue Form von Akademie*, 92–96. On the history of slip-card boxes, see Krajewski, *Paper Machines*.

berg recorded his voice on his Grundig Stenorette instead of having to enter university premises during secretaries' working hours, and mailed in the tapes for their content to be typed up in his absence. If solitary writing was part of the initial appeal of distancing himself from P&H, Blumenberg's lifelong attention to writing processes and writing machinery speaks to their lasting importance not just for publicly staging his disengagement but also for spelling out the complexity of the figure of the spectator as entailing more than simply keeping apart. Blumenberg emphasizes the preconditions for text to appear on the page: the historicity of writing machinery, and the changing social conventions that structure text making. This is a parallel to his conceptual work in poetics, and one that Blumenberg retrospectively places in contrast with Heidegger's stylization of handwriting into a voice of Being. Let me turn to Heidegger briefly to bring out the contrast, before I come back to Blumenberg's historical rather than authorial poetics of writing tools.

As "the purest thinker of the West," Heidegger argues in his lectures on *What Is Called Thinking*, Socrates did not write anything: "Anyone who begins to write out of thoughtfulness must inevitably be like those people who seek refuge from any draft too strong for them." No such fugitive, Heidegger's Socrates did nothing but "place himself into this draft, this current" of "what withdraws"—and "whenever a man is properly drawing that way, he is thinking." But for the fugitives that "all great Western thinkers after Socrates" had to become, the question was not if but rather how they ended up writing: what tools they chose, what literary form they adopted.[21] The question of the material and formal modes of writing preoccupied Heidegger throughout his lifetime. While he continued to experiment with the forms of intellectual composition, his commitment to a single acceptable material mode of text production remained: putting pen to paper.[22] He liked to be pictured pen in hand, as Jacques Derrida noted in his analysis of the "long maneuver that makes of the *path of thinking* and of the question of the sense of Being a long and continuous meditation *of/on* the hand."[23] Heidegger's lifelong practice of handwriting makes its most prominent appearance in *Being and Time* to introduce the vocabulary of ready-to-handness and present-at-handness as modes of being. Quill, ink pot, paper are what first come into the writer's view as he looks up from his desk to develop the notion of equipment, *Zeug*.[24] More than mere illustration, writing equipment plays a "paradigmatic role . . . for the analysis

21. Heidegger, *What Is Called Thinking?*, 17, 26.
22. On Heidegger's experiments with style, see Flatscher, *Logos und Lethe*, 336–85.
23. Derrida, *Geschlecht II*, 177.
24. Heidegger, *Being and Time*, 97.

of equipment," as Michael Schödlbauer sums it up.[25] Set apart by its semiotic character, writing equipment provides an "ontological clue for characterizing any entity whatsoever" in Heidegger's early work.[26]

The reflection on writing equipment continued to inform Heidegger's transition from "metaphysics" to the "history of being." The locus classicus for his attack on the typewriter—or, in Heidegger's words, his discussion of "the modern relation (transformed by the typewriter) of the hand to writing, i.e., to the word, i.e., to the unconcealedness of Being"—are the 1942/43 Parmenides lectures.[27] Having asserted an essential connection between hand and word in his discussion of "action" (*P*, 80), Heidegger's exposition slips within an instant to the manifestation of this connection in writing—and not just an abstract idea of writing, but specifically handwriting as opposed to the use of a typewriter:

> The hand sprang forth only out of the word and together with the word. Man does not "have" hands, but the hand holds the essence of man, because the word as the essential realm of the hand is the ground of the essence of man. The word as what is inscribed and what appears to the regard is the written word, i.e., script. And the word as script is handwriting. It is not accidental that modern man writes "with" the typewriter and "dictates" [*diktiert*] (the same word as "poetize" [*Dichten*]) "into" a machine. This "history" of the kinds of writing is one of the main reasons for the increasing destruction of the word. (*P*, 80–81)

As Schödlbauer argues, Heidegger stylizes the typewriter as the "prototype of the logic of the *Gestell*," his later term for modern technology's demands.[28] In the Parmenides lectures, the typewriter embodies the "irruption of the mechanism in the realm of the word" prefigured in the printing press and its mechanisms of typesetting; it "veils the essence of writing and of the script" (*P*, 85). Effortlessly transporting ancient Greek clouds to modern offices, Heidegger refers to an image from Pindar to describe the typewriter as a "signless cloud of concealment" (*P*, 79). Where Pindar's cloud hides the sky's brightness, the signless cloud of the typewriter, obtrusive as the piece of desktop machinery may be, hides the transformation it allegedly brings about in the "relation of Being to man" (*P*, 85). Where handwriting enacts a relation of Being on the "way toward the unconcealed" (*P*, 79), the use of a typewriter is a sure

25. Schödlbauer, "Diktat," 107.
26. Heidegger, *Being and Time*, 107–8.
27. Heidegger, *Parmenides*, 85 (hereafter cited as *P*).
28. Schödlbauer, "Diktat," 114.

sign of having been led astray: "Writing, from its originating essence, is hand-writing. . . . Being, word, gathering, writing denote an original essential nexus, to which the indicating-writing hand belongs. In handwriting the relation of Being to man, namely the word, is inscribed in beings themselves. The origin and the way of dealing with writing is already in itself a decision about the rela-tion of Being and of the word to man" (*P*, 85). For Heidegger, the typewriter marks an important transformation in the history of the relation of Being to man: the "decision" to withdraw from being. The ubiquitous use of the type-writer appears as a sign of humanity's having chosen a path that is inadequate for relating to Being in its "unconcealedness."

Blumenberg is unconvinced, and uses typewriter and dictation machine to make that clear. Sprinklings of disagreement are scattered across his texts; an example is Socrates the nonwriter, who figures frequently in humorous asides. Xanthippe would have been exasperated with her husband's slackness; the length of Plato's written dialogues is only excusable because it reflects the amount of time left to Socrates to speak (*MS*, 84). In a brief text from the 1980s, "The Seated Blacksmith and Other Thinker Poses," dense despite its jocular tone, Blumenberg counters Heidegger's essentialization of handwrit-ing with a historicization of writing practices. Neither mentioning Heidegger by name nor deigning to enter into any engagement with Heidegger's own alleged relation with Being, Blumenberg's focus is firmly on the materiality of writing tools and text-making processes.

The argument is framed by a deliberation on the "tedious work on self-stylization" (*V*, 147). Blumenberg's opening question is whether to portray himself as working "under the burden of obligation" or instead in the "delight of prowess" (*V*, 147). This distinction echoes his early work on poetics, where the "alternative between inspiration and perspiration [*Anstrengung*]" informed Blumenberg's investigation of the function of poetic language: Does a text betray its author's reliance on the pregiven, inner workings of language, or instead an effort or struggle against linguistic limitation?[29] Here Blumenberg aligns the choice of text-making tools with a historicization of the question of whether thinking amounts to "labor." He starts out by asserting the need, as an aging writer, to hurry and complete the work of self-stylization, since

> the moment is fast approaching when the quill shall be taken from his hand. The quill? That is just the beginning of the embarrassments of assembling one's self-portrait. Is it permissible to admit to having been weaned from the

29. Blumenberg, "Speech Situation," 453 (hereafter cited as SS).

quill long ago, not to write by one's own hand anymore, but to leave the writing to others? For this writer, the last bit of handiwork in the literal sense has gone missing. (*V*, 147)

From this opening dismissal of the essential role of handwriting, Blumenberg moves to dismantle the Heideggerian figure of Socrates the nonwriter. Thirty-five-year-old Immanuel Kant, he observes, was lucky still to be in the early stages of his career when he messed up his self-stylization metaphor in portraying himself as "seated at the anvil of [his] lectern, the heavy hammer of lectures in hand" (*V*, 148). No matter how venerable the figure of the blacksmith pounding the anvil, having him sit down ruins the attempt at conveying how hard the job at hand is. But more important, the rhetorical move of highlighting the laborious effort of philosophical work would have been unacceptable at the time of "the origins of philosophy":

> The sage of antiquity couldn't have claimed that it was labor he was doing with his head and had written up afterwards—for there tended to be a slave available for the tedious process of scripting [*Schreiberei*], except for Socrates, who didn't put anything on the page, busy as he was asking questions. Writing in one's own hand appears to be a mere episode between the wiser epochs of leaving the writing to others. It's just that today's philosopher, were he to reach the surprising insight that what he is doing isn't labor, would have to hide it. After all, one of the last founders of a philosophical school prescribed not just labor but "infinite labor"—except no one could be bothered doing it, given the timely alternative offer of more comfortably waiting out one's time with Being. (*V*, 148)

Against Heidegger's anchoring of hand- versus typewriting in a history of Being, Blumenberg gestures at the social history of writing practices to explain the choice of putting pen to paper oneself.[30] Choosing Husserl, the eager stenographer and founder of the phenomenological school, as his example of a twentieth-century position on the historicized association of philosophizing with labor creates the opportunity for the brief remark on Heidegger's notion of Being as actually stifling such labor.

Turning to his own text production tools, Blumenberg's miniature portrait of the dictation machine absorbs a long history of theory as well as the stereotypical postwar scene of social text production—dictation to a female secretary:

---

30. Sandro Zanetti notes that "the history of writing . . . has primarily been a history of dictation and copying from antiquity into the Middle Ages and modernity" ("Logiken und Praktiken der Schreibkultur," 79).

> The little black box, easily slid into a coat pocket to take along on lonely tracks [*Feldwegen oder Holzwegen*, not missing a chance for further sarcasm for Heidegger], is of harmless appearance: tinny, cheap, disposable. But once its red light is blinking, it turns into a lurking monster. Technology has physiognomically transformed something that already had archaic traits: the secretary with the shorthand pad in her lap, sharpened pencil ready to go, gaze fixed on the thinker's sparsely acting mouth. The longer the thought's stagnation, the more closely the lady's traits begin to resemble the empathetic mockery of the Thracian woman in the *Ur*-scene of theory back in Miletus. Prior to this technological intervention, how much text was dictated for the sole purpose of turning this gaze away and steering it toward the paper? To transform the leniently patient expression into the embarrassed determination to keep up with the moderate speed of thought, relying on the standard number of syllables per minute required to graduate from secretary training. All of this has been transferred to the formalised impatience with the handy *Gestell*. (*V*, 148–49)

The solitary dictation scene still bears traces of the configuration of social text production that it once was. In contrast to Heidegger's manifestation of essential action through the writing hand, the text production process as described by Blumenberg is richly culturally determined. Like the framing alternative of burden or prowess, his emphasis on the historically changing preconditions for producing a text points toward his early work on poetics, where Blumenberg set his historicized concept of reality against Heidegger's notion of Being.

That work—to which I return in the next section—thematized the conceptual prerequisites for the historical emergence of the novel as a literary form. In contrast to an authorial poetics concerned with individual text production processes and principles, Blumenberg's historical poetics aims at conceptual changes that fall outside an individual author's control; thus, the emergence of the novel is predicated on a distinctive change in the concept of reality.[31] In "The Seated Blacksmith" many years later, Blumenberg's focus is on the historicity of material and social writing processes that prefigure a text's constitution. Despite its ironic take on self-portrayal, Blumenberg's text refuses to restrict the discussion of his writing tools of choice to a solely individual

31. Petra Gehring highlights the unusualness of Blumenberg's approach in philosophical terms ("Wirklichkeit," 70). As Haverkamp points out, Blumenberg's concepts of reality can be read to function as historical a prioris ("Nothing Fails Like Success," 1234; see also "Das Skandalon," 197). Blumenberg does not use the term, but his approach could be compared with historical poetics, a critical tradition originating in nineteenth-century Russian scholarship that examines a text's constructive principles—above all, genre—that are beyond authorial control and takes these principles to be historicized and formative of history (Kliger and Maslov, "Introducing Historical Poetics," 15).

matter. A concrete and material aspect of authorial poetics, this choice is subsumed under the historicization of those writing tools and the social conventions of their use. This historical rather than authorial dimension of Blumenberg's poetics is as central to his reflections on his writing machinery as it is to his work on literary genre, and marks his acknowledgment of any writer's historically conditioned position. While there is plenty of room for individual authorial choice in Blumenberg's reflections on the social recluse's text production—whether it is picking a topic, or a Stenorette over a pen—his emphasis is on the space for that choice spanned by historically changing social and material writing conventions.

While Blumenberg maintains the staged indecision between "burden" and "prowess" throughout "The Seated Blacksmith," his concluding claim highlights the hermeneutical advantages of the "epoch of dictation" for solitary text makers like himself (*V*, 151): the technical innovation of the dictation machine enables a form of writing alone that does not amount to a soliloquy lacking the critical potential of interpersonal exchange about the text. The foil for this point is no longer the secretary—who, in Blumenberg's enactment of postwar social stereotypes, is not given any credit in the formation of thought beyond the role of provoking further "mouth action"—but the collective production process of P&H. Dictation, Blumenberg argues, not only turns writers into their own first listener but, more significantly, also turns writers into their own first reader. Crucially, this implies a delay. The term *delay, Verzögerung*, for all its theoretical importance in Blumenberg's work on rhetoric and anthropology, has an eminently practical meaning here.[32] Text dictated to a tape recorder appears before the writer's eyes for the first time only a considerable while later, having been typed up by the secretary and returned by mail. This delay offers the writer "a chance of seeing with different eyes, the objectification of the subjective"; it renders "an author's life with the text" more difficult. That is to the author's benefit: "Leaving the writing to others enforces autohermeneutics. The word is ugly and not indispensable; feel free to forget it once it has done its episodical service" (*V*, 152). Solitary writing is implicitly acknowledged as problematic for its *lack* of distance, of the multiplicity of perspectives that conversation with other readers produces. But Blumenberg's

32. The emphasis on the delay as the decisive function of rhetoric dates back to Blumenberg, "Anthropological Approach"; the classic investigation of the contrast between rhetoric's delaying and technology's accelerating function is Campe, "Von der Theorie der Technik zur Technik der Metapher." In Blumenberg's anthropological writings, the fictional *Urszene* of the origins of humanity revolves around the possibility of delayed action as the prerequisite for the emergence of the human (*Beschreibung des Menschen*, 559).

routines around his dictation tapes are made to stand in for those effects to some extent. He makes no attempt to argue that the temporal distance between the present and past authorial self can approximate other readers' perspectives, but he does credit his writing tools with some degree of compensatory function for the collective text production processes that within P&H, for better or worse, countered the individual voices on the printed page with footnoted challenges, juxtapositions, entanglements in the group's consensus as well as fights: the self-thematizing procedure of theory in action that foregrounded the preconditions for a text to be produced, to resonate with its readers and generate discussion.

No Staying Out: The Writer as Kosmotheōros

"Vous êtes embarqué," Blumenberg quotes Pascal as preamble to his 1979 *Shipwreck with Spectator*, singling out Pascal's take on the shipwreck as a metaphor for existence among the many he surveys in this text. "Remaining in the harbor," he explicates, "is in Pascal's view not an option. The metaphorics of embarkation include the suggestion that living means already being on the high seas, where there is no outcome other than being saved or going down, and no possibility of abstention."[33] The spectator appears as a correlate of the seafaring metaphor for existence that Blumenberg traces from Hesiod to Otto Neurath via Montaigne, Friedrich Nietzsche, and others. From the poetic perspective of constructing a shipwreck narrative, "there must also be the, as it were, emphatic configuration in which the shipwreck at sea is set beside the uninvolved spectator on dry land" (*S*, 10).

Throughout Blumenberg's rich literary and philosophical history of shipwreck and spectator, neither figure ever comes to a standstill. Take the notion of contemplative disengagement, the "theory ideal of classical Greek philosophy, figured by the spectator" (*S*, 26): this ideal is contradicted as early as Lucretius. Even if his spectator's position is still that of an "observer who is secured by philosophy," theoretical contemplation no longer provides happiness, *eudamonia*, but only the "remaining assurance that such a firm ground [as the order of the cosmos] exists at all" (*S*, 26–27). This reassurance relies on human-made knowledge of the material world. Unlike the Greek gods whose image was embodied by the sage, "the spectator of the world cannot be so pure. He needs at least the physics of the atoms to consolidate his own modest existence almost outside the world" (*S*, 27).

Or take the aesthetic dimension of spectatorship in the Abbé Galiani's early modern illustration of the human situation as a theater, from which sea-

---

33. Blumenberg, *Shipwreck*, 19 (hereafter cited as *S*).

faring has vanished altogether: Blumenberg reads it as working against the metaphorical background of security and danger in the contrast of shore and sea. The aesthetic representation accepts that the danger is no longer real; the emphasis shifts to the requirement that the spectator be safely distanced from the drama performed in order to take it in ("The danger is played on stage, and security is a rainproof roof" [*S*, 40]). But because he makes the spectator stand for the ever-changing attempts at measuring out the "boundary values of sayability and unsayability,"[34] the spectator lends itself to Blumenberg's later, personal adoption of a figure oscillating between the "self-understanding" he mocked—but to which he devoted his last collection of essays—and the "self-stylization" that preoccupied him increasingly toward the end of his life (*MS*, 9).

Blumenberg's lifelong focus on the limits of sayability emerged as a counterpart to his historicized concept of reality in his seminal article, "The Concept of Reality and the Possibility of the Novel," for P&H's first published volume. This was the text that first performed Blumenberg's practice of theory by setting his new concept against the preconditions for both the possibility of its articulation as well as the resistances to it following its articulation. Blumenberg argues that the emergence of the new genre of the novel relies on, and is indicative of, changes in underlying concepts of reality to which literary fiction assumes a certain relation (e.g., imitation or deviation). Following the historically evolving constraints on what counts as reality, in the form of implicit assumptions that inform explicit philosophies from Plato through René Descartes into modernity, Blumenberg observes that "it is quite natural that the most deeply hidden implication of an era—namely, its concept of reality—should become explicit only when the awareness of that reality has already been broken."[35]

Blumenberg's early interest in such "deeply hidden" implications unfolded over his lifetime into major projects aimed at "the effort . . . to represent unsayability itself linguistically," namely, his metaphorology, and later the theory of nonconceptuality.[36] Alongside this lifelong concern with inexpressibility, he continued to develop his concept of reality both as positioned against Heidegger's notion of Being and as a historicization of Husserl's notion of the life-world as what remains "hidden in its *contingency*, that is, it is not experienced as something that could also be different."[37] In his final collection of texts,

34. Blumenberg, "Prospect," 248.

35. Blumenberg, "Concept of Reality," 512.

36. Blumenberg, "Prospect," 248.

37. Blumenberg, "Phenomenological Aspects," 374. While Heidegger remained "unnamable at the time" of Blumenberg's first essay on the concept of reality (Haverkamp, "Nothing Fails Like Success,"

A Potential Self-Understanding, the spectator is the figure Blumenberg puts forward, despite much ironic reservation, as embodying the striving to represent unsayability. "Spectators" is the title of one of the collection's sections, and the short essay "How to Become a Spectator" as well as other discussions of spectatorship appear in another section with the title "What Can and Cannot Be Described" (*Das Beschreibliche und das Unbeschreibliche*).

Two important features link the figure of the philosophical spectator presented in those texts back to Blumenberg's performance of theory in P&H as an attempt not to engage in political action but to reform the compromised ways of philosophy. First, the spectatorial perspective is privileged in that it offers insight into what is hidden in its contingency. To the extent—and the qualification is important—that the philosophical spectator of the world shares with the audience of a play the characteristic of being removed from the action being watched, he can benefit from the cathartic effect that, in Blumenberg's reading of Aristotle's poetics, consists in becoming aware of "*his* world" through the contrast with the one being staged (*MS*, 96). For the audiences Aristotle had in mind, for example, staging the chaos emerging from the rivalries between deities meant presenting such chaos as "*no longer* possible" in the *polis*: "That which is disturbing has been enhanced so as to refine the sense for that which otherwise no longer stands out in the 'lifeworld' of the *polis*" (*MS*, 97).

But second, there are important differences. Where the theater stages past reality to cathartic effect, there is no enhancing of contrasting features for the spectator of the world left with the task of bringing presently elusive "reality" into description's grasp. The figure of the philosophical spectator gets a playful name, *kosmotheōros*. Blumenberg offers potential renderings in contemporary German, each with its own set of connotations: the pedantic *Weltbetrachter*; the *Weltanschauer*, carrying with him reminiscences of *Weltanschauung* culminating in the "murderous consequences" of one such worldview, National Socialism (*MS*, 61); and finally the *Weltzuschauer*, the option that is "lightest, frivolous even," and the most appealing one for Blumenberg. It serves as a reminder of the metaphorical roots of the Greek ideal of theory in that "the THEOROS as the audience in a play is older than his THEORIA" (*MS*, 62). In those terms, Blumenberg emphasizes another important yet subtle difference between the audience of a play and the *kosmotheōros*: "The decisive difference is that the spectator of the world (*kosmotheōros*) cannot deny his sub-

---

1233), his "Vorbemerkungen zum Wirklichkeitsbegriff" make its positioning as an alternative to Heidegger's notion of being explicit. See also Haverkamp, *Metapher*, 12.

ject his attention and appreciation, does not have the option of turning his back on the spectacle that is open to a play's spectator. He can withdraw his seriousness from the play so as to be anything but a spectator in his own world" (*MS*, 95). Figured by the spectator, philosophical observation is demarcated from active involvement, but at the same time characterized by the impossibility of distancing oneself entirely.

Quietly but practically, much of Blumenberg's spectatorial "seeing" is a mode of *reading* aimed at the implicit but "real," in Blumenberg's specific and pragmatic sense—a textually mediated parallel to the spectacle that stages what remains hidden in its contingency. When Blumenberg elaborated on his concept of reality a decade after the first P&H volume, he opened provocatively to draw attention to its pragmatic aspect: "*Real [wirklich] is what is not unreal [unwirklich].* I am aware that this sentence must strike a logician as disastrous."[38] The provocation highlights Blumenberg's understanding of reality as an "actuality in consciousness," as effective (*wirksam*) in that it has the ability to affect consciousness[39]—and as distinct from the *ens necessarium* of the metaphysical tradition. The very fact that it is in need of proof demonstrates, according to Blumenberg, that the existence of such a posited entity makes no difference to us. In contrast, Blumenberg's "real that is not unreal" is set apart by its ability to generate action or inaction depending on whether the actuality in consciousness—that is reality—appears in the mode of "reliability," implying not being at risk, or of "urgency," requiring action.[40] A more suitable translation of this concept of reality, *Wirklichkeit*, might be "being at work"; Haverkamp suggests that it points to Blumenberg's engagement with Heidegger's reading of Aristotle's *Rhetoric*.[41] The concept of reality itself had been Blumenberg's earliest example of such an actuality in consciousness, explicated in terms of its effectiveness in opening up the possibility of the novel.

The spectator remained the figure to mark Blumenberg's quest to bring the "real" into view in its effectiveness. When Blumenberg turns from the analysis of historical configurations of spectatorship to "the world we have to do with" (*MS*, 101), one of his examples is the brief text "When there was nothing to be seen." Embedded in Blumenberg's discussion of the dated term *Schutzmann*—"policeman" but more literally "guardian"—is the description of a void: there is a "smoking ruin," lending itself to be read as a reference to the

38. Blumenberg, "Preliminary Remarks," 117.
39. Blumenberg, "Preliminary Remarks," 120.
40. Blumenberg, "Preliminary Remarks," 120.
41. Haverkamp, "Nothing Fails Like Success," 1230.

burning of a synagogue as Blumenberg the high school student might have witnessed it. The Schutzmann turns his back to it and declares that there is nothing to be seen—guarding (*schützen*) both passersby and himself from becoming spectators (*MS*, 81–82). In this opening text to the section "What can and cannot be described," Blumenberg's rendering of the scene homes in on an instance of the unsayable that is in plain sight rather than hidden in its contingency. The both banal and dangerous distortion of reality in the Schutzmann's "understatement" is an element of the quotidian in Nazi Germany that Blumenberg's text dramatizes as lastingly real. Not only would "not having become a spectator render the lives of the passersby easier," but the German fascination with the word *Schutz*, protection, would outlast the term *Schutzmann* despite its association with state-administered protection—not of synagogues, but of those denying their destruction (*MS*, 81).

Blumenberg's concluding discussion of Husserl in the essay "How to Become a Spectator" brings a rare definitive statement: that the spectator is "necessary" (*MS*, 107). This insistence emerges from the contrast with Husserl's assertion of the existential necessity of philosophy for him personally and the suggestion that the spectator can "stay out." Blumenberg traces this assertion back to an element of poetic catharsis by reading two of Husserl's central notions in terms of spectatorship: the phenomenological reduction and the lifeworld. From this perspective, the phenomenological reduction appears as the "*absolute* culmination" of the "art of staying out" that defines the spectator (*MS*, 101–2). The insistence—mistaken, in Blumenberg's view—on the spectator's ability to close off the "world" is predicated on a "cleansing" of the philosophical subject:

> It was a lifelong effort [of Husserl's] to defend the reduction; but it becomes apparent that its defense amounts to defending the spectator's right not to be irritated by the world and its qualities, nor by his own involvement in worldly interests. The decisive novelty lies in the demand for this *catharsis* to precede anything that qualifies as an object worthy of consideration. The burden of the world is exaggerated, like it was in the Aristotelian tragedy, not in order to throw it off in its dramatic enhancement, but so as to never take it up in the first place. For that reason, the fully "cleansed" philosophical subject according to Husserl's formula is the *residue of world annihilation*, which, in spectator fashion, only allows the "essential" to appear to it. (*MS*, 102–3)[42]

On this reading, Husserl's theory of the life world is a philosophical attempt to deal with the difficulties of disentangling the spectator from the "world," diffi-

42. Cf. Möller, "Zuschauer," 391.

culties that turn out to be greater than the "norm of the sole and simple act" of reduction made them out to be (*MS*, 103). "Defined as the world that has no spectators, neither 'from without' nor 'from within,'" the lifeworld stands for what is taken for granted and thus escapes articulation, as well as the challenge to "become aware of our never-ending dependency on it" (*MS*, 104).

Blumenberg's analysis turns into disagreement where he finds Husserl seeking "self-therapy" in his philosophy, claiming to have "cured [him]self" through his *Logical Investigation* after "living from agony to agony" during the fourteen previous years (*MS*, 105)—a gesture Blumenberg aligns with medical understandings of the Aristotelian poetic gesture of cathartic purification from Jacob Bernays to Sigmund Freud. Blumenberg deems the phenomenological project corresponding to self-therapy a failure, inevitably consisting in "being drawn into an unmastered life-world-liness" rather than the desired "reduction of the spectator to a minimum of involvement" (*MS*, 106). But he locates the problem not in this failure but in Husserl's justification for the cathartic move. The latter's personal insistence on the existential need for philosophizing undermines the main poetic function Blumenberg ascribes to the philosophical spectator, namely, the ability to articulate "the essential" through the contrast of historically changing conditions of facticity:

> When the founder of phenomenology summarizes [the function of phenomenological description as a "means for living"] retrospectively (at the occasion of his seventieth birthday in 1929): "I *had* to philosophize, or else I could not have lived in *this* world," this pathos formula fails to go to the trouble of justification that is otherwise always required, and does not dare to generalize that it might have been so in *any* of the worlds that are possible according to the method of free variation, because what required precisely *this* theoretical attitude is not the state or quality of *this* factually given world. It is the essential, not the factual, that proves worthy of contemplation and renders the spectator necessary. (*MS*, 106–7)

Just what is "essential," however, is brought into view poetically rather than philosophically for Blumenberg; it appears not as the result of phenomenological reduction but as a function of the descriptive perspective on the messy, historically layered empirical given. Like Husserl, Blumenberg places a form of contemplative action at the center of his efforts, but it is aimed at "the world" as textually and materially constituted. Not via world annihilation but via engagement with facticity, the contemplative task figured by the spectator consists in bringing into view this world's actuality, in the poetic sense of *wirk-*

sam, as its essential element. "The world, the world, you asses [*ihr Esel*]! is the problem of philosophy, the world and nothing else," Blumenberg quotes Arthur Schopenhauer in the opening to *A Potential Self-Understanding*, immediately adding his regret that "you asses!" did not make it into the published version of Schopenhauer's manuscript (*MS*, 10).

The performative aspect of this invocation encapsulates Blumenberg's approach as a spectator who writes. He will not declare "the world" the target of his own philosophizing but delineate it via the nuanced contrast with predecessors like Schopenhauer and Husserl, and keep the delineation steeped in detail that, in its frequent irrelevance to the main point (such as Blumenberg's disappointment with the deletion of the admonishment "you asses!"), makes apparent the many authorial choices involved in constructing such delineation.[43] If facticity is Blumenberg's means at getting at the essential, his writings perform the demand directed against Husserl's "separation of the factual from the essential." In keeping with the demand that philosophy must rely "on *facts* because of the paucity of the *fictive*," his texts are saturated with detail from "the 'positive sciences' alongside the 'real' fiction of literature *and* culture as conveyed in rites and myths."[44]

The term Blumenberg uses to emphasize this importance of factual detail is *Welthaltigkeit*, "world saturation," stemming from his early work on poetics to characterize the novel as "the most comprehensively 'realistic' genre [*welthaltigste und welthafteste Gattung*]."[45] The challenge that Blumenberg later addresses theoretically in his metaphorology and theory of nonconceptuality is articulated here as the difficulty of methodological justification for the inevitable choice of particulars through which to address such an "overwhelming topic" as "world" or "life."[46] Practically, Blumenberg's slip-card box remained a tool to collect empirical detail from countless contexts and to generate the world-saturatedness of his own writing. The attempt to articulate the prerequisites for the emergence of the world-saturated novel initially led Blumenberg to the development of his concept of reality; decades later the critique of a lack of world saturation united the two extremes on his spectrum of spectatorship. One extreme is marked by Heidegger's merging of theoretical contemplation and action (to which my final section turns), the other by Husserl's "world annihilation" in the attempt to reduce the spectator's object to the essential:

43. Rüdiger Zill discusses Blumenberg's indirect approach in the context of his chosen motto of "detours" ("Auch eine Kritik").
44. Blumenberg, *Zu den Sachen und zurück*, 11.
45. Blumenberg, "Concept of Reality," 516.
46. Blumenberg, "Preliminary Remarks," 119.

> Once a philosopher's examples remain within the tight circle of house and home, mountain and forest, lecture theater and writing equipment—the exception being a hallucinated elephant in the lecture theater—, one must not have too high hopes for their realism, for their philosophy's world saturation [*Welthaltigkeit*]. Remarkable that Husserl and Heidegger should stand in such close proximity to one another in this regard!! (*V*, 50)

Against the Confusion of Thought and Action: Spectatorial Language

Does the philosophical spectator, never quite disentangled from the world being watched, have any effect on it in turn? Characteristically, Blumenberg will not offer any kind of definitive answer, in terms of neither hermeneutics nor a theory of reception, but sarcastically distances himself from simplistic claims about the potential effect of philosophical contemplation on worldly affairs. For instance, the idea that "the present technical era would end if Heidegger's thinking was understood" is merely a "grand gesture" to Blumenberg. Not only are such "effects of thinking unheard of in the history of the world," but positing them is predicated on "recesses of clarity": Who and how many would have to understand Heidegger to bring out this effect? What would it consist of? Would any genuine understanding even be required if those seeking it are already united in the aim of abolishing the present given they dislike? (*MS*, 34). Blumenberg's ostentatious restriction of his own role to that of the *theoros* as spectator stands in contrast to understandings of philosophical contemplation *as* action, above all Heidegger's own.

Blumenberg does not dignify the "fatefully opportunistic glitch" of Heidegger's 1933 rectoral address with discussion of the notion of thinking as action, but directs his critique at Heidegger's use of language (*V*, 56).[47] This demarcation is necessary not least because Blumenberg's phenomenologically inspired spectatorship is distinguished by its attentiveness to language as a site of poetic actuality that is not to be confused with Heidegger's caricature (in Blumenberg's view) of the linguistically mediated effects of thought. Taking up the task of bringing the elusive "actual" into view, Blumenberg's spectatorial writing explicitly traces the linguistic articulation of conceptual shifts, and it performs the attention to the unsayable in following metaphors and the associative threads they generate. In contrast, Heidegger misleadingly asserts, rather than genuinely performs, a reliance on linguistic structure—or so Blumenberg charges. Initially formulated in terms of poetics, this charge takes on

---

47. On the intersections between Blumenberg's and Adorno's critique of language as partly directed against Heidegger, see Tränkle, "Die Vernunft und ihre Umwege." On the difficult relations between Adorno and Blumenberg, see Voller, "Kommunikation verweigert."

political significance as Blumenberg's hopes for reforming the postwar academic landscape shift from his involvement with P&H to his spectatorial practice of theory.

To put Blumenberg's point bluntly, the constraints imposed by Heidegger's idiolect on his reception do indeed work to produce a certain effect, but that effect is the imitation of a pose rather than intellectual engagement: social and professional compulsion disguised as the effect of a text. Rather than participate in the many discussions about the philosophical function of Heidegger's idiolect, from the assertion that his use of language sets "a new standard for thinking" to accusations of "linguistic fascism" in which humans simply act as instruments of language's machinations,[48] Blumenberg's critique is formulated in terms of poetics and takes on a distinctly sharper tone as he connects Heidegger's "alleged obedience to language" with its social effect of practically requiring imitation.[49] It is through the contrast with this critique, to which I turn now, that Blumenberg's own language appears as an attempt to leave open the text as a site of the "real," not in virtue of reflecting a special relation to "Being," but as a register of historically contingent processes.

The core of Blumenberg's criticism appears in his 1966 P&H essay "Speech Situation and Immanent Poetics," where he characterizes Heidegger's use of language as a "prior decision for the inspirational" (trans. adapted from SS, 453): the *claim* to linguistic guidance of thought precedes any reliance on linguistic structure performed by the text, and therefore appears as an element of authorial stylization rather than a product of the actual work process. Slipped into a brief aside, Blumenberg's critique relies on both the context of his essay and what he demonstratively leaves unsaid about Heidegger's conception of language. Revisiting Blumenberg's early essay shows the continuities between his early and later critique of Heidegger's language in terms of poetics. Blumenberg's spectatorial position depends on its attentiveness to linguistic registrations of the unsayable, but it emphatically does not stylize the author into a privileged "listener." This demarcation from Heidegger is significant, in that it continues to mark the critical function of "theory" for interrogating authorial positions.

Blumenberg's essay lays the groundwork for P&H's investigation of the function of language as an element of "immanent poetics." He distinguishes between three "basic ideas of the relationship between language and thought"

---

48. Gadamer, "Der Denker Martin Heidegger," 60; Edwards quoted in Flatscher, *Logos und Lethe*, 288.

49. Blumenberg, *Lebensthemen*, 139 (hereafter cited as *L*).

(SS, 452). First, there is the idea of "an essential surplus of thought beyond language," corresponding to the "experience of a 'poverty of language'"—never quite adequate for articulating the achievements of thought (SS, 450); second, the idea of an "exact language" grounded in the belief of a universal coincidence between speech and thinking; and third, the reversal of the first idea, which consists in "declaring language mightier than thought" (SS, 451). Blumenberg loosely historizes the three notions, introducing the idea of the poverty of language by reference to Cicero, while Descartes's criteria of clarity and distinctness exemplify the early modern introduction of the idea of exact language. "Modern language philosophy," in contrast, is characterized by the idea that language "preforms the latitude of what is possible and impossible for thought" (SS, 452).

In this context, the aside on Heidegger serves as a negative example that sets the stage for Blumenberg's main discussion of poetic "trust" or "confidence" in "a language that speaks itself" (SS, 454). Such trust, for instance, in language's musicality, he argues,

> need not be connected with a prior decision for the inspirational [*Vorentscheidung für das Inspiratorische*]; it need not mean that one has to listen to the appeal of "being" that acts not *within* language but that itself *is* language. This is only the shape and premise of the modern critique of language that has been reversed positively, which nonetheless assumes the supremacy of language over thought, only with the difference that it, as it were, prohibits the "listening" and strives to exorcise its appeal as a type of bedevilment. (trans. adapted from SS, 453–54)

It is noteworthy that Blumenberg subsumes Heidegger's conception of language squarely under the idea that language is mightier than thought, the third basic idea of the relation between language and thought in Blumenberg's list.[50] The sole difference with "modern language philosophy" is the positive or negative sign: Heidegger advocates what is otherwise "prohibited," namely, "listening" to "the excess of language beyond real, verifiable, and justifiable thought," whereas most "modern philosophy of language," as Blumenberg has characterized it (dangerously summarily), strives to "reveal and dismantle" that excess (SS, 452, 454). This classification signals Blumenberg's dismissal of

---

50. Heidegger framed his early project of overcoming metaphysics as facing the poverty of language. This raises the question of whether his early conception of language falls into the first of Blumenberg's basic ideas, but the only element of Heidegger's conception of language that Blumenberg engages with here is that of an inspiring, leading function ascribed to language in guiding thought.

Heidegger's assertions of a decisive break with a tradition reaching back to Aristotle in Heidegger's conception of language defined by "Being," understood to "eventuate" in language.[51] With the straightforward categorization of Heidegger's conception of language under the third basic idea that "thought can only follow the anticipation of language," little more remains of Heidegger's claim to radicalness than the now common commitment to the linguistic constitution of thought (SS, 451). The distinctive difference lies in Heidegger's "prior decision for the inspirational": before it has even begun, the text production process is qualified as one that will necessarily be led by "being" qua language.

But because of the prior emphasis on the understanding of the text as the result of "listening," Heidegger's use of language appears as a negative example of "trust in language" in Blumenberg's essay, an authorial gesture rather than a feature of the text. Far from mentioning—let alone endorsing—any of Heidegger's claims of a responsiveness to the "appeal of Being" bound up with his notion of listening, Blumenberg opposes it to examples of genuine "trust in language" that a given text may display, for example, in its reliance on association, sound, or rhyme (SS, 453). To use Blumenberg's distinction, these examples are elements of an "immanent poetics" to be explicated by investigating the function of a given text's language. In contrast, Heidegger's authorial assertion about a text's relation to language is an example of "exogenous poetics," an articulated authorial comment, for instance, in self-observation and other forms of authorial testimony. Heidegger, in Blumenberg's assessment, *declares* the verbal thinking process to be one of "inspiration" rather than "perspiration" (the set of alternatives that Blumenberg used many years later to frame his discussion in "The Seated Blacksmith"). With this sharp but brief highlight on Heidegger's authorial gesture of taking his lead from "a Being" (to keep Blumenberg's ironic indefinite article), Blumenberg leaves the matter of Heidegger's use of language in this early text.[52]

Witnessing Heidegger's elaborate retrospective self-stylization as a misunderstood great thinker rather than active supporter of National Socialism, the focus of Blumenberg's criticism scattered across the posthumously

51. On Heidegger's conception of language as positioned against the distinction between mental and symbolic realms that is Blumenberg's starting point here, see Flatscher, *Logos und Lethe*, 52–73; see Flatscher throughout on Heidegger's conception of language as invested in the question of the actuality, *Wirksamkeit*, of language within human existence—the problem that Blumenberg took as his initial point of inspiration from Heidegger but that also turned into his point of departure via the concept of reality.

52. Blumenberg, "Sprachsituation," 141.

published collections *The Philosopher's Seducibility, A Possible Self-Understanding*, and *Life Themes* remains on the poetic function of language that is at the core of his concept of spectatorship. Heidegger's "alleged obedience to language" appears as a perversion of attentiveness to the linguistic shifts that indicate the actuality Blumenberg is after (*L*, 139). The one-page text "Belated Deletion," for instance, singles out an example of Heidegger's asserted reliance on linguistic guidance, in this case a twist on a proverb, that instead marks little more than the rhetorical alignment of his philosophy with the political context of rising fascism. As Blumenberg observes, Heidegger has found his "new faith in language's thinking ahead" by the time he gives his 1930 talk "The Essence of Truth," but there is a telling discrepancy between the talk and its printed version from 1943. It consists in the omission of the concluding proverb that Heidegger had modified significantly to read *Nicht auf das Biegen, auf das Brechen kommt es an* ("Not the bending, the breaking is what matters"): "Here is an instance of the play with a turn of phrase readily provided by language. *Auf Biegen und Brechen*, 'by hook or crook,' is being split and sharpened antithetically. Even in 1930 that had already become a reckless thing to say. Philosophy began to participate in brazenness. In 1943, it was much too late to no longer have it printed" (*V*, 85). What is portrayed as "play" with language is really participation in political "brazenness"; as Heidegger's belated suppression of the phrase in the print version shows, the alleged obedience to language did not suffice to deny responsibility for this alignment even in his own judgment.

Beyond such rhetorical alignments with fascism masked as plays with language, Blumenberg's critique is aimed at the social constraints imposed by Heidegger's use of language. Blumenberg distinguishes between the "artificial prose" of *Being and Time* and the later language of "divining being" (*Seinsorakelei*) (*L*, 139; *V*, 100). Although he deems the early attempt at an artificial prose a failure, since even that early language of Heidegger's "could only be imitated but not understood," he does grant what he calls the "existential idiom" a constructive role. It offered the possibility of philosophical engagement for those (few, according to Blumenberg) who could *avoid* adopting it in their own work and thematize instead of imitate it. Because the "orientating intention of the artificiality of language was comprehensible," the struggles with the limitations of language that Heidegger's idiom performed could be made explicit, and so allowed productive philosophical exchanges. In contrast, the language of Heidegger's history of being—"that which Heidegger, in the alleged obedience to language, claimed to divine about being and the history of being after his 'turn'" (*L*, 139)—lacks such a comprehensible intention. In the absence of the possibility of productive engagement, the reception of the *Seinsorakelei* is reduced to the need to imitate Heidegger's language.

The implications of this required imitation are serious for Blumenberg. As he argues in "The Suggestion of the Nearly Achievable," the seductive possibility to confuse mere posing-as-a-thinker with genuine attempts at engagement with philosophical thought was the decisive factor in the "conversion" from Husserl to Heidegger—a confusion that preceded explicitly political choices. This essay starts out as a sarcastic take on academic philosophy, suggesting that professional success is facilitated by a philosophical text's "quality of lending itself to parody": The easier it is to confuse parody and reception (intentionally or not), the quicker adherents may multiply (*MS*, 89). As counterexamples to this rule, Blumenberg discusses two thinkers he takes to be impossible to parody for different reasons: Kant and Husserl. But the tone of academic satire vanishes with Blumenberg's claim that this impossibility was the reason for the many "conversions" from Husserl to Heidegger:

> [Heidegger] offered a Dorado for the delights of parody, and only very few of his most tasteful disciples have been able to resist the resulting temptation to demonstrate "understanding." The disloyalty to Husserl and the loyalty to Heidegger as local phenomena in Freiburg were not procedural or even political hazards. It was impossible to be loyal to Husserl since there was no *habitus* for that, and it was impossible *not* to be loyal to Heidegger, since there was no other relation to this demand [*Anspruch*] than imitation [*Nachspruch*]. (*MS*, 91–92)

Blumenberg's charge is leveled at those choosing to follow the mode of engagement Heidegger's philosophy requires, "imitation" (*Nachspruch*, in Blumenberg's parody of Heidegger that performs his point of the impossibility to operate outside the latter's jargon). Not primarily "politics" but the acceptance of this alleged relation between language and thought explains the loyalties and disloyalties of his philosophical colleagues in Freiburg for Blumenberg: the surrender to a gesture of profundity. Philosophical "tastelessness" came first, but resulted in choices of loyalty that had significant consequences at the personal level for Husserl and in the political compromising of most of the profession. If Blumenberg was reluctant to judge individual colleagues' support of National Socialism publicly, his condemnation of the profession's failure could not be clearer, and it is not limited to the period prior to 1945.

If Heidegger's language, according to Blumenberg, "could only be imitated but not understood," Blumenberg's can instead be understood but barely imitated, reflecting the critique both of the authorial gesture of an alleged obedience to language and of the trading of intelligibility for followers. From *Shipwreck with Spectator* on, much of Blumenberg's writing performs his "trust in language" in his texts' reliance on associative threads produced by the focus on, say, "shipwrecks" or "lions," dragging with them the world-saturated detail Blumenberg demands. These contingent, empirically produced threads have their motivation in Blumenberg's metaphorology and theory of nonconceptuality, but his willingness to rely on them as structuring elements for his texts—frustrating those of his readers who take them to be more or less disjointed sequences of note card entries—is one distinctive element of Blumenberg's own authorial poetics. It is the performative counterpart to the conceptual continuity between Blumenberg's turn toward the problem of the "real" in his work with P&H and his notion of spectatorship.

Despite his well-publicized qualms about the very point of writing, Blumenberg kept doing it in his demonstrative reclusiveness, with volumes of text still being published under his name years after his death (e.g., *L*, 29–33, 67–79). The figure of the spectator that corresponds to this reclusiveness is aimed at the often implicit or hidden "real," but bringing the real into view does not necessarily require its articulation in turn, certainly not its written articulation. Yet Blumenberg shows no signs of being content with Socratic ephemerality. His practice of theory in his first P&H article had failed to set a more widely accepted standard, and his departure from the group signaled his abandonment of the attempt at the social reorganization of such practice. But the quickly growing body of Blumenberg's texts does reflect his lasting commitment to the historical poetics that his early P&H text first conceptualized and performed. The constant articulation of the conditions of possibility of the spectatorial act aimed at the "real," of the shifting and contingent historical constellations that prefigure human lifeworlds and that become visible thanks to the hermeneutic privilege of temporal distance, has been an exasperating feature for those of Blumenberg's readers who wish to "trade in positions."[53] From the historical perspective I have adopted here, this feature of Blumenberg's texts appears as a continuation of his postwar ambition to set the authorial voice against the preconditions for its possibility and potential actuality. Instead of—on the extreme part of the spectrum of authoritative philosophical

53. Haverkamp, "Das Skandalon," 204.

traditions—the performance of a listening to Being and the corresponding stylization of the author-listener as a voice of individually privileged insight and therefore authority, Blumenberg's texts perform the necessity to bring into view the constitutive features of texts themselves, and of the philosophical positions they articulate, that are beyond individual authors' control. His writing is not an attempt to convince readers of any given position but a practical performance of his theoretical foregrounding of the conditions for the possibility of "seeing more; no more than seeing."[54]

Daniela K. Helbig teaches in the School for History and Philosophy of Science at the University of Sydney.

---

54. Blumenberg, *Zu den Sachen und zurück*, 350.

References

Amslinger, Julia. *Eine neue Form von Akademie: "Poetik und Hermeneutik"—die Anfänge.* Paderborn: Fink, 2017.

Blumenberg, Hans. "An Anthropological Approach to the Contemporary Significance of Rhetoric (1971)," translated by Hannes Bajohr. In *History, Metaphor, Fables: A Hans Blumenberg Reader*, edited by Hannes Bajohr, Florian Fuchs, and Joe Paul Kroll, 177–208. Ithaca, NY: Cornell University Press, 2020.

Blumenberg, Hans. *Beschreibung des Menschen: Aus dem Nachlass*, edited by Manfred Sommer. Frankfurt am Main: Suhrkamp, 2006.

Blumenberg, Hans. "The Concept of Reality and the Possibility of the Novel (1964)," translated by David H. Wilson. In *History, Metaphor, Fables: A Hans Blumenberg Reader*, edited by Hannes Bajohr, Florian Fuchs, and Joe Paul Kroll, 499–524. Ithaca, NY: Cornell University Press, 2020.

Blumenberg, Hans. *Die Verführbarkeit des Philosophen.* Frankfurt am Main: Suhrkamp, 2005.

Blumenberg, Hans. *Ein mögliches Selbstverständnis: Aus dem Nachlaß.* Stuttgart: Reclam, 1996.

Blumenberg, Hans. *The Genesis of the Copernican World*, translated by Robert M. Wallace. Cambridge, MA: MIT Press, 1987.

Blumenberg, Hans. *Lebensthemen: Aus dem Nachlaß.* Stuttgart: Reclam, 1998.

Blumenberg, Hans. "Phenomenological Aspects on Life-World and Technization (1963)," translated by Hannes Bajohr. In *History, Metaphor, Fables: A Hans Blumenberg Reader*, edited by Hannes Bajohr, Florian Fuchs, and Joe Paul Kroll, 358–99. Ithaca, NY: Cornell University Press, 2020.

Blumenberg, Hans. "Preliminary Remarks on the Concept of Reality (1974)," translated by Hannes Bajohr. In *History, Metaphor, Fables: A Hans Blumenberg Reader*, edited by Hannes Bajohr, Florian Fuchs, and Joe Paul Kroll, 117–26. Ithaca, NY: Cornell University Press, 2020.

Blumenberg, Hans. "Prospect for a Theory of Nonconceptuality (1979)," translated by Hannes Bajohr. In *History, Metaphor, Fables: A Hans Blumenberg Reader*, edited by Hannes Bajohr, Florian Fuchs, and Joe Paul Kroll, 239–58. Ithaca, NY: Cornell University Press, 2020.

Blumenberg, Hans. *Shipwreck with Spectator: Paradigm for a Metaphor for Existence*, translated by Steven Randall. Cambridge, MA: MIT Press, 1997.

Blumenberg, Hans. "Speech Situation and Immanent Poetics," translated by Hannes Bajohr. In *History, Metaphor, Fables: A Hans Blumenberg Reader*, edited by Hannes Bajohr, Florian Fuchs, and Joe Paul Kroll, 449–68. Ithaca, NY: Cornell University Press, 2020.

Blumenberg, Hans. "Sprachsituation und immanente Poetik." In *Wirklichkeiten in denen wir leben: Aufsätze und eine Rede*, 137–56. Stuttgart: Reclam, 1981.

Blumenberg, Hans. "Vorbemerkungen zum Wirklichkeitsbegriff." In *Zum Wirklichkeitsbegriff*, by Günter Bandmann et al., 3–10. Mainz: Akademie der Wissenschaften und der Literatur, 1974.

Blumenberg, Hans. *Zu den Sachen und zurück*, edited by Manfred Sommer. Frankfurt am Main: Suhrkamp, 2007.

Bülow, Ulrich von, and Dorit Krusche. "Nachrichten an sich selbst: Der Zettelkasten von Hans Blumenberg." In *Zettelkästen: Maschinen der Phantasie*, edited by Heike Gfrereis and Ellen Strittmatter, 113–19. Marbach: Deutsche Schillergesellschaft, 2013.

Campe, Rüdiger. "Von der Theorie der Technik zur Technik der Metapher: Blumenbergs systematische Eröffnung." In *Metaphorologie: Zur Praxis von Theorie*, edited by Anselm Haverkamp and Dirk Mende, 283–315. Frankfurt am Main: Suhrkamp, 2009.

Derrida, Jacques. "Geschlecht II: Heidegger's Hand," translated by John P. Leavey Jr. In *Deconstruction and Philosophy*, edited by John Sallis, 161–96. Chicago: University of Chicago Press, 1987.

Flatscher, Matthias. *Logos und Lethe: Zur phänomenologischen Sprachauffassung im Spätwerk von Heidegger und Wittgenstein*. Freiburg im Breisgau: Alber, 2014.

Gadamer, Hans-Georg. "Der Denker Martin Heidegger." In *Heideggers Wege: Studien zum Spätwerk*, 55–60. Tübingen: Mohr, 1983.

Gehring, Petra. "Wirklichkeit: Blumenbergs Überlegungen zu einer Form." *Journal Phänomenologie* 35 (2011): 66–81.

Haverkamp, Anselm. "Das Skandalon der Metaphorologie: Hans Blumenbergs philosophische Initiative." *Deutsche Zeitschrift für Philosophie* 57, no. 2 (2009): 187–205.

Haverkamp, Anselm. *Metapher-Mythos-Halbzeug: Metaphorologie nach Hans Blumenberg*. Berlin: de Gruyter, 2018.

Haverkamp, Anselm. "Nothing Fails Like Success: Poetics and Hermeneutics—a Postwar Initiative by Hans Blumenberg." *MLN* 130, no. 5 (2015): 1221–41.

Heidegger, Martin. *Being and Time*, translated by John Macquarrie and Edward Robinson. Oxford: Blackwell, 1962.

Heidegger, Martin. *Parmenides*, translated by André Schuwer and Richard Rojcewicz. Bloomington: Indiana University Press, 1992.

Heidegger, Martin. *What Is Called Thinking?*, translated by Fred D. Wieck and J. Glenn Gray. New York: Harper and Row, 1986.

Heinz, Marion. "Politisierung der Philosophie: Heideggers Vorlesung 'Welt, Endlichkeit, Einsamkeit' (WS 1929/30)." In *Philosophie und Zeitgeist im Nationalsozialismus*, edited by Marion Heinz and Goran Gretić, 269–90. Würzburg: Königshausen und Neumann, 2006.

Helbig, Daniela K. "Denktagebücher? Zur textuellen Form der *Schwarzen Hefte*." In *Martin Heideggers "Schwarze Hefte": Eine philosophisch-politische Debatte*, edited by Marion Heinz and Sidonie Kellerer, 310–25. Berlin: Suhrkamp, 2016.

Helbig, Daniela K. "Life without Toothache: Hans Blumenberg's *Zettelkasten* and History of Science as Theoretical Attitude." *Journal of the History of Ideas* 80, no. 1 (2019): 91–112.

Kliger, Ilya, and Boris Maslov. "Introducing Historical Poetics: History, Experience, Form." In *Persistent Forms: Explorations in Historical Poetics*, edited by Ilya Kliger, Boris Maslov, and Eric Hayot, 1–36. New York: Fordham University Press, 2016.

Krajewski, Markus. *Paper Machines: About Cards and Catalogs, 1548–1929*. Cambridge, MA: MIT Press, 2011.

Krauthausen, Karin. "Hans Blumenbergs präparierter Valéry." *Zeitschrift für Kulturphilosophie* 6, no. 1 (2012): 211–24.

Love, Jeff, and Michael Meng. "The Political Myths of Martin Heidegger." *New German Critique*, no. 124 (2015): 45–66.

Meyer, Ahlrich. "Hans Blumenberg, oder: Die Kunst, sich herauszuhalten." In *Fliegende Fische: Eine Soziologie des Intellektuellen in Zwanzig Porträts*, edited by Thomas Jung and Stefan Müller-Doohm, 337–62. Frankfurt am Main: Fischer, 2009.

Möller, Melanie. "Zuschauer." In *Blumenberg lesen: Ein Glossar*, edited by Robert Buch and Daniel Weidner, 379–94. Berlin: Suhrkamp, 2014.

Müller, Oliver. "Martin Heideggers Verführbarkeit: Zu Lesarten, Deutungen und Distanznahmen Hans Blumenbergs." In *Heideggers Weg in die Moderne: Eine Verortung der "Schwarzen Hefte,"* edited by Hans-Helmuth Gander and Magnus Striet, 135–64. Frankfurt am Main: Klostermann, 2017.

Müller, Oliver. *Sorge um die Vernunft: Hans Blumenbergs phänomenologische Anthropologie*. Paderborn: mentis, 2005.

Müller, Oliver. "Subtile Stiche: Hans Blumenberg und die Forschungsgruppe 'Poetik und Hermeneutik.'" In *Kontroversen in der Literaturtheorie / Literaturtheorie in der Kontroverse*, edited by Ralf Klausnitzer and Carlos Spoerhase, 249–64. Bern: Lang, 2007.

Schödlbauer, Michael. "Diktat des Ge-stells: Vom Schreibzeug zur Schreibmaschine." In *"In die Höhe fallen": Grenzgänge zwischen Literatur und Philosophie*, edited by Anja Lemke and Martin Schierbaum, 99–122. Würzburg: Königshausen und Neumann, 2000.

Tränkle, Sebastian. "Die Vernunft und ihre Umwege: Zur Rettung der Rhetorik bei Hans Blumenberg und Theodor W. Adorno." In *Permanentes Provisorium: Hans Blumenbergs Umwege*, edited by Michael Heidgen, Matthias Koch, and Christian Köhler, 123–43. Paderborn: Fink, 2015.

Voller, Christian. "Die Erfindung des Rades: Eine Beobachtung an Hans Blumenbergs Zettelkasten." In *Wörter aus der Fremde: Begriffsgeschichte als Übersetzungsgeschichte*, edited by Falko Schmieder and Georg Toepfer, 315–20. Berlin: Kadmos, 2018.

Voller, Christian. "Kommunikation verweigert: Schwierige Beziehungen zwischen Blumenberg und Adorno." *Zeitschrift für Kulturphilosophie* 7, no. 2 (2013): 381–405.

Zanetti, Sandro. "Logiken und Praktiken der Schreibkultur: Zum analytischen Potential der Literatur." In *Logiken und Praktiken der Kulturforschung*, edited by Uwe Wirth, 75–88. Berlin: Kadmos, 2009.

Zill, Rüdiger. "Auch eine Kritik der reinen Rationalität: Hans Blumenbergs Anti-Methodologie." In *Permanentes Provisorium: Hans Blumenbergs Umwege*, edited by Michael Heidgen, Matthias Koch, and Christian Köhler, 53–74. Paderborn: Fink, 2015.

In Memory of Ernst Cassirer: Speech Delivered in Acceptance of the Kuno Fischer Prize of the University of Heidelberg, 1974

Hans Blumenberg

If you will permit me to steer clear of the obvious—that is, addressing the *last* recipient of the Kuno Fischer Prize and the body of work thus honored[1]—I shall instead cleave to something only slightly less obvious: to speak in memory of its *first* recipient. To do so is obvious not least because in a few days, on July 28, we should have occasion to commemorate the one hundredth birthday of Ernst Cassirer. It is exactly sixty years ago that Cassirer became the first recipient of this prize, which was founded in 1904.[2]

Please be assured that I shall not read out an essay in commemoration of somebody whom I never even knew personally. I should much prefer to inquire into the state of that matter which was important to the man and whose associ-

Originally published as "Ernst Cassirers gedenkend: Rede bei Entgegennahme des Kuno-Fischer-Preises der Universität Heidelberg im Juli 1974," *Revue internationale de philosophie* 28, no. 11 (1974): 456–63; from Hans Blumenberg, *Wirklichkeiten in denen wir leben: Aufsätze und eine Rede* (Stuttgart: Reclam, 1981), 163–72. Translated with the kind permission of Bettina Blumenberg. The bracketed footnotes have been added by the translator.

1. [Wilhelm Nestle received the Kuno Fischer Prize for an outstanding work in the history of philosophy in 1947 for his book *Vom Mythos zum Logos*; Hans Blumenberg was the first recipient after a twenty-seven-year hiatus, during which the prize was not awarded.]

2. [Ernst Cassirer received the prize in 1914.]

New German Critique 145, Vol. 49, No. 1, February 2022
DOI 10.1215/0094033X-9439713   © 2022 by New German Critique, Inc.

ation with which was accorded prominence by awarding him the prize. We must ask, that is to say, how his conception of the historiography of philosophy has fared. Did he—and if so, how—put his own twist on that great maxim of Kuno Fischer himself, whose name this prize bears and who, in his "History of Philosophy as a Science,"[3] claimed that to engage in the history of philosophy was already to philosophize?

When Cassirer was awarded the prize, the first two volumes of what was to become his four-volume history of the problem of knowledge (*The Problem of Knowledge: Philosophy, Science, and History since Hegel*, 1906–50)[4] had already run to their second editions. Nonetheless, the further course of his thought is determined by the very decline of epistemology as the theme at the core of philosophy. Though as late as 1929, in his debate with Martin Heidegger at Davos, Cassirer could say, "I do not conceive of my own development as a defection from Cohen,"[5] he added that to him, mathematical natural science no longer stood for the whole, but merely its paradigm.

We have reason to follow in Cassirer's intellectual biography the all-encompassing process that is this loss of the primacy of epistemology. This process denotes an elementary shift in the relations between philosophy and the sciences. The desire for reassurance from which all theory of knowledge springs could not but change in proportion to the increasing difficulty of still making theoretical certainty the central concern of thought at a time when everything else seemed more uncertain than knowledge. Especially to the kind of reflection that is far from being historically unsophisticated, the time-honored question of what we *can* know becomes increasing transformed into another, which asks what it even was that we *wanted* to know. What is more, the repercussions of science on the lifeworld had intensified to the point at which it seems surprising that anyone should doubt the demonstrability of scientific theories. In each technological push of a button is the reliability of science manifested, even where what it produces or enables is perceived as threatening. Such trivial experiences were alien to Kant and indeed still largely to the neo-Kantians, to whom the mechanism of the heavens and the sporadic sensations of confirmation it yielded were the prototype of theoretical vindication.

Cassirer's first major theme was thus a monumental historical obituary, but as such, it refused to join in the denigration: through its history and the

---

3. [Fischer, "Die Geschichte der Philosophie als Wissenschaft."]

4. [Cassirer, *Erkenntnisproblem*, 4 vols.; only the fourth volume is available in English: *Problem of Knowledge*.]

5. [Cassirer and Heidegger, "Davos Disputation," 194.]

comprehensive and conclusive gaze cast on it, the theory of knowledge becomes the thread to guide historical-theoretical reflection.

Cassirer's second major theme was the theory of concept formation, which he elaborated in what to this day remains, to my mind, a work that has yet to be fully understood and nonetheless has been largely and unjustly forgotten: *Substance and Function* of 1910.[6] *Forgotten* is an apposite word in considering Cassirer's influence or lack thereof in its astonishing proportions. For fifteen years Cassirer taught at a university that could safely be called "unphilosophical," though I speak in the past tense so as not to make a benchmark of my experience of two years in a Hamburg chair.[7] Nonetheless, his time at Hamburg compelled Cassirer's thought—and this was by no means against his own inclinations—to take on an aptitude for the world [*Weltfähigkeit*] by which he, alone among all the German emigrants to the United States, exerted an influence palpable to this day, the unrivaled organ of which is the *Journal of the History of Ideas.*

In Hamburg there was the Warburg Library, a singular dossier of the undiscovered. The library's theory, if one may say so, and later that of the eponymous institute, was Cassirer's three-volume *Philosophy of Symbolic Forms* (1923–29).[8] It may be that this system of symbolic function was the keystone of the intentions, implicit or explicit, of neo-Kantianism as such, according to which the table of categories of natural objects is to be considered merely a special case of the system of categories of cultural objects, among which, in the end, the methodically prepared objects of nature once again reappear. Yet the effect of the mesh of symbolic forms and its vertical structure was to open up a new world of objects and topics to philosophical theory, or to discover new ways by which they might be distinguished and integrated.

Putting to the test the performance of the concept of symbolic forms led Cassirer to consider noncanonical, exotic, and obscure material. The ubiquity of the symbolic form is the impossibility of prelogical primitivity. Cassirer was fascinated by Hermann Usener's notion of "momentary gods" [*Augenblicksgötter*],[9] in which he saw exemplified the elementary achievements of name giving and system formation. It was henceforth to be impossible to make scientific progress the indicator of all differentiation of consciousness, as is proved by the comprehensive reappraisal of findings made by linguistics, ethnography,

6. [Cassirer, *Substanzbegriff und Funktionsbegriff.*]

7. [Blumenberg was professor of philosophy at the University of Hamburg from 1958 to 1960.]

8. [Cassirer, *Philosophie der symbolischen Formen*, 3 vols.; 4 vols. in English, the last volume a collection of drafts.]

9. [Usener, *Götternamen.*]

and the history of religion. History appears as but one of the relations in which what is foreign may be perceived as something potentially our own. Time and space are accorded equal rank as the dimensions of this fundamental experience, from which arises the task of seeing and assessing what is foreign not by measure of what we consider our own, nor the past by measure of the present.

Accordingly, the historian of philosophy continued to deepen his study of the seemingly obscure. Light was cast on the no-man's-land that the philosophy of history left behind between Scholasticism and Cartesianism in Cassirer's book on the Renaissance (*The Individual and the Cosmos in Renaissance Philosophy*, 1927);[10] moreover, it was dignified as a worthy subject of understanding. Something similar applies to the account of the Platonism of the Cambridge school (*The Platonic Renaissance in England*, 1932).[11]

For its part, the theory of symbolic forms is rooted in everyday—that is, no longer scientific—experience. Yet what is brought to mind in this everyday experience is seen through the medium of Gestalt psychology. Cassirer wanted to consider the "intuitive world,"[12] its phenomena of expression, as the foundation of all theoretical achievements, and the latter only as the execution of the former. That, however, is too easily said to be able to dispel the suspicion of its being the most difficult thing indeed. It is the theme to which Edmund Husserl, at nearly the same time, was led under the rubric of "life-world."[13] In turning to this subject, Husserl finally eliminated the neo-Kantian element from his philosophy: the beginning of philosophizing cannot lie in reducing everything to a single fact, even if that fact is science. The lifeworld is not "all that is the case."[14] Indeed, it is quite possibly nothing of what is the case. But can what it is be grasped and described in the mode of scientificity without moderating the object down to the objecthood of science?

No less than for the phenomenological "lifeworld," an uneasy question arises with regard to Cassirer's de facto departure from the premises of neo-Kantianism according to the criterion of the world of intuition and expression: Was it really possible to leave behind the teleology of neo-Kantianism in the direction of norm-regulated scientificity by transferring the ideal of the categories to the theory of symbolic forms? It is all very well in retrospect to measure the degree to which this task, ever susceptible to despair, failed. A harder task is

10. [Cassirer, *Individuum und Kosmos*.]

11. [Cassirer, *Platonische Renaissance in England*.]

12. [This term appears frequently in Cassirer, for instance, *Philosophy of Symbolic Forms*, 1:111.]

13. [Husserl, *Crisis*, pt. 3. See on this topic Blumenberg, "Phenomenological Aspects on Life-World and Technization."]

14. [Wittgenstein, *Tractatus Logico-philosophicus*, 5.]

nonetheless to perceive the extent to which its completion was approached. Yet more important still is not to lose sight of the liability it imposes, which no degree of failure can mitigate.

There is a mismatch to be found in Cassirer's work between the autonomous value of each discrete system of symbolic forms—myth, language, religion, art—and the consistent intentionality of the overall system, which is directed toward knowledge of a kind resembling science and its unsurpassable finality. To make this observation is not to doubt science as a factor in progress. I find such doubt, so widespread today, to be reckless and improper, but also self-defeating, for it can only ever appear in the form of science. But is the *Philosophy of Symbolic Forms* ultimately not just a history of science, albeit expanded in both space and time? Which is to say: does it not see in the purpose of knowledge the suspension of all other purposes of world-understanding as mere preliminaries?

That we should be able to notice this focus at all is something we owe to the philosophical process, to which such different minds as Dilthey, Simmel, Husserl, Cassirer, and Heidegger each contributed in his fashion. In his work, in attempting to make an exit from neo-Kantianism, Cassirer himself created the aspect in which we can still recognize in him what we ourselves will be accused of a few decades hence: that the present remains the salient point, the criterion that serves to justify the newly presented phenomena and indeed history all the way back to its mythical horizons. This may not describe Cassirer's optics in points of detail or regional description, but it does apply to his overall construction. It would be wrong to assume facile airs of superiority. Not only those who speak of progress, but no less those who would find the last redoubt against antihistoricism in instrumentalizing all "the plenitude of the past to enlighten the present" have not yet thought any differently by so much as a jot. They have only put it another way.

What remains to be learned from Cassirer resides precisely in what he did not succeed in yet is discernible as an urgent impulse throughout his life's work and beyond: not to make the history of philosophy, of the sciences, of the systems of symbolic forms subservient to the self-confirmation of present states, to the criterion of success—or indeed to their relevance to consciousness formation. Nowhere did Cassirer let us know whether it was as a Kantian that he resisted—successfully or not—the imperative to use humanity, even in a single person, as a means to an end, even to that of functionalizing history with a view to the present's need for topical relevance. Yet this is nothing if not an ethos of understanding, one that refuses to limit itself to validating history's mechanisms of selection, valuable though they may be. This ethos, so proper to the historian, denies that any present state might ever be something like the goal of history or the preferred means by which such a goal might be approached. It is this ethos that demolishes [*destruieren*] the mediatization of history. And we are better off for it, for there being no goal to history preserves us from remaining in "anticipation" of such a goal, of being a means subservient to its fulfillment. Ideas of the kind that seek to promote "the Education of the Human Race"[15] defend the meaning of history at the expense of those born too early already to be "well-brought-up."

Christian dogmatics, though never shy of positing that salvation might be forfeit, could nonetheless not bear the contingency of the moment at which redemption was brought to the world. The wonderful mythologem that is [the phrase] *descensus ad inferos*[16] was the means by which foregoing generations were made to benefit from the belated salvatory act.

What today touches a distinct nerve is the arrogance of those who simultaneously inhabit the space of a world grown narrow, the right of the firstborn claimed by those comfortable in progress over the unfortunate in need of a helping hand. In the dimension of time, it is taken as an obvious form of self-understanding that progress, putative though it may be, inevitably causes earlier generations to fall behind later ones, and that every temporal guise under which the cunning of reason appears includes and demands indifference toward all intermediate and transitional stages, and not least toward the present as such a stage.

Ethnography has long proscribed an attitude that remains commonplace in the history of science: to make the point in time and space at which the observer stands the reference point for the facts selected and the judgments passed—though we are only gradually coming to understand the pervasiveness of ethnocentrism. In Claude Lévi-Strauss's *Race et histoire* (1952),[17] structural anthropology went too far in its acceptance of the postulate of descriptive equality, to the point even of conceiving of history as the mere cumulation of heterogeneous ethnic and cultural substrata and, in doing so, allowing time to fade into unreality. The history of science has almost always joined in the mockery of those who were proved right. But what about Sizzi, Magini, and Cremonini, of whom we so often hear as not wanting to look through Galileo's

15. [Lessing, *Education*, originally published in 1780.]

16. ["The Harrowing of Hell," that is, Christ's descent into hell one night after his crucifixion to free the souls of the righteous trapped since the creation of the world. See on this topic Blumenberg, *Matthäuspassion*, 57, 149, 252.]

17. [Lévi-Strauss, *Race and History.*]

telescope or, when they did, claiming to see reflections rather than the moons of Jupiter?[18] They were quite right, for looking through Galileo's telescope is worth nothing if done but once. That those were not reflections is something that cannot be perceived but only observed by the regularity with which their positions shift over the course of days and weeks, and finally removed from doubt by predicting their constellations. So overcome was Galileo by the heliocentric analogy of what he saw that he did not even offer his opponents that verification of reality. To the history of philosophy, the character of Simplicio in Galileo's *Dialogue concerning the Two Chief World Systems* is no longer just an amusing personage but a polemical caricature. The history of science, which by its subject is tied to the notion of success, finds itself in awkward straits when it comes to according respect to those who have fallen into obscurity.

Such inequity in the dimension of time may no longer be of concern to those whom time has passed over. But it corrupts in a more subtle and pervasive fashion, regardless of who might be its agent. It is manifested above all in mediatizing the past for the benefit of the present, of *a* present and its demands of relevance and measures of timeliness, which give a hearing only to what can claim palpable relevance for that present. Perhaps history really does have lessons to teach us—or perhaps not. That is a secondary consideration when set against the elementary obligation of forsaking nothing that is human.

I have always felt the charge of "historicism" to be an honor. I reject the idea that it should be our "interest" and our interest alone that is entitled to motivate and give legitimacy to our understanding in time and space. The aborigines of Patagonia or the Kwakiutl, who have so recently been dignified with scholarly attention,[19] have a right not just to be allowed to live but also not to be theoretically forgotten by those who engage in theory, that is, to see their share in humanity respected and preserved in their persons.

Of course, such an *officium nobile* [noble office] derives from our having theory as an attitude, as a capacity for perception, in the first place. Under this admittedly historical condition, however, we quite literally have "no choice." It may be that we can discard this *officium* which has come down to us through history, but we cannot do so as we may choose, in parts, without falling prey to the corruption of clinging to what some "interest" or other might have us preserve. It is not a matter of our choosing but of the claim to which we are subject that we should preserve and remain aware of the ubiquity of the human. It is

18. [See on this topic Blumenberg, *Genesis*, 657–74.]

19. [This may refer to Erich Fromm's *Anatomy of Human Destructiveness* (1973), in which the Kwakiutl First Nation forms a case study.]

precisely by thinking we know what is important and worth knowing "to us" in time and space that we fall prey to the precondition that we wished to avoid, that of the arbitrariness of the knowable.

The religious and metaphysical tradition of the idea of immortality, all the way to Kant's postulate, has led to be obscured and forgotten what was contained in such old institutions as *gloria* [glory] and *memoria* [memory], and negatively even in that most terrible one, *damnatio memoriae*:[20] a claim to remembrance, not just of the active but no less of the passive kind, to the contemporaneity of those who are themselves noncontemporaries, to the effort of not capitulating before the contingency of time and space. "Humankind" is not some sort of super subject, for there is no way of integrating oneself into this *universale*. Antihistoricism, in its various iterations, is the attempt at least to forget the contingency of one's own position in time, to simulate—since it cannot be fulfilled—the postulate of equality in time. That, it should be added, is the best-case scenario, for it may also occur that *history* [*Geschichte*] is pushed aside by *a story* [*Geschichte*]. Those who speak *against* history may not wish it to be known straight away what story it is that they are *for.* To live with the vexation to which the contingency of time and space gives rise means not only to forgo the use of the present and its proximate future as a yardstick but at the same time to retain the indelible consciousness of its unbearableness.

Continuing to engage in the history of philosophy and furthermore the history of science can only be one form of making a claim to the respect of those who are yet to come—by extending that respect to those who preceded us.

Translated by Joe Paul Kroll

20. ["Condemnation of memory," that is, the Roman practice of ordering someone's removal from official records.]

References

Blumenberg, Hans. *The Genesis of the Copernican World*, translated by Robert M. Wallace. Cambridge, MA: MIT Press, 1987.

Blumenberg, Hans. *Matthäuspassion*. Frankfurt am Main: Suhrkamp, 1988.

Blumenberg, Hans. "Phenomenological Aspects on Life-World and Technization." In *History, Metaphors, Fables: A Hans Blumenberg Reader*, edited by Hannes Bajohr, Florian Fuchs, and Joe Paul Kroll, 358–99. Ithaca, NY: Cornell University Press, 2020.

Cassirer, Ernst. *Das Erkenntnisproblem in der Philosophie und Wissenschaft der neueren Zeit*. 4 vols. Berlin: Cassirer, 1906–20.

Cassirer, Ernst. *Die platonische Renaissance in England und die Schule von Cambridge*. Leipzig: Teubner, 1932.

Cassirer, Ernst. *The Individual and the Cosmos in Renaissance Philosophy*, translated by Mario Domandi. Oxford: Blackwell, 1963.

Cassirer, Ernst. *Individuum und Kosmos in der Philosophie der Renaissance*. Leipzig: Teubner, 1927.

Cassirer, Ernst. *Philosophie der symbolischen Formen*. 3 vols. Berlin: Cassirer, 1923–29.

Cassirer, Ernst. *Philosophy of Symbolic Forms*, translated by Ralph Mannheim. 4 vols. New Haven, CT: Yale University Press, 1953–57.

Cassirer, Ernst. *Philosophy of Symbolic Forms*, translated by Ralph Manheim, John Michael Krois, and Donald Phillip Verene. 4 vols. New Haven, CT: Yale University Press, 1965–96.

Cassirer, Ernst. *The Platonic Renaissance in England*, translated by James P. Pettegrove. Austin: University of Texas Press, 1953.

Cassirer, Ernst. *The Problem of Knowledge: Philosophy, Science, and History since Hegel*, translated by William H. Woglom and Charles Handel. New Haven, CT: Yale University Press, 1950.

Cassirer, Ernst. "Substance and Function." In *"Substance and Function" and "Einstein's Theory of Relativity,"* translated by William C. Swabey and Marie C. Swabey, 1–350. Chicago: Open Court, 1923.

Cassirer, Ernst. *Substanzbegriff und Funktionsbegriff: Untersuchung über die Grundlagen der Erkenntniskritik*. Berlin: Cassirer, 1910.

Cassirer, Ernst, and Martin Heidegger. "Davos Disputation between Ernst Cassirer and Martin Heidegger." In *Kant and the Problem of Metaphysics*, by Martin Heidegger, translated by Richard Taft, 193–207. Bloomington: Indiana University Press, 1990.

Fischer, Kuno. "Die Geschichte der Philosophie als Wissenschaft." In *Einleitung in die Geschichte der neuern Philosophie*, 1–14. Heidelberg, 1897.

Fromm, Erich. *The Anatomy of Human Destructiveness*. New York: Holt, Rinehart and Winston, 1973.

Husserl, Edmund. *The Crisis of European Sciences and Transcendental Phenomenology: An Introduction to Phenomenological Philosophy*, translated by David Carr. Evanston, IL: Northwestern University Press, 1970.

Lessing, Gotthold Ephraim. *The Education of the Human Race*, translated by Fred W. Robertson. London, 1881.

Lévi-Strauss, Claude. *Race and History.* Paris: UNESCO, 1952.

Nestle, Wilhelm. *Vom Mythos zum Logos.* Stuttgart: Kröner, 1940.

Usener, Hermann. *Götternamen: Versuch einer Lehre von der religiösen Begriffsbildung.* Bonn, 1896.

Wittgenstein, Ludwig. *Tractatus Logico-philosophicus*, translated by D. F. Pears and B. R. McGuinness. London: Routledge, 1974.

Unburdening from the Absolute:
In Memory of Hans Blumenberg

Odo Marquard

Hans Blumenberg, who died on March 28, 1996, in Altenberge near Münster, was born on July 13, 1920, in Lübeck. He was a man whom I not only held in exceedingly high esteem as a philosopher but also liked as a human being. Here I would like to give, in addition to some personal memories of him, a brief characteristic of his work, which I, like many intellectuals and philosophers worldwide, consider one of the most fascinating oeuvres of German philosophy after the Second World War. "What contemporary philosopher do you consider important?" Hans Jonas was once asked; he replied: "Hans Blumenberg."

First Approach
My contribution is not that of a Blumenberg expert, for that is not what I am. And although I learned more than just a good deal from him, I am not a student of Blumenberg's either: I am eight years younger than him, but am still too much a member of his generation; and what is more, I met him in the early to mid-1960s, too late for me to become his student. Nor am I a Blumenberg scholar, whose intention it was or is to have read, interpreted, and thought through as much of his work as possible and to know as much as can be known about the

Originally published as "Entlastung vom Absoluten: *In Memoriam*," in Wetz and Timm, *Die Kunst des Überlebens*, 17–27. Translated with the kind permission of Edeltraud Luise Marquard. The bracketed footnotes have been added by the translator.

New German Critique 145, Vol. 49, No. 1, February 2022
DOI 10.1215/0094033X-9439699   © 2022 by New German Critique, Inc.

circumstances of his life. To be sure, I have encouraged my own students—Franz Josef Wetz, for example, who would have thought of doing so almost at the same time without my involvement—to read up on Blumenberg and write about him.[1] I have also spoken and written about Blumenberg myself, first in the 1968 Poetics and Hermeneutics volume on myth,[2] and I have written and spoken in appreciation of him, for example, when he was awarded the Sigmund Freud Prize for Academic Prose by the German Academy for Language and Literature in 1980,[3] and when he was awarded an honorary doctorate in the philological faculties of the Justus Liebig University of Giessen in 1982. But I am no Blumenberg expert, which I must repeat so that you know what you can and cannot expect from my remarks. My approach to his work—which is admittedly a constant presence in my own, for it fascinates and inspires me—was made for different reasons because it arose from different situations. The reasons being:

1. I got to know Blumenberg better when I, albeit only briefly, became his closest colleague in 1965 at the University of Giessen after being appointed to the second chair of philosophy, which he established in the Department of Philosophy. I gratefully remember the help he offered to me, a then still very inexperienced young professor of philosophy, for example, by showing me how to run a university department. On that occasion he confessed: "You are the head here; for in 1960"—that was when he, coming from an associate professorship in Hamburg, himself became full professor in Giessen—"they forgot to appoint me head of the department. I did not complain about that," he added, "you never know what something like that can be good for." I was thus able—which I took for granted anyway—to allow his secretary to continue typing his Dictaphone tapes (Stenorette brand) even after his official move to Bochum. In this way, *The Legitimacy of the Modern Age* was written at Ludwigstrasse 12 in Giessen; and since then, I have known that at least his big books are dictated books.

2. Also in 1965, Blumenberg, Hermann Lübbe, and I were, at the suggestion of Helmut Schelsky, appointed members of the founding committee of the East Westphalian University, later to be known as the University of Bielefeld. Blumenberg's interests—and this too was characteristic of him—were not

1. Wetz, *Blumenberg zur Einführung.*

2. [Fuhrmann, *Terror und Spiel.*]

3. [Marquard, "Laudatio auf Hans Blumenberg." For Blumenberg's acceptance speech, see Blumenberg, "Pensiveness."]

aimed at the subject of philosophy in the narrower sense but focused on the Center for Interdisciplinary Research. And finally:

3. Blumenberg was one of the four founders of the pioneeringly interdisciplinary research group Poetics and Hermeneutics, which began in 1963 in Giessen and to which, since 1966, I also belonged. Its pacemaker was Hans Robert Jauss, but its dominant philosopher was undoubtedly Blumenberg. His formative influence reaches far beyond the seventh colloquium of Poetics and Hermeneutics in 1974, after which he—who would have liked it to have become a corresponding society, communicating only by letter—withdrew from the research group. But it was also due to these activities that he was one of the decisive initiators of interdisciplinary work in philosophy.

In all three situations—as a colleague in the same department, through coexistence in the same founding team, and through cooperation in the same research group—it was indispensable for me to know him and his philosophy, and to know him so well that fruitful interplay became possible, so much so that, speaking in the technical language of soccer, one could play the game in blind understanding and make moves even without the ball and into the gaps of the field. This did not require a scholarly and detailed knowledge of Blumenberg, but rather a pragmatic and compact understanding of his philosophy, which, of course, became more difficult to keep up with as his work grew more and more voluminous. Because at that time—after the unpublished Kiel dissertation and postdoctoral thesis, his Copernicus studies, his works on the history of concepts, and his *Paradigms for a Metaphorology* (1960)—his big books were published: *The Legitimacy of the Modern Age* (1966), *The Genesis of the Copernican World* (1975), *Work on Myth* (1979), *The Readability of the World* (1981), *Life-Time and World-Time* (1986), and *Cave Exits* (1989), as well as the numerous smaller volumes, such as *Shipwreck with Spectator* (1979), *The Laughter of the Thracian Woman* (1987), *Care Crosses the River* (1987), and *St. Matthew Passion* (1988).[4] These books—extensive and thematically varied by virtue of Blumenberg's stupendous erudition—can only be absorbed (at least in my case) for purposes of pragmatic compact knowledge by reducing their complexity in a manner not unlike the reduction that interests artists today: How much picture can one leave out of a painting without it ceasing to be a picture? How much theater can one subtract from a play without it ceasing to be theater? How much music can one omit in music without its ceas-

---

4. [Blumenberg, *Paradigms*; Blumenberg, *Legitimacy*; Blumenberg, *Genesis*; Blumenberg, *Work on Myth*; Blumenberg, *Lesbarkeit*; Blumenberg, *Lebenszeit und Weltzeit*; Blumenberg, *Höhlenausgänge*; Blumenberg, *Shipwreck with Spectator*; Blumenberg, *Laughter of the Thracian Woman*; Blumenberg, *St. Matthew Passion*.]

ing to be music? The question is analogous: How much of Blumenberg's work can be omitted without the remainder of this textual destruction ceasing to be Blumenberg? For this reduction—and here my Germanist colleague Ulrich Karthaus reminded me of an apt couplet of Christian Morgenstern's—it would be advantageous to be possessed of one of Korf's inventions, "spectacles whose focal strength / shortens texts of any length."[5] By means of such spectacles, we might condense the whole Blumenberg corpus perhaps, if not quite (although this would be philosophically honorable too) into just "one question mark," then into something quite equivalent: a basic idea.

Basic Idea

This basic idea of Blumenberg's philosophy seemed and seems to me to be the idea of an unburdening from the absolute [*Entlastung vom Absoluten*].[6] Humans cannot bear the absolute. They must, in various forms, gain distance from it. I first formulated this in my speech at the Freud Prize ceremony in Darmstadt in 1980, and afterward asked Blumenberg: "Are you very dissatisfied with this interpretation?" He, who could be very polite, answered: "I am dissatisfied only with the fact that it is possible so quickly to notice that everything more or less comes down to that idea."

Humans' lifelong task is to ease the burden of the absolute, and culture is work on that distance. That, I think, is what Blumenberg's philosophy is about. It is what *The Legitimacy of the Modern Age* is about. Humans cannot bear God; that is why they invented, as the first overcoming of Gnosticism, the Middle Ages, and, as the second overcoming of Gnosticism, the modern age. They protect themselves from the "theological absolutism" of an all-too-almighty God by inventing the culture of self-preservation and self-assertion as well as the modern age's scientific culture of curiosity.

And it is also this unburdening from the absolute that Blumenberg's *Genesis of the Copernican World* is about: humans cannot stand the suffering of the world and try, by means of the "theory" that the Greeks invented at the same time as tragedy, to forget it, instead gazing into the distant and fascinating cosmos. But this fascinating cosmos, after its Copernican disenchantment, proves to be a forbidding desert, of which humans for their part must unburden themselves by affirming the earth as an oasis amid this desert, the earth as a human lifeworld. And Blumenberg's book *Work on Myth* is also about an unburdening from the absolute. In the beginning, which historically is always already

5. [Morgenstern, "Spectacles."]

6. [The concept of *Entlastung* goes back to Arnold Gehlen's anthropology. The term is usually translated as "relief" or, closer to the German, "unburdening." See Gehlen, *Man*.]

beyond time, the "absolutism of reality" prevails. Humans have alleviated their dependence on this threatening superiority called reality through work, above all also through the work on myth—by transforming reality through an "archaic" and "mythical separation of powers" into a multitude of stories, and by transforming its horrors into play.[7] We humans cannot do without this. We remain— says this book, which for Blumenberg ultimately becomes a book on Goethe— liable to myth. Myth cannot be "brought to an end."[8] The stories, the images, the myths are never behind us.

Likewise, Blumenberg's book *Readability of the World* asserts this: humans unburden themselves of absolute reality through the distancing feat of transforming it into a book-like corpus of reading matter, with the book of books always in the background. Even our most advanced natural scientists— when they decipher the "genetic code,"[9] for example—remain philologists and exegetes. *Cave Exits*, too, continues this concept of the unburdening from the absolute. Humans need, find, and build caves to find unburdening from the absolute deadliness of the outside world. As living beings inevitably exposed and endangered by visibility, they seek shelter in these caves and their successor forms, the institutions, and develop culture, inwardness, and reflection there, through which they keep the absolute and dangerously direct reality at bay. Thus, by these manifold steps, Blumenberg shows that humans live by relieving themselves of that unendurable absolute and immediate reality to which even God belongs. But by relieving humans of God, God at the same time relieves himself of humans and leaves them: God is dead. This is why Blumenberg listens to Bach, in 1988 in a new interpretation of the *St. Matthew Passion*, as a kind of Nietzsche before Nietzsche, by focusing on the words that in this Passion story are the last words of the Son of man on the cross: "My God, my God, why hast thou forsaken me?" Therefore, I think, this late book by Blumenberg is what his early books were, a radicalized question about theodicy that finds no answer.

I repeat: the basic idea of Blumenberg's philosophy seemed and seems to me to be the idea of unburdening from the absolute. Humans cannot bear the absolute, as reality and as God; they must gain distance from it. And their life-long task, culture, is the work on this distance, which is always and simultaneously the mitigation of simplicity [*Einfalt*] by plurality [*Vielfalt*]: by unburdening ourselves of the one absolute that we cannot bear—as reality and as

---

7. [Blumenberg, *Work on Myth*, pt. 1, chap. 1.]

8. [Blumenberg, *Work on Myth*, pt. 2, chap. 4.]

9. [Blumenberg, *Lesbarkeit*, chap. 22.]

God—in its undivided might and endure only by putting it at a distance by manifold ways of coping with it, by "the proclamation of the plural," as Eckard Nordhofen called it.[10] We lack the phenomenological and anthropological book by Blumenberg that might have given us the possibility to grasp this basic idea of his philosophy even more vividly: precisely that humans need to be unburdened of the absolute.[11] This basic thesis, I think, also characterizes his literary process, about which I would now like to make a few comments.

Way of Writing

For it was also through the literary form of his works that he, who argued by narrating discursively or aphoristically, sought this unburdening from the absolute.

As a philosopher, Blumenberg was also an eminent writer. Not only had he the gift of discerning problems in the sharpest manner, but he also explicated them most thrillingly. He wrote an impressive scholarly prose, which one could think of as a kind of prose geared to increasing the pressure of a problem [*Problemdrucksteigerungsprosa*], that and philosophical problems capable of inducing nightmares. His problem thrillers [*Problemkrimis*], as I have called them, disguised as scholarly tomes make us more aware of what is going on. But Blumenberg not only wrote it, he also said what scientific and philosophical prose is. Moving from the *Paradigms for a Metaphorology* of 1960 to the more general "Theory of Nonconceptuality" in the appendix of *Shipwreck with Spectator* of 1979,[12] he emphasizes that exact conceptual language is not the unsurpassable form of the language of science. The Cartesian program of terminologization and formalization of the sciences is insufficient. No science and no philosophy can do without images and myths. Each is subject to metaphors. Allow me to put it crudely. As with grog—water can, sugar should, rum must be added—so with philosophy: formalization can, terminology should, metaphor must be added. Otherwise it is not worth drinking, in the one case, and philosophizing, in the other.

That is why—says Blumenberg, hermeneuticist that he is—neither philosophical systematics nor philosophical concepts and metaphors must be separated from their history. For him, who here followed in the footsteps of Ernst Cassirer,[13] this includes the step from substance thinking to function thinking

10. [Nordhofen, "Die Proklamation des Plurals."]

11. [This book, also mentioned in the last paragraph of this text, was posthumously published as Blumenberg, *Beschreibung des Menschen.*]

12. [Blumenberg, "Prospect for a Theory of Nonconceptuality."]

13. [Cassirer, "Substance and Function."]

in the history of philosophy, the history of ideas, and the history of science. History, says Blumenberg, is not an avenue along which unchanging traditional substances are hauled, so that historians can then argue over which accident and which robbery—such as the act of highway robbery termed "secularization"—had occurred at which tree. Rather, history is a budgetary system of positions into which answers or other vital arrangements enter as carriers of functions. When they disappear, they leave behind vacancies and needs for reoccupation, the fulfillment of which—since almost everything is connected with everything else—entails consequential problems; thus everything is in open-ended motion. This is Blumenberg's "historicism," and he understood this to be an honorific title.[14] This model of historical reoccupation—operating with the metaphor of the staff budget—sharpens the eye for historical follow-up costs and is therefore, in my opinion, eminently suitable for the beneficial replacement of a mentality of conviction with a mentality of responsibility.

At the same time, however, Blumenberg did not allow himself to be frightened by the prohibitions on metaphysics that are common today. He held on to the great questions of philosophy: God, world and man, death, evil. For instance, to the question: Does death come into the world through sin, or rather the other way round, does sin come into the world through death? Maybe also because man—the being that "hesitates" and can therefore be "pensive"—has too little life-time to hesitate enough? He cleaves (and Wetz underlined this in his book on Blumenberg) to these great questions and refuses to relinquish them. Indeed: I know of no contemporary philosophy that, while deeply aware of the critique of metaphysics and its history, pursues metaphysics as impartially and fruitfully as Blumenberg's. He has never accepted restrictions on thought, and so everything becomes philosophically important to him, from phenomenologically describable quotidian findings to anecdotes to literature and poetry as well as the Bible. That is also why he refuses to accept that any stylistic genre might be out of bounds: from the historico-conceptual or historico-metaphorical miscellany to the philosophical treatise, from the systematic-historical fundamental work to the essay, from the poetic narrative to the fable and the aphorism. As an author, too, he cultivated the stylistic separation of powers and, as he advanced in age, divided the single author Hans Blumenberg into that variety of authors that he, the multiple philosopher, united within himself. Finally, in concluding my attempt at characterizing him, I will try to point out a problem that moved Blumenberg in a special way.

---

14. [Blumenberg, "In Memory of Ernst Cassirer," in this special issue, 221.]

Finitude

My favorite book by Blumenberg is *Life-Time and World-Time*, which he published in 1986. In it Blumenberg developed—on the basis of an idiosyncratic and brilliant interpretation of the late Edmund Husserl's "genetic phenomenology"—the shortness of human life as a central problem of time. The more humans, after their expulsion from the world of immediate obviousness, discover the so-called "objective" world with its incredibly expansive "world-time," the more they inevitably also discover that their "life-time" is an ultra-short "episode," limited by death, the inexorable boundary to their vital and cognitive appetite for the world. The "congruence" of "life-time and world-time" proves to be a delusion; the "opening of the time gap" between "life-time and world-time" proves to be reality. Thus the character of our life-time as limited by time becomes central for Blumenberg: our time is finite, for everyone's most certain future is death. This, and here I must correct an earlier interpretation of mine and take Blumenberg's written objection into account, is not an indignant protest against death as limiting our access to the world. Rather, Blumenberg sees death—for example, in his 1983 essay about his self-understanding and in his recourse to Seneca[15]—as a condition of freedom. Quote: "Qui potest mori non potest cogi." Perhaps to be rendered as: "He who knows how to get away cannot be oppressed." (This is how Blumenberg puts it.)[16] Yet what is also true is this: the scarcest of our scarce resources is our life-time. So we experience ourselves as an episode, and the book *Life-Time and World-Time* becomes a temporal phenomenology of human finitude. There are signs of this temporal finitude for humans: diseases. Blumenberg interpreted this in 1982 in his essay "Goethe's Mortality" in view of the strokes of fate and crises of illness that befell the poet with whom he had engaged so closely—not only in his book on myth—that he is said to have referred to Goethe's birthday as more important to him than his own.[17] It was only logical that finitude as mortality should in this way also become the focus of Blumenberg's philosophical attention. For unburdening oneself of the absolute leads to finitude gaining importance.

Blumenberg responded to the experience of having no time, which was philosophically explained above all in *Life-Time and World-Time*, in his own life practice with those characteristics that earned him the reputation of being "difficult." My own experience with him was mostly nothing of the kind: I

---

15. [Blumenberg, "Einleitung."]
16. ["Wer sich davonzumachen weiß, ist nicht bedrückbar" (Blumenberg, "Einleitung," 18).]
17. [Blumenberg, "Goethes Sterblichkeit."]

found him helpful, stimulating, loyal, of course also challenging, and someone with whom one could get along quite well. This was also due to his humor and his pronounced sense of playfulness, through which he particularly rewarded intelligent moves and sometimes allowed himself to be disarmed by them. What I mean is this: his peculiarities arose from the fact that he arranged his life—especially in view of the scarcity of his life-time—more consciously and rationally than most of his peers. I remember stimulating discussions with him on October 16, 1980, when he received the Freud Prize in Darmstadt. He said to me: "You have lost no time in your life. I have lost eight years that I must make up for." Quite obviously he had in mind, without saying it, that he—a "half Jew" in Nazi terminology—was not allowed to enter a university in 1939 after his graduation from school, so that he took recourse to the church's theological-philosophical seminaries in Paderborn and Frankfurt am Main. When he was barred from them as well, he worked in the Dräger factory in Lübeck and was thus temporarily protected. Afterward he was put in a camp, from which he escaped, and went into hiding in Lübeck until, after the end of the war, he was finally allowed to study in Hamburg, and then in Kiel. To make up for this lost time in his life (this is how it was told to me), he from then on slept only six times a week and thus gained one working day: this was possible only because he also worked at night. This—which did not make it any easier to get through to him—was the life-practical answer to his experience of the lack of time, whose roots he described philosophically in *Life-Time and World-Time*. In this context, it is also worth mentioning that, to make up for the lost life-time, he withdrew from public life at the end of the 1960s at the latest: away from the lectures, the academic tourism with its discursive orgies, and the large administrative tournaments of the reform university so that he could devote himself completely to the work on his texts through an "economical" use of the scarce resource of life-time, focusing on enormous reading lists and the dia-logue with his Dictaphone. This was, one tends to forget, not the case from the very beginning. He initially, beyond research and teaching, invested a great deal of energy in working for the university—as a long-standing member of the Senate of the German Research Foundation and, for example, also for the institutional restoration of the University of Giessen.[18] But then—and what had been done to the university since 1968 may have played a role in this—he rightly had the impression that he had done more than most in his institutional duties, so that, at last, it was for others to take their turn. That is why, to make up for lost life-time, he finally retreated in 1970, when he was a professor in

18. [See Blumenberg, "World Pictures and World Models."]

Münster, and after 1985 as an emeritus, into his very private cave, his writing cave in Altenberge in the countryside near Münster—and, so to speak, turned off the doorbell at the cave exit. Hans Robert Jauss, Henning Ritter, and Martin Meyer have had the courage to overcome this barrier every now and then, and not only through phone conversations. The rest of us, and I certainly reproach myself for this, had so much respect for him that we also respected his methodical loneliness, which, although he wanted it, probably also made him sad. He—this stimulating, impressive, great man, whose special characteristic was to have only special characteristics—perhaps underestimated how strongly he was nevertheless present and influential as a philosopher and writer. He did not publish his last works, reflections on Thomas Mann's diaries as well as a phenomenological anthropology, of which he spoke as early as 1982, when my wife and I last saw him at our home after he had received the honorary doctorate from Giessen. "For whom, actually?" he is said to have asked. I believe I know an answer that, beyond his death, objects to this resignation. For whom, actually? I believe: for us and for him, whom we cannot allow to be taken away from us, even by Blumenberg himself.

Translated by Hannes Bajohr

References

Blumenberg, Hans. *Beschreibung des Menschen*, edited by Manfred Sommer. Frankfurt am Main: Suhrkamp, 2006.

Blumenberg, Hans. *Die Lesbarkeit der Welt*. Frankfurt am Main: Suhrkamp, 1981.

Blumenberg, Hans. "Einleitung: Das Unselbstverständliche." In *Ein mögliches Selbstverständnis: Aus dem Nachlaß*, 9–18. Stuttgart: Reclam, 1997.

Blumenberg, Hans. *The Genesis of the Copernican World*, translated by Robert M. Wallace. Cambridge, MA: MIT Press, 1987.

Blumenberg, Hans. "Goethes Sterblichkeit." *Neue Zürcher Zeitung*, March 20, 1982.

Blumenberg, Hans. *Höhlenausgänge*. Frankfurt am Main: Suhrkamp, 1989.

Blumenberg, Hans. *The Laughter of the Thracian Woman: A Protohistory of Theory*, translated by Spencer Hawkins. New York: Bloomsbury, 2015.

Blumenberg, Hans. *Lebenszeit und Weltzeit*. Frankfurt am Main: Suhrkamp, 1986.

Blumenberg, Hans. *The Legitimacy of the Modern Age*, translated by Robert M. Wallace. Cambridge, MA: MIT Press, 1983.

Blumenberg, Hans. *Paradigms for a Metaphorology*, translated by Robert Savage. Ithaca, NY: Cornell University Press, 2010.

Blumenberg, Hans. "Pensiveness." In *History, Metaphors, Fables: A Hans Blumenberg Reader*, edited by Hannes Bajohr, Florian Fuchs, and Joe Paul Kroll, 525–30. Ithaca, NY: Cornell University Press, 2020.

Blumenberg, Hans. "Prospect for a Theory of Nonconceptuality." In *History, Metaphors, Fables: A Hans Blumenberg Reader*, edited by Hannes Bajohr, Florian Fuchs, and Joe Paul Kroll, 239–58. Ithaca, NY: Cornell University Press, 2020.

Blumenberg, Hans. *Shipwreck with Spectator: Paradigm of a Metaphor for Existence*, translated by Steven Rendall. Cambridge, MA: MIT Press, 1997.

Blumenberg, Hans. *St. Matthew Passion*, translated by Paul Fleming and Helmut Müller-Sievers. Ithaca, NY: Cornell University Press.

Blumenberg, Hans. *Work on Myth*, translated by Robert M. Wallace. Cambridge, MA: MIT Press, 1985.

Blumenberg, Hans. "World Pictures and World Models." In *History, Metaphors, Fables: A Hans Blumenberg Reader*, edited by Hannes Bajohr, Florian Fuchs, and Joe Paul Kroll, 40–52. Ithaca, NY: Cornell University Press, 2020.

Cassirer, Ernst. "Substance and Function." In *Substance and Function and Einstein's Theory of Relativity*, 3–346. New York: Dover, 1953.

Fuhrmann, Manfred, ed. *Terror und Spiel: Probleme der Mythenrezeption*. Munich: Fink, 1971.

Gehlen, Arnold. *Man: His Nature and Place in the World*, translated by Clare McMillan and Karl Pillemer. New York: Columbia University Press, 1988.

Marquard, Odo. "Laudatio auf Hans Blumenberg." *Deutsche Akademie für Sprache und Dichtung*. www.deutscheakademie.de/de/auszeichnungen/sigmund-freud-preis/hans -blumenberg/laudatio.

Morgenstern, Christian. "The Spectacles." In *Galgenlieder: A Selection*, edited by Max Knight, 169. Berkeley: University of California Press, 1969.

Nordhofen, Eckard. "Die Proklamation des Plurals: Zum Tode des Philosophen Hans Blumenberg." *Die Zeit*, April 12, 1996.

Wetz, Franz Josef. *Hans Blumenberg zur Einführung*. Hamburg: Junius, 2004.

Wetz, Franz Josef, and Hermann Timm. *Die Kunst des Überlebens: Nachdenken über Hans Blumenberg*. Frankfurt am Main: Suhrkamp, 1999.

Keep up to date on new scholarship

Issue alerts are a great way to stay current on all the cutting-edge scholarship from your favorite Duke University Press journals. This free service delivers tables of contents directly to your inbox, informing you of the latest groundbreaking work as soon as it is published.

To sign up for issue alerts:

1. Visit **dukeu.press/register** and register for an account. You do not need to provide a customer number.

2. After registering, visit **dukeu.press/alerts**.

3. Go to "Latest Issue Alerts" and click on "Add Alerts."

4. Select as many publications as you would like from the pop-up window and click "Add Alerts."

Printed and bound by CPI Group (UK) Ltd, Croydon, CR0 4YY

13/04/2025

14656471-0006

Intermittent Legitimacy:
Hans Blumenberg and Artificial Intelligence

Leif Weatherby

Hans Blumenberg's only known treatment of the topic of artificial intelligence comes in the form of a fragmentary meditation on the first chatbot, Joseph Weizenbaum's ELIZA. Blumenberg compares this program to the philosophy of Edmund Husserl, arguing that both AI and phenomenology make a false assumption about intelligence or consciousness. This article argues that Blumenberg's brush with digital systems is crucial in updating our own critique of AI as it proliferates in a new, dynamic form today. Drawing on and shifting the account of technology in the phenomenological tradition, Blumenberg includes machines in the constitution of meaning through rhetoric and points the way to a new wave of digital critique.

Intermittent Legitimacy:
Hans Blumenberg and Artificial Intelligence

Leif Weatherby

Keywords   Hans Blumenberg, artificial intelligence, phenomenology, Joseph Weizenbaum, ELIZA program

A Well-Tempered Modernist

Colin Lang

In the vast archive of literature from, and on, Hans Blumenberg, there are few mentions of theories of modern or contemporary art. Two exceptions exist, which both took place in 1966. One deals with the topic more obliquely: a lecture on Paul Valéry given at the Akademie der Künste in West Berlin. The second takes the topic of pop and op art head-on in a discussion led by Blumenberg for the research group Poetik und Hermeneutik. In neither does Blumenberg offer anything like a working theory of contemporary art, but his lecture enacts a performative contemporary reading of Valéry's attempt to make Leonardo da Vinci relevant for the French poet's age. Comparing Blumenberg's comments on contemporary art with those in US formalist art criticism (Clement Greenberg, Michael Fried) provides a unique constellation of later modernist thinking on the plastic arts (painting and sculpture, chiefly). This article attempts to read Blumenberg as a contemporary thinker for art, an attempt that revisits the provocation that Blumenberg set for himself in 1966 when considering the stakes for contemporary art forms. Can one say that Blumenberg was himself a modernist?

A Well-Tempered Modernist

Colin Lang

Keywords   Michael Fried, Clement Greenberg, modernism, formalist criticism, pop art

Hans Blumenberg and Leonardo

Johannes Endres

Hans Blumenberg's, frequently oblique, reflections on art rank among the most erudite in twentieth-century theories of art. The following investigations focus especially on his views on the visual arts as they unfold from his critical reception of Leonardo da Vinci's art and science. At the center of such a reception stands a preeminent image concept of the Renaissance, the "window image," and its epistemological implications, which Blumenberg counters with a skeptical attitude toward the mimetic aesthetics of images. In doing so, he contradicts Paul Valéry's influential interpretation of Leonardo's "method," which Blumenberg discusses at great length, just to cut short the ambiguities of Renaissance perspective as a "symbolic form."

Hans Blumenberg and Leonardo

Johannes Endres

Keywords   Hans Blumenberg, Leonardo da Vinci, Paul Valéry, mimesis, theory of the image

Working on the Myth of the Anthropocene: Blumenberg and the Need for Philosophical Anthropology

Vida Pavesich

The Anthropocene concept emerged from questions raised by scientists about whether human activity has ushered in a new and perilous geological age. The term migrated into the humanities and social sciences and now involves a proliferation of metanarratives about anthropogenic disruptions to systems that support life on this planet. This article develops an interpretive framework drawn from Hans Blumenberg's theories of myth and metaphor, philosophical anthropology, and philosophy of history to address how Immanuel Kant's fourth question, "What is the human being?," has reemerged in the Anthropocene, and to assess which narratives tend to best reflect realistic responses to the current crisis. In contrast to the mythical species-subject *Anthropos*, Blumenberg's minimal anthropology characterizes humans as having a permanent bioanthropological need for orientation that requires cultural compensation, including partial reliance on metaphor and myth. As an interpretive optic, this anthropology has the resources to deflate narrative excess. In addition, Blumenberg's philosophy of history can shed light on how the Anthropocene is both unprecedented yet not entirely new insofar as it addresses problems or questions suppressed by modernist progress myths. Through the prism of a minimal anthropology and an application of Blumenberg's philosophy of history, this article explores those questions and presents criteria for distinguishing between harmless narratives and unrealistic, dangerous myths, such as ecomodernist fantasies of controlling the Earth system.

Working on the Myth of the Anthropocene: Blumenberg and the Need for Philosophical Anthropology

Vida Pavesich

Keywords   Hans Blumenberg, philosophical anthropology, myth, metaphor, Anthropocene

The Vanishing Reality of the State: On Hans Blumenberg's Political Theory

Hannes Bajohr

While many interpreters of Hans Blumenberg have searched *The Legitimacy of the Modern Age* or *Work on Myth* for hints of a political theory, there is still no in-depth discussion of the only essay published during his lifetime that deals directly with political theory, "The Concept of Reality and the Theory of the State," which appeared in May 1968. This article reconstructs that essay's main arguments and contextualizes it in the "historical phenomenology" Blumenberg developed in his middle period. Arguing that we are witnessing a slow dissolution of the state, he suggests that politics is supplanted by rhetoric and the state by supranational structures. Setting apart this historical approach from the anthropological one of his later work, the article argues for a break in Blumenberg's oeuvre around 1968.

The Vanishing Reality of the State:
On Hans Blumenberg's Political Theory

Hannes Bajohr

Keywords   Hans Blumenberg, Carl Schmitt, Jürgen Habermas, political theory, reality

Decoding Aesop:
Blumenberg's Fabulistic Turn

Florian Fuchs

This article develops Hans Blumenberg's intensifying interest in fables during the 1970s and 1980s and argues that it marked his decisive turn away from academic philosophy toward a rethinking of storytelling as a philosophical practice. Blumenberg's simultaneous writings on anecdotes are thus reframed as a testing ground and subsequent application of a philosophy of fabulistic storytelling. The systematic reach of this fabulistic turn is exhibited by tracing a set of concepts—pensiveness (*Nachdenklichkeit*), nonunderstanding (*Unverstand*), and disturbance (*Störung*)—that Blumenberg coined to define the specific phenomenological conditions of being interrupted by a fable-type story. Though no actual "fabulology" ensued from these plans, the fabulistic turn can be contextualized with Blumenberg's metaphorology as it represents his ultimate attempt to study the role of language for philosophy, however, with a shift from analysis to pragmatism: while metaphorology demanded, retroactively, that absolute metaphors be revisited throughout the history of philosophy to gauge the plasticity lost by philosophical language, Blumenberg's fabulology proposes, proactively, to change philosophical language itself by conducting narratological experiments with the lifeworld to rethink the relation between lifeworld, reality, and storytelling.

Decoding Aesop:
Blumenberg's Fabulistic Turn

Florian Fuchs

Keywords   Hans Blumenberg, Aesop, fables, anecdotes, metaphorology

No More Than Seeing:
Hans Blumenberg's Poetics of Spectatorship

Daniela K. Helbig

Hans Blumenberg is known as much for his theoretical focus on unsayability as he is for his ostentatious reclusiveness. This article argues that Blumenberg's figure of the spectator connects these two elements. Blumenberg's social and theoretical retreat to a spectatorial position bears distinctive traces of his attempt at finding new ways to do philosophy after 1945. As much a departure from as a legacy of his early attempts to critically renew scholarly practice with the working group Poetics and Hermeneutics, the figure of the spectator served Blumenberg as a means of self-stylization and embodied his striving at the descriptive representation of unsayability. Blumenberg's theoretical figure of the distanced yet critically engaged spectator is distinguished both from Martin Heidegger's notion of thinking *as* action and from Edmund Husserl's positioning of the philosophical spectator as removed from the empirical world. The figure of the *theoros*, the spectator, absorbs the ambition of bringing into view the unsayable and of articulating the conditions for this spectatorial act.

No More Than Seeing:
Hans Blumenberg's Poetics of Spectatorship

Daniela K. Helbig

Keywords Hans Blumenberg, Poetics and Hermeneutics, spectator, *Wirklichkeit*, writing practices

In Memory of Ernst Cassirer:
Speech Delivered in Acceptance of the Kuno Fischer Prize
of the University of Heidelberg, 1974

Hans Blumenberg

On the occasion of receiving a prize first awarded to Ernst Cassirer (1874–1945), Hans Blumenberg assesses Cassirer's legacy and influence. Blumenberg underlines Cassirer's contribution to epistemology in the neo-Kantian tradition as well as his pioneering work in the history of ideas before discussing how his celebrated *Philosophy of Symbolic Forms* led Cassirer to reappraise the problem of history more generally. Blumenberg reads Cassirer as having tried to establish the independence of history with regard to the imperatives of the present and from this derives a defense of his own idea of historicism, which Blumenberg understands as the claim to equal consideration by historians on the part of those eras, peoples, and subjects that may not serve present interests. Historians must be aware of the contingency of their own position and preserve the memory even of those aspects of humanity that fail to meet their criteria of progress.

In Memory of Ernst Cassirer:
Speech Delivered in Acceptance of the Kuno Fischer Prize
of the University of Heidelberg, 1974

Hans Blumenberg

Keywords   neo-Kantianism, philosophy of symbolic forms, historicism, uses of history

Unburdening from the Absolute:
In Memory of Hans Blumenberg

Odo Marquard

First delivered as a short laudatory speech on the occasion of Hans Blumenberg receiving the Sigmund Freud Prize for Academic Prose in 1980, this essay by the German philosopher Odo Marquard served as a eulogy at a memorial event for Blumenberg after his death in 1996. Marquard, who was a colleague of Blumenberg's at the University of Giessen between 1965 and 1970, offers one of the first and still most influential attempts at condensing Blumenberg's thought to a basic idea: willfully reductive, Marquard argues that all of Blumenberg's books can be read as a variation on the theme of "unburdening from the absolute"—the task of human beings to keep an overwhelming reality at bay. Marquard thus interprets him mainly as a proponent of the German current of "philosophical anthropology." The text also sheds light on Blumenberg's relationship to finitude, his life and reclusiveness, and his writing technique.

Unburdening from the Absolute: In Memory of Hans Blumenberg

Odo Marquard

Keywords   Hans Blumenberg, Odo Marquard, philosophical anthropology, absolutism, finitude